THE WARSAW TREATY ORGANIZATION

The Warsaw Treaty Organization

A Political and Organizational Analysis

Neil Fodor

MACMILLAN

First published 1990

Published by

THE MACMILLAN PRESS LTD
Houndmills, Basingstoke, Hampshire RG21 2XS
and London
Companies and representatives
throughout the world

Printed in Hong Kong

British Library Cataloguing in Publication Data
Fodor, Neil, *1959* –
The Warsaw Treaty Organization : a political and
organizational analysis.
1. Organizatsiya Varshavskogo Dogovora
I. Title
335'.031'091717
ISBN 0–333–51475–0

Contents

List of Figures and Tables

List of Figures and Tables

Abbreviations

ABM Treaty	Anti-Ballistic Missile Treaty
APL	Albanian Party of Labour
BCP	Bulgarian Communist Party
CBMs	Confidence-Building Measures
CC	Central Committee
CDM	Committee of Ministers of Defence
CECSPSE	Conference of European Countries for Safeguarding Peace and Security in Europe
CFM	Committee of Ministers of Foreign Affairs
CMEA	Council for Mutual Economic Assistance
CPC	Communist Party of China
CPCz	Communist Party of Czechoslovakia
CPSU	Communist Party of the Soviet Union
CSCE	Conference on Security and Co-operation in Europe
CzR	Czechoslovak Republic
CzSR	Czechoslovak Socialist Republic
C-in-C	Commander-in-Chief
C-of-S	Chief of Staff
EDC	European Defence Community
FMs	Foreign Ministers (meeting prior to the CFM)
FRG	Federal Republic of Germany
GDR	German Democratic Republic
GSFG	Group of Soviet Forces Germany
HPA	Hungarian People's Army
HPR	Hungarian People's Republic
HSWP	Hungarian Socialist Workers' Party
INFs	Intermediate-range Nuclear Forces
JAFs	Joint Armed Forces

KGB	'Committee of State Security'; the Soviet secret service
MC	Military Council
MPA	Main Political Administration
NATO	North Atlantic Treaty Organization
PCC	Political Consultative Committee
PRA	People's Republic of Albania
PRB	People's Republic of Bulgaria
PRC	People's Republic of China
PUWP	Polish United Workers' Party
RCP	Romanian Communist Party
RPA	Romanian People's Army
RPR	Rumanian People's Republic
RSFSR	Russian Soviet Federal Socialist Republic
RWP	Rumanian Workers' Party
SED	Sozialistische Einheitspartei Deutschland – the 'Socialist Unity Party of Germany'
SRR	Socialist Republic of Romania
SWB	BBC Monitoring Service's Summary of World Broadcasts
TNFs	Theatre-range Nuclear Forces
UK	United Kingdom
UN	United Nations
US/USA	United States of America
USSR	Union of Soviet Socialist Republics
WEU	Western European Union
WTO	Warsaw Treaty Organization

Preface

I first studied the Warsaw Treaty Organization in an honours option on 'International Communism' at Dundee University, as part of my degree course in Political Science. Full acknowledgement must go to my then tutor, Alex Reid, for allowing me to pursue this topic, and generously aiding and encouraging my interest in it.

In that early reading I was fascinated that open academic sources presented such a different view of the WTO from that seen in the West's media. In particular they did not adopt the image of a 'war-fighting, war-winning' military machine used by the West's political leaders. In my resolve to develop my understanding of the subject beyond the undergraduate level, I was happily awarded a Social Science Research Council (now Economic and Social Research Council), grant to take to the Institute of Soviet and East European Studies (ISEES), Glasgow University, which had offered me the expertise and resources to carry out advanced research into this topic. Under the guidance and supervision of Professor William V. Wallace, the Director of ISEES, and Dr Stephen L. White, that research was carried out and completed. This book has developed and updated that doctoral research.

While my conclusions do not necessarily show the opposite of the image of the WTO commonly seen in the West, my researches do show a political-military alliance that is very different from such an image. While I cannot claim to have produced the ultimate handbook on the WTO, I hope I throw some light on many of the things that seemed so puzzling and contradictory to me when I first looked at the Organization, and I trust that this book offers insight into practical aspects of the body. I would like to think that I have provided at least some of the groundwork for the further study and assessment of the WTO.

In the course of my studies, I was steadily drawn to the conclusion that the political rather than the military aspects of the WTO were the more important, and the more fruitful for research. This is not to deny substance to the military factors. Rather I have been forced into dividing between what I have found to take place within the formal structure of the WTO, and what takes place in the name of the WTO. Of the two, the political and the military, it is my analysis that the former takes precedence over the latter in the formal context of the Organization. Where there are formal military ties, I have indicated their scope and significance. My conclusion is that the actual miltary relationships within the formal alliance are extremely limited. The content of this book reflects such an analysis.

My policy throughout has been to base my research on open original sources, not just from the Soviet Union but where possible from the non-Soviet members of the alliance. While I have consulted Western sources, they have played a peripheral part in my analysis. The aim has been to explain the WTO in the words of its own documents; I have generally quoted Western sources only to add substance to my own conclusions based on the original sources. I have adopted the term 'Central Europe' to denote the European allies of the USSR. My contacts in those countries confirmed a preference for this description, considering 'East' Europe to refer geographically to the Soviet Union's European territories.

During the period of my doctoral research the opportunity arose for me to visit the Hungarian People's Republic, on a British Council scholarship. I was thus able to consult several published sources not available in Britain, but above all had the opportunity to talk at length with a variety of academics from several disciplines (and also not just from Hungary). This will explain why Hungarian sources may be seen to figure disproportionately in this work. I also greatly benefitted from conversations with academics from many of the Warsaw Treaty states who visited Glasgow during the period of my study. While often providing me with useful unpublished information, these people, together with research in Hungary, served to confirm many of the conclusions I had reached from my reading of the published materials. In the text, when I have quoted these sources, I have marked them with a superscript [N]. I have also used this method to show non-attributable remarks gained from situations similar to those governed by Chatham House rules. All responsibility for the interpretation I have placed on my sources, both published and confidential, remains with me. The book is accurate to the end of 1988. The effect of the events of 1989 on the WTO must await further study

Apart from the continuous help and support I received from Professor Wallace and Dr White as my supervisors, I must acknowledge the further academic help and encouragement I received from the rest of the staff at ISEES. The secretaries were also of immense support in the supply of sundry assistance and humour. External to the Institute, Gerard Holden, Boris Meissner, Dan Nelson, and Condoleezza Rice also helped my research. The National Library of Scotland and the Newcastle Polytechnic Library provided sources not available at ISEES. Thank you also to Mrs C. Tyler for compiling the index to this volume.

In personal terms, I must not forget the many other students at the

Institute and beyond. Amongst them, Richard Berry was of inestimable support, both in Glasgow and Budapest. Peter Anghelides also made an appearance in Glasgow, only this time he did not have to lend me his typewriter. A special mention must go to Susan Lamb, who entered my life early in the proceedings and has not yet left it. Whilst revising and updating the original research, Vicki Griffey provided unforgettable encouragement, and the Griffey-Rose attic unprecedented seclusion. Hello also to the Kirkby family for their continuing diversions during and after the revision, and to Liz for her own special contribution.

1 The Early Post-war Period

INTRODUCTION

It is not the purpose of this chapter to discuss the post-war years and the origins of the Cold War. Such aspects of the political and military division of Europe are amply covered elsewhere in the academic literature of both East and West. However, in their discussion of the origins of the Warsaw Treaty Organization (WTO), Soviet historians do briefly mention events prior to 1954–55. As an introduction to the analysis of the WTO proper, this chapter will outline how the Soviet literature introduces the topic of this thesis.

By comparison, the Central European literature does not really cover this period; the Czechoslovak writer Josef Urban, for example, goes straight into discussing the threat of German militarism as the origin of the WTO. The Central European analysis of the 30th Anniversary (see Chapter 5), unlike the Soviet analysis, again ignores any events prior to the perceived growing threat of anti-socialist imperialism and the need for the peace-loving states of Europe to defend their revolutionary gains with a political-military defensive alliance.

It is probable that the need to justify the roots of a multilateral socialist alliance is felt much more keenly by the USSR, if only for ideological and propaganda purposes, for the self-styled kudos of the first socialist state. The original claim was that the WTO was to be open for accession by any state, regardless of social or political system (see the Treaty text, Appendix 1; and Chapter 2). As this chapter shows, the USSR has since argued that the WTO was, rather, a natural progression for its members, and its members alone – in other words an example of the scientific materialist development of history. The assessments of historians, both East and West, is thus avoided, in favour of this 'more-political' analysis.

THE ROOTS PRIOR TO 1945

Grechko (1977, p. 326) argues that, 'The comradeship-in-arms among [the] armies of the fraternal countries dates back to the first years of Soviet power . . . [when] a quarter of a million fighter-internationalists' helped the Red Army against foreign intervention and the Civil War. In a book marking the 30th Anniversary of the Warsaw Treaty, Viktor Shkarovskii (1985, p. 10a) goes even further back in time, and claims that 'The basis of a military-political defensive co-operation of the fraternal countries of socialism was laid down by the Great October Socialist Revolution'.

Both these writers include lists of nationalities that helped in the battles of the young socialist state, but they are not quite the same. They both mention Hungarians, Poles, Serbs, Czechs, Slovaks, and Bulgarians (all, bar the Serbs, now active in the WTO), but then Grechko adds Finns, Chinese, Koreans, 'and representatives of many other peoples' while Shkarovskii adds Croats, Romanians 'and representatives of other peoples' – of whom only the Romanians are active in the WTO (Grechko, 1977, p. 326; Shkarovskii, 1985, p. 10a).

Such lists, of course, stress the contribution of the USSR's allies, but the inclusion of even other nationalities is presumably to show an international support for socialism. Why, though, should Grechko, one-time Commander-in-Chief of the WTO and Soviet Minister of Defence, omit to mention the Romanians? Was it a subtle snub at a time when the Romanians were asserting a measure of military independence? But in 1976 the Romanians had hosted a session of the WTO's Political Consultative Committee (PCC) that had significantly extended the formal political mechanisms of the Organization (see Chapter 3). The reasoning for Grechko's action must remain obscure.

As the next stage of co-operation, Grechko goes on to discuss the aid sent by both the USSR and the Soviet Party to revolutions that occurred in the inter-war years, citing Hungary, Mongolia, China, and the Spanish Civil War, as examples of international solidarity. As a much more fundamental example of military co-operation, Soviet writers excel in their treatment of the years of the Second World War, and the Soviet Union's role in this. For example:

> In the fire of battle against fascism took shape and was baptised the military-political co-operation of the Soviet people with the patriotic forces of a number of European countries. Together with the Soviet Army . . . (Shkarovskii, 1985, p. 10b)

Shkarovskii lists 'Yugoslavia, Poland, Czechoslovakia, patriots of Bulgaria, Albania, Romania, Hungary' as recipients of Soviet equipment and stores, and for whom 'The Soviet Union rendered great help' in the creation of their armies (p. 10b). For such a reason Shtemenko (1976) was able to claim that the WTO was 'A brotherhood, born in battle'.

The significance of these earliest years is explained by Shkarovskii

(p. 11b) when he writes about the defence of 'the gains of the Great October' and its role in the development of the world revolutionary processes (p. 11b). He also states that, 'The traditions of the armed friendship, born in the years of the Second World War, serve today the affairs of the training of the soldiers of the state-participants of the Warsaw Treaty' (ibid.).

THE END OF THE WARTIME ALLIANCE

The participation of the Soviet Union as an equal partner on the world arena during what it calls the Great Patriotic War seems to have had great importance for the Soviet leaders. According to one history of the WTO, this great wartime alliance could and should have been carried on into the post-war period, in order 'to channel the course of historical development towards peace and co-operation, and [to ensure] that mankind's centuries-old dream of eliminating wars and military conflicts from inter-state relations and from the life of society would finally come true' (*The Warsaw* . . . , p. 7). On this basis the Potsdam decisions were to be seen as the grounding for the continued co-operation of the 'states in the anti-Hitler coalition', in order that Germany would never again threaten the peace of Europe (ibid., pp. 7–8).

Such a future did not occur because, as is officially argued in Warsaw Treaty historiography, the imperialists did not want such a world. The West, led by the US Joint Staff, created 'aggressive military blocs' in Europe and around the world (Bakhov, 1971, p. 3) and began to work out plans 'for a preventive war against the USSR' (Zhilin *et al.*, 1984, p. 15). Rather than construct peace, the US military leadership sought to use the West's economic and human resources for its own aggressive aims (Bakhov, p. 3). This caused the 'objective necessity for the armed defence of the achievements of the socialist revolutions' in Europe (Zhilin *et al.*, p. 14).

THE CREATION OF 'ARMIES OF A NEW TYPE'

With the establishment of people's democracies in much of the Soviet zone of liberated Europe came the problem of the defence of those states. As the volume *Marxism–Leninism on War and Army* puts it, the new socialist armies were different from 'the armies of exploiter states' because of the 'class-historical laws' of 'historical purpose and moral make-up' that were behind them. This meant that 'in order to consolidate their power, to uphold their revolutionary gains and to defend the socialist country, the working class [had] to create powerful armed forces' (p. 167). In other words, maintaining defences against an imperialist threat defends 'the achievements of building socialism and communism, the freedom and independence of the socialist countries . . . ' (ibid., p. 168). Such developments in the armed forces, as with the establishment of a socialist state as such, are considered to be an expression of the general laws of the transition from capitalism to socialism (ibid., p. 169). The establishment of armed forces as 'an instrument of the socialist state of the whole people' thus results in an army of a new type. These armies are determined by social and historical laws and guided by a Marxist–Leninist ideology (ibid.).

Such deep social transformations of the post-war years led, according to Grechko (1977, p. 330) to the 1945–55 period being seen as the 'first stage' of development[1] where 'the countries which embarked on the socialist road almost completely solved the problem of forming national armies'. The problem had been that of forming 'armies of the dictatorship of the proletariat' (ibid., p. 331) – in other words, where they supported the new socio-political regimes, and guaranteed defence against a hostile imperialism. In practical terms, a multilateral alliance could not have been possible in this 'first stage' because, presumably, the armies did *not* support the new regimes. The confrontation with hostile imperialism was being maintained by the Soviet armed forces or by the groups of Soviet military advisers which arrived in Central Europe 'On the request of the governments of the fraternal countries and their armies' (Yakubovskii, 1975b, p. 63).

The main mechanism for securing the support of the armed forces for the new regimes seems to have been the development of officer corps loyal to the new political leaderships, generally by encouraging membership of the ruling parties and the promotion of politically-reliable officers. The quotation of figures showing the growth of this party membership features prominently in several of the writings on the WTO (e.g. Yakubovskii, 1975b, pp. 60–2; Shtemenko, 1976; Kulikov *et al.*, 1980b, p. 53). Kulikov, citing problems in Hungary, Romania, and Bulgaria in the eradication of 'anti-national elements' from the armed forces, concluded that 'To the end of the 1940s the communist and workers' parties completely secured for [themselves] the leadership of the armed forces' (ibid.). Yakubovskii (1975b, p. 60) explained that a major element in achieving this, and overcoming 'anti-popular conspiracies', was the activity of a party-political apparatus in the new armies, using the experience of the political work in the Soviet Army. In his discussion of the construction of the armies of the

European countries of the socialist community, Zhilin *et al.* (1984, p. 3), began by claiming that, 'The creation and strengthening of the armies of a new, socialist type is one of the important results of the activities of the Marxist–Leninist parties, and of the people of the socialist countries.'

The aim of this party work was, according to Kulikov *et al.* (1980b, p. 53) to help ensure the 'democratization of the army, and the conversion of it into the reliable instrument of the defence of the dictatorship of the proletariat.' where old customs had to be broken, the army and the people drawn together, the mood of the officers and men brought round to the socialist revolution; the communist staff [*komsostava*] was purified of enemies and fellow-travellers.

Grechko (1977, p. 330) explained what the new military type amounted to: 'the fundamental principles of their construction were the same: community of political aims and tasks, Marxist–Leninist ideology, and . . . the interests of the people and the army, and the principles of organizing political education and training of the armed forces.' The Soviet Union was credited with giving much material and training aid to this process (ibid., p. 331). Kulikov *et al.* (1980b, p. 56), explained that it was on 'the request of the governments of the fraternal countries' that Soviet military advisers arrived in their armies, giving weapons experience, helping to master new military techniques, reorganize military structures and institute military and political training. He concluded that 'The effectiveness of the Soviet military aid above all brought about the firm decisions of the leaderships of the fraternal communist and workers' parties to construct their armed forces according to the experience of the Soviet Army' (ibid.). This suggests that the post-war Soviet leadership was satisfied with developing a string of national armies in Central Europe. Either it did not want or could not attain a collective socialist army. Were the Soviet advisers sufficient to ensure whatever military might would prove necessary? Or did the Soviet leadership consider that national armies could better rally each nation to its new political leaderships?

THE CONCLUSION OF THE NETWORK OF BILATERAL TREATIES

The 'first stage' of military construction was also the period when the network of bilateral treaties was established, the only formal system of military alliance of the Stalin era. (For a fuller discussion of the bilateral treaties, see Appendix 4.) Bakhov (1971) explains that these treaties were signed by the socialist countries 'in the interest of guaranteeing their security' (p. 4), though security mainly against 'the rebirth of German imperialism and the repetition of German . . . aggression' (pp. 4–5). Bakhov compares them to the wartime Anglo-Soviet and Franco-Soviet treaties (p. 4) – (which were ceremoniously revoked by the Soviet Union in 1955, after the ratification of the Paris Agreements of 1954 – see Chapter 2 on the specific origins of the WTO). Writing only four years later, Yakubovskii (1975b, p. 62), in a book originating from the WTO Joint Staff (according to the publishing and production notes), argued that the rôle of the bilateral treaties was for security of the socialist community in the face of the wider aggression of international imperialism .

In practice, the bilateral treaties became the justification, if not the mechanism, for measures of mutual military assistance, and consultation and co-ordination of defensive capacities – activities which were later developed and co-ordinated in relation to the Warsaw Treaty (see *Marxism–Leninism* . . . , p. 171). This seems to confirm a general progression, a stage-by-stage development, of the Soviet Union binding its allies into a political-military alliance.

THE POLITICS OF THE POST-WAR YEARS

In popular western political and media presentation, the post-war years and the establishment of people's democracies resulted in a uniform political, economic, and social system in a Central Europe in thrall to the Soviet Union and above all to the personality of Stalin. Views expressed by Central European academics[N] recently, and with hindsight, totally rejected such an interpretation. These views should be treated with circumspection, but they seem to confirm that the 1945–55 period was one of bilateral links, and not just in military terms, between individual states and the Soviet Union. They argue that there was in fact a marked differentiation in the Soviet Union's links with each state. The main factors determining these relations were whether or not the Central European state was a 'winner' or 'loser' in the war, the strengths of the national ruling party and of popular feelings or antipathy to the Soviet Union, the existing industrial level, and the intensity of Soviet occupation. Cultural, political, geographic, and internal factors all had an influence.

The Soviet Union itself must not be seen as monolithic or uniform, since factionalism is to be found in all aspects of its political system.[2] The death of Stalin can be seen as a major influence on the foreign policy of the region. Internal Soviet debates covered not just attitudes towards Central Europe, and Germany in particular, but also economic factors and their influence on the conventional or nuclear military balance. It is still being suggested by some Central Europeans[N] that the internal Soviet factionalism after Stalin's death even included debate over whether or not to reduce the USSR's hold over Central Europe. It may even have been made effectively neutral in exchange for a reduction of US influence in Europe and a general rapprochement all round (ibid.).

The move to a broader and multilateral alliance through the Warsaw Treaty is not to be seen as such a marked change or innovation, even within the post-Stalin context. There had been a move towards greater military cohesion from 1951, as a response to the superpower confrontation in Korea. Military spending and construction increased as part of a greater integration of foreign policy. By the early 1950s, the Soviet Union had realized that it had lost the Cold War and would lose its traditional predominance in the European conventional military balance, and there would be an inexorable growth of the western part of Europe.[3]

According to this analysis, the creation of the Warsaw Treaty Organization did not in itself change anything in *military* terms. In East–West political terms it could have been a symbol of the new policy, an image to raise the conventional confrontation. At the moment of founding, the WTO was just 'a fiction'.[N] It could have been seen as no more than another aspect of the internal Soviet factionalism, dependent more on Khrushchev's line of the moment than its inherent political or military utility. It was, at this level, a factor of a superpower, not European, politics.

In superpower terms, official Soviet writers on the WTO generally chart public actions by western leaders, such as Winston Churchill's iron curtain speech, the Marshall Plan, the creation of the Brussels Treaty Organization, the establishment of NATO and the accession to it of Greece and Turkey, and the creation of the ANZUS ('Australia, New Zealand, US') alliance, the South East Asia Treaty Organization, and the Baghdad Pact (see, e.g., Bakhov, 1971, p. 3; Grechko, 1977, p. 332; Zhilin *et al.*, 1984, p. 15). Having faced this threat with no more than the bilateral treaties and the Stalinist military hegemony over Central Europe, it took, in the early post-Stalin period, the single continuing issue of the division of Germany and the new moves towards the rearmament of West Germany, to produce the formal establishment of the Warsaw Treaty.

2 The Specific Origins of the Warsaw Treaty

INTRODUCTION

The Warsaw Treaty explicity states that it was formed on 14 May 1955 as a response to the so-called Paris Agreements of nine Western powers (of 23 October 1954). Among other things, West Germany was remilitarized and integrated into NATO, through the formation of the Western European Union (WEU – as a successor to the Brussels Treaty Organization of 1948) military alliance.

The Preamble to the Warsaw Treaty states that the ultimate aim is

> to create a system of collective security in Europe based on the participation of all European states, irrespective of their social and political structure, whereby the said states may be enabled to combine their efforts in the interests of ensuring peace in Europe . . . (see Appendix 1)

The seven signatory states claimed that the Paris Agreements had created a new situation. Describing themselves as the peaceable European states, they claimed that such moves in the West warranted their taking 'the necessary steps to safeguard their security and to promote the maintenance of peace in Europe' as described in the Treaty.

This places the formation of an East-bloc multilateral political-military alliance within the ideological East–West confrontation and what amounts to the Cold War. The Treaty is specifically linked to the issue of Germany, politically still under zonal division.

THE GERMAN QUESTION AND EUROPEAN SECURITY

In the absence of a post-war treaty, Germany was still divided in accordance with the wartime conferences. The German administrations were still not given full autonomy or sovereignty. The Four Powers were putatively still attempting to agree on a scheme that would unite Germany under one independent government. The Potsdam Conference of 1945 had agreed an Allied Attitude to Germany that had specified that

> the Allies will take in agreement together, now and in the future, the . . . measures necessary to assure that Germany will never again threaten her neighbours or the peace of the world . . . It is their intention that the German people be given the opportunity to prepare for the eventual reconstruction of their life on a democratic and peaceful basis. If their own efforts are steadily directed to this end, it will be possible for them in due course to take their place among the free and peaceful peoples of the world. (*Keesings* 7361A, p. 7362)

Germany was to have been treated as a single economic unit, with parallel political development in the four occupation zones (Banks *et al.*, 1985 p. 180a,b).

It is not the purpose of this book to participate in the historiography of the Cold War, and argue which events and actions on which side led to the failure, by the 1950s, of the implementation of the unspecific, unfocused particulars of the Potsdam Accords. Even taking into account that the two sides may or may not have usefully been adhering to the formal ties of a united Germany, their ultimate purposes may have been different. On the Eastern side, a Soviet-style system of administration, including a reorganized form of district and local government, with a revised judicial system and collectivized agriculture, had been introduced in 1952; the USSR 'announced the attainment of full sovereignty by the GDR on March 25, 1954' (ibid., p. 181b).

On the other side, the three Western powers had agreed on a scheme that would give West Germany limited military forces, involved in the proposed European Defence Community (EDC), in a Treaty signed in Paris on 27 May 1952. The EDC included a proposal for a European Army in which West German troops would be involved. There was to be a European Defence Minister as a solution to the problem of rearming West Germany, and so it was to be 'a European solution to the question of Germany's contribution to the organization of European defence' (*Keesings* 11037A). The USSR had from the outset objected to such a Western military alliance, and in particular to the West German involvement in it. The USSR's prime concern was the resurgence of German militarism which, at least from the point of view of an armed West Germany, it saw as a major threat to Soviet security.

On 25 January 1954, at the opening of the Berlin Conference of Foreign Ministers, convened after a long period of stalemate without negotiation between the four powers, Soviet Foreign Minister Molotov stated that:

> The reunion of Germany and the creation of an all-German Government is indissolubly bound up with the question of whether a united Germany is going to be a peaceful democratic state or whether it once more becomes a militarised and aggressive state. (*Keesings* 13434)

Molotov went on to object to the EDC as 'a military bloc of European countries directed against other European states', and argued that such an action would make German reunification impossible (ibid.).

The Soviet Union saw any European military grouping from which it was excluded as anti-Soviet, claiming that divisive military blocs were adding to international tensions and heralding a new European war. It also claimed that observance of the Potsdam Accords would be a satisfactory basis for the solution of the German question. During the discussions on Germany at the Berlin Conference, Molotov repeated the Soviet assertion that NATO was responsible for the division of Europe, and rejected Western offers of guarantees to the USSR that German militarism would not be revived (ibid., 13437).

To the USSR, German militarism seemed to mean a West German military force (East Germany had a Soviet-controlled paramilitary police force), especially if it was included in a mutual defence agreement of restricted membership. Molotov put forward proposals during the Berlin Conference (10 February 1954) for a Programme for Germany and a European Security Pact, which amounted to a pan-European collective security system that would control any German military resurgence. This would lead the way to German reunification. In his closing speech (18 February 1954), he said that: 'During the discussion of the German problem we all stated that the settlement of this [German] question was inseparably bound up with safeguarding security in Europe' (*SWB* SU/495, 22 February 1954).

In other words, there could be no post-war settlement, no peace treaty, without a solution to the German problem, which in itself could not be resolved without a long-term rapprochement between East and West, or even an end to the Cold War. To the USSR, security was paramount; security meant a system of collective security, proposed at Berlin as a Draft General Treaty on Collective Security in Europe. This would involve limits or controls to the military structure of a unified German state, a state which the USSR would only then be willing to countenance. The USSR had fought against Nazi Germany with the Western allies, and was therefore seeking a role in a post-war security system involving Germany.

That the German issue was paramount to Soviet foreign policy can be seen from the fact that, although the Berlin Conference discussed Germany, Austria, and European security, and reached agreement to hold talks in Geneva to settle the Korean dispute, the BBC's *Summary of World Broadcasts* noted that the great bulk of Soviet commentary 'dealt with the German question – and, in particular, with the proposals put forward by Molotov on 10th February' (*SWB* SU/494, 19 February 1954).

SOVIET SECURITY CONCERNS IN 1954

The two Soviet concerns that continued throughout the period were thus European security in general, and a guarantee against the remilitarization of Germany in particular. Soviet leaders expressed concern at any aspect of international affairs which they felt had a bearing on these issues.

On 31 March 1954, the Soviet Government sent a Note to the Governments of France, Britain, and the United States, which in general reiterated Soviet proposals to establish a general European system of collective security, and reiterated concern against the EDC and German militarism. The Note concluded:

> The position of the Soviet Government as regards the North Atlantic Treaty is well known. The Government of the USSR has not shared and cannot share at the present time, the point of view that this treaty is of a defensive character. In this, the Soviet Government proceeds from the fact that the North Atlantic Treaty creates an exclusive grouping of states, ignores the task of preventing new German aggression and, since of the great powers which belonged to the anti-Hitler coalition only the Soviet Union is not participating in this treaty, the North Atlantic Treaty cannot but be regarded as an aggressive treaty, directed against the Soviet Union.
>
> It is perfectly obvious that in appropriate circumstances the North Atlantic Treaty Organization could lose its aggressive nature, provided that all the great powers which belonged to the anti-Hitler coalition become parties to it. In accordance with this . . . the Soviet Government expresses its readiness to examine, together with the governments concerned, the question of the Soviet Union's participation in the North Atlantic Treaty. (*Pravda*, 1 April 1954)

It is interesting that the Soviet Union waited for five years before applying for membership of NATO, but to do so was part of its renewed drive on the issues of European security and the question of Germany, precipitated by the proposed EDC. The Note indicates how the USSR sought to transform the Western concept of security (armed defence of a limited number of states united on ideological grounds), into its own version of big power alliance and policing. (One wonders if the USSR would have encouraged the future members of the Warsaw Treaty to apply for membership of NATO at a later date.) When, on 7 May 1954, NATO rejected the Soviet application, the USSR claimed proof that NATO was 'a closed military group of an aggressive character aimed against the Soviet Union' (*SWB* SU/508, 9 April 1954). It continued to press for its preferred version of security, a collective treaty guaranteeing the non-militarization of Germany. In a further Note, dated 24 July 1954, to Britain, France, and the United States, again opposing closed military groupings (and naming NATO and the EDC), the Soviet Government proposed that a conference be convened for European countries and the USA to 'exchange views' on 'the question of setting up a system of collective security in Europe' (*Pravda*, 25 July 1954.).

The *Summary of World Broadcasts* noted that European security was the most extensively treated topic in Soviet foreign policy output during the summer of 1954, centring on German militarism and the EDC (*SWB*, SU/545, 16 August 1954).

On 29 August 1954 the French Parliament, for internal reasons, rejected ratification of the EDC Treaty, and threw the whole West European defence policy into disarray. Both before and after this event the Soviet Union's policy was to promote its own concept of European security. Prior to the French action the USSR was calling for the EDC to be scrapped;[1] afterwards it was counselling against any new move to replace the EDC, and a statement was released from the Soviet Foreign Ministry on 9 September to this effect. Paragraph 14 of this noted plans for West Germany to join NATO directly. After pointing to Western silence on Soviet proposals to convene a Four-Power conference to discuss the German question [cf. the 24 July note discussed above] (para. 18), the statement concluded that 'The interests of safeguarding general European security demand that a system of collective security with the participation of all European countries irrespective of their social systems should be established instead of building closed military alignments in Europe' (*SWB* SU/553, 13 September 1954).

In other words, the USSR was once again stressing its policy of a pan-European security system as the basis of international relations, going on to call for a general European conference to examine appropriate proposals. Within a few days, after visits by both Sir Anthony Eden of Britain and John Foster Dulles of the USA to Bonn, the USSR was objecting not only to a proposed integration of West Germany into NATO, but also to the proposal to integrate West Germany into the Brussels Treaty Organization, an alliance which it saw as overtly against German aggression but covertly anti-Soviet (*SWB* SU/555, 20 September 1954).

THE LONDON NINE-POWER CONFERENCE, 28 SEPTEMBER–3 OCTOBER 1954

The Paris Agreements which were cited in the Preamble to the Warsaw Treaty were the endorsement of a set of wide-ranging documents embodied in a Final Act, agreed on by the foreign ministers of the same states at an earlier London Conference.[2]

The scope of the London conference broadly covered various aspects of the Western approach to European security. When the signatories spoke of European unification they were limiting themselves to the area understood as West Europe. The conference made six recommendations. First of all it proposed ending the occupation status of West Germany; it also proposed that West Germany and Italy join the Brussels Treaty Organization (the statement included a West German declaration undertaking not to manufacture atomic, biological, or chemical weapons). Thirdly Britain, the USA, and Canada declared their support for European unity and the maintenance of their military forces in Europe. A declaration was included recommending West German accession to NATO and also covering the future deployment of NATO forces in Europe. Fifthly, West Germany promised to conduct its policies in accordance with the UN Charter, renouncing the use of force to achieve German reunification or the changing of its frontiers, while Britain, France, and the USA attached a declaration defining their relationship with the German Federal Republic. Finally came a declaration announcing that the detailed agreements to implement the provisions of the London Conference would be worked out by the respective governments and submitted for the approval of the North Atlantic Council [i.e., NATO] (*Keesings* 13809).

> [The London conference declared that it had] dealt with the most important issues facing the Western World – security and European integration within the framework of a developing Atlantic community dedicated to peace and freedom . . . [it had] considered how to assure

> the full association of the German Federal Republic within the West, and the German defence contribution . . . (Ibid.)

Thus the explicit aim of the London Conference was to cement the West European political and military bloc, which had as its pretext the common defence through NATO, an organization that had a restrictive membership which, at least by implication, placed it in opposition to the Soviet bloc. The conclusion of the London Final Act explicitly stated that the agreements and arrangements were to 'reinforce the Atlantic community' in the interests of 'world peace' (ibid.).

The USSR continued to object both to the plans to rearm West Germany and the effect the London decisions would have on European security. Commenting on the conclusion of the Conference, the Soviet Union rejected the controls and guarantees against West German militarism that the agreements promised, and saw the threat of a German 'aggressive military grouping' (*SWB* SU/560, 8 October 1954). The USSR continued to lobby for the adoption of the position it had expressed at the Berlin Conference, its call for a pan-European security system that would neutralize the German military structure. In objecting to the divisive moves by the West and preferring its own solution, 'Moscow continued to devote a very substantial proportion of its output to a detailed consideration of the various problems connected with European security – particularly that of German rearmament' (ibid., SU/562, 15 October 1954). In this way, the Soviet response to the events in the West continued along the same path that it had taken for several years without managing to alter the West's position.

THE PARIS CONFERENCE, 20–23 OCTOBER 1954

The Foreign Ministers of the states which had convened in London met again in Paris, and confirmed their previous recommendations. They agreed to end the occupation status of West Germany, modified the Brussels Treaty Organization to be a general defence forum (rather than being anti-German) called the Western European Union (WEU). West Germany and Italy were invited to join. In conjunction with the 14 NATO powers they invited West Germany to join NATO, and agreed on measures for the further strengthening of the NATO structure (*Keesings* 13850) A month later they revealed that they had also agreed on 'a convention on the presence of foreign forces in the German Federal Republic' (ibid., 13869) which converted the post-war occupation forces into mutual defence forces.

Both the termination of the Occupation Regime and the establishment of the WEU referred to the EDC proposals as being the basis of the agreements, highlighting the fact that the Paris Agreements were a continuation of the 1952 policies for Western defence, and were in fact a response to the French Parliament's rejection of that scheme. Thus despite all the lobbying and representations of the USSR, its preferred action of a pan-European collective security system was once again being ignored and rebuffed. The West was not interested even in talking about these proposals. It had a concept of security incompatible with that of the USSR. The Final Act of the London Conference, endorsed and implemented (subject to ratification) by the Paris Conference, was a development of the 1952 proposals envisaging a European Defence Community, but took no consideration of Soviet views of its own post-war defence and security needs. The Soviet view of the Paris Conference was that it was the same as the 1952 proposals for the 'militarisation of Western Germany and the permanent occupation of that part of the country' (*SWB* SU/566, 29 October 1954).

On 23 October 1954, the USSR issued another Note to Britain, France, and the United States, on opposition to the agreements of the London and Paris Conferences, but limiting its concern to the role of Germany in European defence arrangements, and including a call for their attendance at a Conference to be held in Moscow in November of that year (*Pravda*, 24 October 1954). Once again the USSR was using tried and failed techniques to influence the West. It was this limited response that dominated Soviet objections to the agreements. While considering that the end to the occupation of West Germany was spurious since the agreements also permitted troops to remain on German soil as allies, the USSR did not seem to object to Italian inclusion in the WEU, even though Italy had been an ally of Nazi Germany. Though the USSR was itself party to the UN Charter, it claimed that it could not trust West German adherence to Article 2 (peaceful settlement of disputes) (ibid.).

SOVIET EUROPEAN POLICY, NOVEMBER 1954

During the celebrations for the October Revolution, Soviet Presidium (Politburo) member Maksim Zakharovich Saburov made a speech with a section detailing the Soviet foreign policy positions on a number of issues. The overall call for peaceful co-existence and co-operation between socialists and capitalists to their mutual advantage was repeated. The London and Paris Nine-Power Agreements were specifically dealt with, reiterating Soviet objections to the perceived Western 'positions of strength' policy, which was seen to be characterized by the organization of aggressive miltary blocs directed against the USSR. In particular, Saburov spoke out against the arming of 'revenge-seeking forces' in Germany, who would be 'resurrecting German militarism'. This action was seen to be particularly objectionable, since the USSR considered that extant agreements between the Soviet Union and France, Britain, and the United States, were supposed to prevent the resurgence of German militarism. West Germany was seen to be militarized, and given access, through the London and Paris agreements, to nuclear weapons (*SWB*, SU/570, 12 November 1954). Saburov concluded that there was a need for a collective security system in Europe (ibid.).

The reference to German possession of nuclear weapons is interesting, since Annex 1 of the London Final Act, a statement covering German and Italian accession to the Brussels Treaty Organization, 'included a declaration under which the German Federal Republic undertook not to manufacture any atomic, biological, or chemical weapons' (*Keesings* 13809). This commitment was specifically reaffirmed in Protocol II of the Paris Agreements relating to the conversion of the Brussels Treaty Organization into the Western European Union (ibid., 13871).

However, at a later date, in a Note to various European governments[3] dated 13 January 1955, the USSR argued that:

> The Paris Agreements provide that the member-countries of the Western European military alliance shall conduct preparations for chemical and bacteriological warfare, accumulating stocks of chemical, bacteriological, and atomic weapons and using them in the armaments of their armies.
>
> The Soviet Government considers it its duty to issue in warning, in particular, that the Paris Agreements give chemical and bacteriological weapons, alongside atomic weapons, to the West German Army whose establishment is stipulated by these agreements. (*Pravda*, 14 January 1955)

Although confusing, the wording in this instance could be said to argue that the West German army would have access to such weapons *by association*. In other words, the USSR may have been objecting to West German involvement in military alliances (the WEU or NATO) which included nuclear powers. It could be argued that this was just another aspect of Soviet objections to the remilitarization of the western part of Germany, which was central to its European security policy.[4]

The Soviet Union was well informed as to the proceedings and decisions of both the London and Paris Conferences (see, for example, *SWB* SU/565, 25 October 1954). It must have been well-versed in the wordings of the West German renunciation of nuclear and mass destruction weapons. Therefore either the USSR did not give due credence to such a declaration, or chose to ignore it for propaganda purposes, both internally (as in the case of Saburov's speech) or externally.

THE SOVIET NOTE AND THE MOSCOW CONFERENCE, NOVEMBER 1954

The Soviet Union dealt with the German Question and European security yet again in a Note dated 13 November 1954,[5] which was much less compromising in its language concerning the Western defence systems.

Taking as its starting-point the London and Paris Agreements, the USSR expanded on its view that West Germany was being dangerously militarized within exclusive alliances 'of certain states pitted against other European states' (*Pravda*, 14 November 1954).

> All this testifies that a policy is being pursued towards Western Germany which is incompatible both with the promotion of peace in Europe and with the national reunification of Germany. The carrying out of the London and Paris Agreements will mean that the reunification of Germany through free all-German elections is sacrificed to the present plans of resurrecting German militarism, that mortal enemy of the nations of Europe, including the German nation itself. (Ibid.)

Once again the USSR proposed solving the German problem by means of a system of collective European security. Also contained in the Note were two threats.

The first was the claim that the London and Paris Agreements were incompatible with previous treaty commitments against German aggression, as had been suggested during the October Revolution celebrations. The Note referred specifically to the 1942 Anglo-Soviet Treaty of Collaboration and Mutual Assistance, and the 1944 Franco-Soviet Treaty of Alliance and Mutual Assistance. It implied once again that since the USSR saw France, Britain, and the USA as having complicity in the remilitarization of Germany, the need for action in line with the formal war-time ties.

The main threat was towards the end of the Note. Reiterating that the London and Paris plans 'cannot but complicate the system in Europe' by leading to an arms race and strained international relations, the Note declared that, 'It will therefore be quite natural if the peace-loving European nations find themselves obliged to adopt new measures for safeguarding their security' (ibid.). The term new measures for the peace-loving European states would often recur, including in the formal declarations surrounding the Warsaw Treaty.

The object of the Note was to announce that, due to the issues raised, the Soviet Government was convening a conference to be held in Moscow from November 29, 'to consider the establishment of a European system of collective security' (ibid.).[6]

Such a conference had been referred to in the Soviet Note of 23 October 1954 (see above) to Britain, France, and the USA, which had been the first response to the Paris declaration, but the USSR had not openly pursued the idea immediately. The *Summary of World Broadcasts* noted again that the main preoccupation of the USSR's media output was European security after the London and Paris Conferences, and 'the fallacy of the Western Powers' reasoning that East–West negotiations could profitably be held after ratification' of those Agreements (*SWB* SU/572, 19 November 1954).

Did the Soviet Union truly believe that the West would attend a conference explicitly geared towards a policy that had already been rejected by the West? In view of the aggressive wording in the publicized replies from the future signatories of the Warsaw Treaty, it seems that the USSR was, in sending the invitation to the West, merely keeping up the public façade of its preferred policy of being an innocently maligned participant on the European stage. Even taking into account that the West handed in their notes of non-attendance on the day the Conference opened, the tone of the speeches at the Moscow Conference, and the resolutions agreed to there, that must have been written and arranged before the event, indicated that the Conference of European Countries for Safeguarding Peace and Security in Europe was conceived of and carried out as an East-bloc riposte to the London and Paris Conferences. The USSR cannot have believed that the West would accept the Soviet proposals on Germany and European security as proposed by Molotov at the Berlin Conference of Foreign Ministers ten months before. However, even after the event, Bakhov (1971, p. 5) argued that this non-attendance was evidence that 'The imperialist states refused to co-operate with the socialist countries in the cause of the organization of a system of all-European security'.

The Moscow Conference was attended by the eight Soviet-bloc countries which eventually signed the Warsaw Treaty, with an observer from the People's Republic of China. The tone and scope of the gathering was set by Molotov, as head of the Soviet delegation, in his introductory speech:

> The fact should not be lost sight of that the aggressive elements in certain countries well known to all, are resorting to every means of pressure to expedite the remilitarization of Western Germany and its inclusion in their imperialist military alignments. This being the case, the peace-loving countries cannot confine themselves to the measures hitherto taken by them to safeguard their peace and security. (*Pravda*, 30 November 1954)

The Soviet Union, in objecting to the Paris Agreements, had evidently decided that there was no chance of causing the West's defence policies to be amended or scrapped. The various states present were already linked by the network of bilateral defence treaties originating in the early post-war years, which Soviet defence policy had until then considered to be a sufficient safeguard. The new measures were thus to go beyond this.

Molotov outlined the proposed new measures in his introductory statement, also given on 29 November. The peaceful states would have to 'cement their forces and strengthen them considerably' if the Paris Agreements were ratified. They would take 'joint measures in the sphere of the organization of their armed forces and their command, as well as other measures' in order to guarantee their peaceful labour and their frontiers against possible aggression (ibid.).

This implies that the USSR had already decided on some form of multilateral alliance incorporating joint armed forces and a joint command. Molotov had stated on 25 January 1954, in his opening address to the Berlin Conference of Foreign Ministers, that the creation of a European army through the EDC 'may lead to the creation of a defensive alliance of other European countries for the purpose of safeguarding their security' (*Keesings* 13434), but the Moscow Conference, following the collapse of the EDC project and the formation of the Paris Agreements, was the first overt move that the USSR had taken to implement such a view. The threat at Berlin does not seem to have been raised again within the Four-Power talks, and was not raised again in all the earlier propaganda and lobbying against the London and Paris Agreements. The Note of 13 November 1954, being sent also to the Western powers, had only mentioned the discussion of a European collective security system. At Berlin, Molotov had claimed that only if an Eastern bloc was set up would 'the countries of Europe be split into two opposing military groupings of states . . . ' (ibid.), implying that he did not consider the bilteral treaty network as a military bloc; the Moscow Conference, in anticipating the conclusion of just such a bloc system, could not then in reality have been pursuing the Soviet policy of a collective security system, unless both sides were giving limited delineations of Europe.

The *Summary of World Broadcasts*, in commenting on the non-Soviet speeches at the Moscow Conference, wrote:

> [They] followed a set pattern. All stressed their people's will to peace, the dangers of German militarism as demonstrated by historic precedent, the worthlessness of Western 'guarantees', the need for a European collective security system as proposed by the Soviet Union, the possibility of general European co-operation only if the West abandoned the policy of rearming Germany, and the intention – embodied in the [final] Declaration – to take joint defensive counter-measures in the event of ratification [of the Paris Agreements]. (*SWB* SU/577, 6 December 1954)

The Statement by Hungarian premier András Hegedüs, for example,[7] thanked the Soviet Union for convening the Conference (Hegedüs, 1955, p. 15), and endorsed the Soviet Union's draft European collective security pact, which he said would lead to a peaceful solution to the German question (ibid.). The USA and 'responsible quarters in England [*sic*] and France' were, through the Paris Agreements, acting 'to prolong bellicose tension' (ibid., p. 16).

Hegedüs effectively endorsed a division of Europe, by justifying Hungary's alignment with 'the Soviet people and with other fraternal peoples who have given the Hungarian people a helping hand since liberation, assisting them in their progress' (ibid., p. 19). In several extended passages of diatribe against West Germany, he justified this foreign policy, and its endorsement of the Soviet proposals, on the grounds of Hungary's historic 'experience of German militarism' (ibid., pp. 16–18, 20–1). The ultimate aim was to permit peaceful economic construction in Europe (ibid., p. 22–3).

Perhaps drawing on Hungary's own historic experience rather than the specific issue of the Conference, Hegedüs also mentioned that 'A peaceful solution to the Austrian question within the system of European collective security is another vital point of interest for the Hungarian people' (ibid., p. 23). Overall, however, 'The Hungarian Government delegation fully endorses and accepts Comrade Molotov's analysis of the European situation . . . ' (ibid., p. 24). This underlines the point that, certainly in the early years of the WTO, the Central European countries had no autonomous foreign policy role.

The concluding Declaration from the Moscow meeting, dated 2 December 1954, reiterated the call for collective European security. It confirmed the threat, in Molotov's opening statement, that the ratification of the Paris Agreements would lead to East-bloc countermeasures, which were justified as self-defence under the UN Charter (*Pravda*, 3 December 1954). It could be argued, then, that the Moscow Conference and Declaration indicate the first formal, or at least overt, start to the process that led to the signing of the Warsaw Treaty five and a half months later.[8]

On 9 December 1954, the Soviet Government issued a further Note, addressed to the British, French, and US Governments, expressing regret at their non-attendance at the Moscow Conference, and reiterating concern over the Paris Agreements (*Pravda*, 10 December 1954). No mention was made of the other Western states invited to attend. While the French note of refusal (which was almost identical to the British and US notes) had been reprinted in full in the Soviet press on 2 December, there was likewise no mention of what responses to the invitation and to Soviet concern had been made by the other Western states.

THE WARTIME TREATIES

A further example of the finality of the Soviet reactions to the Paris Agreements can be seen in the treatment given to the wartime Anglo-Soviet and Franco-Soviet Treaties. During the October Revolution celebrations (see above), it had been stated that the USSR saw French, British, and US actions on the rearming of West Germany as contrary to their wartime commitments against German aggression. The Soviet Note of 13 November 1954 (see above) had specifically mentioned the Anglo-Soviet Treaty of 1942 and the Franco-Soviet Treaty of 1944.

From just after the Moscow Conference through to May 1955, the Soviet press gave blow-by-blow details of Soviet Government notes and Western responses on the question of the Paris Agreements and the wartime treaties. The Soviet press then gave blow-by-blow details of the various state commissions and bodies that considered and approved the annulment of the wartime treaties, culminating in a Decree from the Presidium of the Supreme Soviet of 7 May 1955 (*Pravda*, 8 May 1955). The justification for such a move was argued in a *Pravda* editorial. Discussing the Paris Agreements, it stated that: 'One cannot fail to see that the revival of German militarism would create a new situation in Europe and change the existing position of Britain and France: instead of allies of the USSR these powers are becoming the allies of German militarism' (*Pravda*, 10 April 1955).

Once again, the whole basis of Soviet foreign policy was the German question. Italy was being invited to join NATO and the WEU, Hungary and Romania had also been allies of Nazi Germany, but the Soviet Union was not objecting these countries being involved in military alliances. It would seem that the chain of events leading up to the formation of the Warsaw Treaty was dependent on Soviet policy towards Germany.

THE WARSAW CONFERENCE

The USSR Ministry of Foreign Affairs issued the following statement:

> Consultations with regard to the conclusion of a treaty of friendship, co-operation, and mutual assistance between the eight countries which participated in the Moscow Conference have taken place recently between the governments . . . (*Pravda*, 22 March 1955)

This appears to be the first public intimation that the new measures for joint defence would take the form of a multilateral treaty. The statement had an opt-out, in that the proposed treaty would be formed 'in the event of ratification of the Paris Agreements' (ibid.). In the event, those Agreements were fully ratified early in April 1955.

Following further consultations, a communique was issued on 3 May 1955 announcing the convocation of a second Conference of European Countries for Safeguarding Peace and Security in Europe, to be attended by the 'State-participants of the Moscow Declaration of December 2, 1954' (*Pravda*, 3 May 1955). The limitation on the countries associated with the further conference indicates that no others had seen the light or been influenced by the Soviet politicking with its notes, statements, and so on, concerning European security and the German problem. The Cold War division of Europe remained intact. The communique also stated that the consultations leading to the second conference had concurred the conclusion of a treaty, and also the 'organization of a joint command' for the participants in the proposed treaty (ibid.). The justification for such a move was that the Paris Agreements had been ratified.

This second conference was to be held in Warsaw, and thus the first and only multilateral treaty limited to and binding together the Soviet bloc was to become the Warsaw Treaty. Why Warsaw? After all, the process began with a Moscow conference. Why did the USSR wish to associate such an alliance with Poland? Certainly Poland has primary geostrategic importance as the main historic route for invasions of Russia and the USSR, and in modern terms Poland has the largest non-Soviet military force within the WTO. But in terms of 1955 the choice was curious. Perhaps the USSR wished to emphasize that the measures were to be seen as definitely European, even though it was obvious that the non-Soviet participants were merely agreeing with the Soviet line throughout. This is all mere speculation.

N. A. Bulganin, the new Soviet Prime Minister, headed the Soviet delegation rather than Foreign Minister Molotov, who had been the chief representative at the Moscow Conference.[10] While the various notes and so on leading up to the Warsaw Conference had been restricted in general to European security, Bulganin's opening statement placed the proposed founding of a new European military alliance in the context of Soviet worldwide policies, citing international tensions throughout Europe, the Near and Middle East, the Far East, Asia, and Africa. He argued that the aggressive rearming of West Germany was just one more example of the US-inspired Western positions of strength policy that sought to encircle the Soviet bloc with military bases and alliances (*Pravda*, 12 May 1955). The bulk of the speech was still concerned with the Paris Agreements, the call for a European collective security system, and the fact that the Moscow Conference and its ensuing discussions, with the proposed military alliance, were broadening the co-operation of the socialist states to include the sphere of joint defence. The general Soviet justification was that the climate of international relations, in its broadest senses, demanded that a multilateral defence alliance be formed – 'The treaty of friendship, co-operation and mutual assistance, for the conclusion of which the conference was meeting in Warsaw, was to serve the aim of safeguarding security' (ibid.).

The main Soviet reasoning remained: Bulganin's opening speech once again reiterated the Soviet view that a remilitarized Germany was a threat to Europe and the Soviet Union, and that 'the remilitarization constituted the chief obstacle to the restoration of Germany's national unity on peace-loving and democratic principles' (ibid.). The founding of the Warsaw Treaty put the seal on the post-war division of Germany, giving a Soviet de facto acceptance of the Western move to militarize its own sector.

As with the Moscow Conference, the speeches and proceedings were standardized. The communique of the fourth and final session of the Warsaw Conference stated that 'The meeting examined, paragraph by paragraph, the Treaty . . . All the delegations of the states represented at the conference declared their agreement with the text of this treaty' (*Pravda*, 14 May 1955). This session also 'adopted a decision to form a joint command of the armed forces of the state-participants to the treaty' (ibid.). The Treaty was formally signed on May 14, along with the resolution for the creation of a Joint Command. The states ratified the Treaty, and it came into force on 4 June 1955.

Krasnaya Zvezda, on 15 May 1955, covered the conclusion of the Treaty with the title 'Reliable basis for the guaranteeing of the security of the peaceloving states' above the text of the final communique and a photograph of Bulganin signing the Treaty, all on page one. After placing on page two the texts of the Treaty and the resolution creating the Joint Command, plus a report of the ceremonial dinner that followed, page three had an article ('Meeting in Warsaw') which claimed that '200 000 workers of the capital's enterprises, representatives of communal organizations, activists of science, culture, and the arts' had gathered in Felix Dzerzhinskii Square, and spontaneously applauded the chief delegates and leaders of the Polish United Workers' Party involved in the Warsaw Conference, with the flags of the allies adorning the rostrum. Such an ecstatic welcome (if it did in fact take place) seems somewhat out of place, not just in view of how little the WTO affected the individual countries for several years after its creation, but also since the documents directly emerging from the meeting did not cover party participation in the proceedings at all.

The general justification for having created the Warsaw Treaty Organization was that it exemplified

> the unanimity and might of the peace camp, the indivisibility of peace and security as illustrated by the [Chinese People's Republic's] pledge of support, the full conformity of the Treaty with the UN Charter and the defensive and peaceful character of the countermeasures taken as borne out by the provisions for accession to the Treaty by other states and for its invalidation in the event of the establishment of an all European system of collective security. These points were frequently linked with references to the support expressed at Warsaw and throughout the world for the Soviet disarmament proposals. (*SWB* SU/626, 31 May 1955)

However, by the 30th Anniversary, it was argued that 'The signing of the Warsaw Treaty was an objective necessity brought about by the conditions in which the European socialist countries had to live and act . . . ' (Nezhinsky, 1985, p. 162).

An editorial in *Kommunist* (1955/8) also covered the Warsaw Conference. Titled 'In the interests of strengthening peace and the security of peoples', in three pages out of nine it covered only joint defence against a West German and imperialist threat. After referring to the Joint Command and Joint Armed Forces, it added that 'The participants of the Treaty will also take other co-ordinated measures for strengthening their defence potential . . . ' (p. 13) which implied immediately that the formal military structure was not going to be the limit of military co-operation. The editorial did not refer at all to the Political Consultative Committee, or the *political* co-operation called for in the Treaty. Overall, the significance of the Warsaw Treaty was minimized, since the editorial went on to discuss, as quite separate events, the Austrian State Treaty, Soviet co-operation with Yugoslavia, the German question, Taiwan and the People's Republic of China, the United Nations, and other world issues. (In the majority of Soviet journals of the period there was virtually no coverage of the Warsaw Treaty.)

POST HOC EXPLANATIONS

Ignoring the press coverage of the main speeches and Declarations, the first Soviet apologia (intended for Western consumption) for the creation of the WTO was in *International Affairs*, in an article by M. Slavyanov (1955/6), entitled 'Firm Foundation of European and International Security (the Warsaw Conference)'. The purpose of the article was to set the foundation of the WTO, by summarizing the Treaty, in the context of the Paris Agreements and what amounted to a Cold War ethos. It was argued that the Paris and Warsaw proceedings 'reflect the existence and struggle of two opposing policies in world affairs, but largely predetermine further developments in the international situation' (p. 17). While stressing the German question and the new situation of NATO policy in Europe, Slavyanov also brought in the wider international context of the 'imperialist camp''s positions of strength policy, the arms race and the balance of power, and the 'capitalist encirclement' of the 'socialist camp' due to which 'The Warsaw Treaty lays an even more reliable foundation for the policy of co-existence of different social systems . . . ' (p. 25). In its widest context, Slavyanov claimed that 'The Warsaw Treaty strengthens the international positions of socialism as a dependable and indestructible bulwark of the peoples, who are fighting for peace, freedom, and progress' (p. 23). However, unlike its coverage of the Austrian State Treaty, *International Affairs* did not publish the text of the Warsaw Treaty, which would seem to play down the importance of the new Organization.

The October issue of *International Affairs* also carried an article on the Warsaw Treaty, this time by the Polish expert on international law, Professor M. Lachs. This also placed the Treaty in the context of the Paris Agreements, but argued that the latter were merely an expression of a broader policy of Western aggression (Lachs, 1955, p. 55). To Lachs, the Treaty was an extension of socialist bilateral co-operation to a multilateral level, creating mutual political obligations made necessary by the 'conclusions regarding the international situation' recognized in the Treaty (ibid.). As with the speeches and declarations of the Warsaw Conference, he argued that there was a need for a collective security system in Europe, but claimed that the Warsaw Treaty was a contribution to this policy since it was not an 'exclusive bloc' along the lines of NATO, the WEU, and the South East Asia Treaty Organization, all of which he named.

His article was the basis for an anti-Soviet article in the *New York Times* (12 December 1955, p. 30) by its Moscow correspondent, S. L. Sulzberger. In a further article in *International Affairs*, which mis-initialed Sulzberger as 'C. L.', Lachs (1956) was given the opportunity to reiterate his basic foreign policy points.

> The *New York Times* correspondent calls the Warsaw Treaty a reply to the North Atlantic Treaty, in short – 'anti-NATO'. We do not deny that. We have always declared that if there had been no North Atlantic Treaty and no Western European Union, there would have been no need for the Warsaw Treaty. The latter took shape under definite international circumstances, and was necessitated by the aggressive international policy of the Western Powers, particularly the United States. (Ibid., p. 113)

And, in the context of the Paris Agreements:

> [The Warsaw Treaty] is a defensive arrangement open to anyone who wants to co-operate for European peace. The Warsaw Treaty organization [*sic lower case*] will cease to exist the moment there is a general European collective security system. (Ibid., p. 115)

This seems to indicate a slight modification of the reasoning for the Warsaw Treaty, with the Paris Agreements, and therefore German rearmament, being seen not as an issue in themselves, which is the way they were presented prior to the Warsaw Conference and in the Treaty, but as an important factor within the Western defence policy as responded to by the Soviet Union.

CONCURRENT INTERNATIONAL ISSUES

The analysis so far has shown that the Warsaw Treaty appears to have been created as a direct result of the militarization of West Germany within the context of the London and Paris Agreements. This was not the only foreign policy issue that the USSR was campaigning about at the time. On 13 May 1955, during the Warsaw Conference, the Soviet Union made a major set of proposals to the UN Disarmament Commission, a move praised after the event by the Central European leaders but apparently made independently of the multilateral discussions going on within the Soviet bloc. This indicates that the Moscow and Warsaw meetings were just one strand of Soviet thinking on its security.

Western analysts have put forward a variety of reasons for the formation of the WTO, in which the Paris Agreements and the German accession to NATO (treated as independent actions by those citing them), figure prominently, though not in the context of the Soviet concept of a general European security system.

Several Western sources cite a Soviet desire for 'military integration', which was indeed mentioned by the contemporary sources, but is placed by Western analysts in the context of a consolidation of the East-bloc bilateral military treaties. In Bulganin's opening statement to the Warsaw Conference, however, he argued that:

> Nearly all our countries are bound with one another by bilateral treaties of friendship and mutual assistance, which have played and *continue to play* an important part in safeguarding European peace and security.
>
> But in the new situation this is no longer enough. (*Pravda*, 12 May 1955; my italics)

This indicates that the USSR conceived of the multilateral alliance as complementary to the bilateral treaties, which still exist and play a part in Soviet defence thinking to this day.

Soviet fears of encirclement are cited by few of the Western analysts. This reason was explicitly stated by the Soviet Union, but was first mentioned only during the Warsaw Conference, rather than in the propaganda campaign leading up to the establishment of the WTO. This could indicate that such a fear was intended primarily for internal consumption, or that the Soviets did not want to admit the point in public.

Very few Western writers suggest that the WTO was formed as a bargaining chip with the West, despite the repeated claims by the original sources that the WTO would cease to exist if a collective security system acceptable to the Soviet Union was created in Europe (i.e. replacing the WEU and NATO also), and as stated in Article 2 of the Treaty. The Soviet Union only seemed to use the WTO as such at the Four-Power Geneva Conferences later in 1955, but the offer of mutual dissolution still continues to appear in official WTO documents.

The main Western reason given for the founding of the WTO was that it was a justification for the continued Soviet military presence in Central Europe after the successful negotiation of the Austrian State Treaty (ending the post-war occupied status of Austria), which was signed on 15 May 1955, the day after the signing of the Warsaw Treaty. This reason should probably be discounted.

The Four-Power Moscow Declaration of 1943 had promised an Austrian peace treaty, but by as late as November 1954 the three Western powers were still accusing the USSR of obfuscation and delay, both at the Four-Power and at the UN levels, in refusing to negotiate let alone ratify such a treaty. The main Soviet excuse was that, without a satisfactory solution to the *German* problem, there would always be the chance of another *Anschluss*, which Soviet security needs would not tolerate.

The Soviet shift of policy on the Austrian problem seems to date from a speech to the Supreme Soviet by Molotov, on 8 February 1955. This was followed by Soviet-Austrian discussions to clarify the Soviet statement, and the resultant Soviet declaration that it would no longer insist on retaining occupation troops in Austria even though there was still no peace treaty with Germany (*Keesings* 14059, 14154). Agreement was concluded in April 1955, allowing the Soviet Union to draw up a peace treaty with the Western powers (ibid., 14155). The terms of the Austrian State Treaty were agreed by a Four Power meeting in Vienna between 2 and 11 May 1955, and were given final consideration by the Big Four foreign ministers on May 14, being signed the next day (ibid., 14193, 14194).

Under the terms of the Austrian State Treaty, occupation forces would be removed by 25 October 1955 (Part III Article 20[3] – *Keesings* 14194). In the event, the Soviet Union had removed all its forces by 19 September (ibid., 14561) a fact which would not indicate any feeling that it was trying to maintain a military position in Central Europe up to the last moment. Only British troops remained longer than the Soviet ones, being finally removed on 24 October (ibid.). In fact, Jain (1973, p. 17) points out that the Western powers which signed the Austrian State Treaty never invited the USSR to withdraw its troops from the rest of Europe once its position in Austria no longer had to be maintained.

The USSR could claim that the bilateral treaties, which dated from the early post-war years, permitted the stationing of its forces in Europe. If there was a problem, the Soviet Union did not need a multilateral treaty to solve it. Soviet troops still stationed in Europe are in any case there through individual bilateral agreements which do not need the Warsaw Treaty as justification, a point acknowledged by Central European specialists.[N]

In other words, it seems that since the Moscow Conference put in motion the multilateral events that led to the Warsaw Treaty, two months *before* the Soviet Union gave any indication that it was prepared to negotiate an Austrian settlement, and since it did not need to occupy Austria in order to justify its presence on its allies' soil, the Austrian question had no bearing on its policy to develop the WTO. (As pointed out in footnote 8 of this chapter, the decision to form the WTO was taken even before the Moscow Conference – further evidence that it was an independent issue for the USSR.)

In arguing that the USSR feared encirclement and felt the need to bind Albania closer to the rest of the socialist community, Szawlowski (1976, p. 6) seems to be the first Western writer to argue that the Soviet Union specifically feared the 'Balkan Pact'. This Treaty of Alliance, Political Co-operation and Mutual Assistance, a collective security alliance overtly aligned with NATO, was signed by Greece, Turkey, and Yugoslavia on 9 August 1954, though the preamble describes it as extending and strengthening the 1953 Treaty of Friendship and Co-operation of the same three countries, which was not a mutual defence treaty (*Keesings*, 1952–54 volume). While this treaty falls within the lead-in time to the Moscow Conference, it was never mentioned by name or even by implication in any of the speeches surrounding the WTO, or the diplomatic moves of the Soviet Union leading up to the Treaty. The USSR and Yugoslavia had in fact undergone a rapprochement from June 1953 (Fejtö, 1974, p. 13), and Yugoslavia had signed treaties with Hungary (Hegedüs, 1955, p. 19). Thus it would seem that Yugoslavia would not have been engaging in activities likely to harm that rapprochement with the USSR, and the Balkan Pact would not have been seen by the USSR as a threat.

There was another mutual defence pact of this period not mentioned by Western sources, the Baghdad Treaty, originally signed by Turkey and Iraq on 24 February 1955, but later acceded to by Britain, Pakistan, and Persia, with close military and political liaisons on the part of the USA. It was explicitly a military alliance, explicitly an Arab alliance, and implicitly anti-Soviet and anti-Israeli (*Keesings*, 1955 volume).

The first suggestion that the Baghdad Treaty was of concern to the WTO was in the declaration issued by the first session of the PCC (1956). In expressing concern about the growing US influence around the USSR's borders, the declaration mentioned by name the 'North Atlantic Bloc', the 'Baghdad Bloc', and the South East Asia Treaty Organization. Fear of the Baghdad Treaty can therefore not be seen as a *particular* threat to the USSR, but just as another aspect of the East–West division of influence. This is how the Baghdad Pact continued to be referred to, for example by Grechko (1977, p. 331).

In expressing its feeling encircled, the Soviet Union observed specific NATO pressures in Europe. For example, part of Bulganin's opening remarks to the Warsaw Conference were to do with a decision by NATO 'to prepare for atomic war' (*Pravda*, 12 May 1955). He was apparently referring to a regular meeting of the North Atlantic Council held in Paris on 17–18 December 1954. Hidden within the various resolutions covering the full scope of NATO affairs, it was decided that SHAPE (NATO's military wing) 'should be given authority to plan its defensive strategy "taking into account modern developments in weapons and techniques", but that the decision on the use of these weapons should be left in civilian hands' (*Keesings* 13988). This move was understood to be the go-ahead for the development of military strategies based on emerging theatre nuclear weapon technologies, which is certainly how the USSR interpreted it. However, the NATO policy agreed on at the session of the NATO Council was based on the North Atlantic Council directives adopted in December 1953 (ibid.). Once again, though, this issue emerged after the London and Paris Agreements had set in motion the events that led to the Moscow Conference and after.

CONCLUSIONS

The formation of the Warsaw Treaty Organization lies squarely in the Cold War confrontation of the mid-1950s. It was a further aspect of the continuing Cold War division of Germany referred to at the start of this chapter. The USSR did back down over Austria, and accepted the assurances on Austrian neutrality and the limitation of its military policies. But then Austria was not so geostrategically important as Germany, was not being incorporated into the West's military policies, and above all the Soviet Union was fully involved in the discussions on the fate of Austria.

Things that cannot be calculated or even accounted for are, of course, the internal Soviet debates and factionalism on all areas related directly or indirectly with security and defence, and the influence Khrushchev, as party leader, had on this and on the policies that actually emerged. Soviet reactions to the EDC proposals of 1952 were limited by the lack of action on the matter taken when Stalin was alive. Even before the EDC project emerged in the West, there were moves, noted in Chapter 1, to a greater co-ordination of Soviet defence policy with its allies, but this was contained within the existing bilateral relationships. Concern that a rearmed West Germany represented a new situation for the socialist countries could, therefore, only be publicly voiced after the collapse of the EDC. The London and Paris Agreements gave the new Soviet leadership the excuse they needed to do something publicly with their allies, even something as unsophisticated and moribund as the WTO was in its earliest years.

But the question remains as to why, in its earliest manifestation, the WTO was so obviously an inter-state body. Khrushchev did not officially participate in the WTO until the PCC sesion of 1960. The main state representatives, from the Moscow Conference of 1954 onwards, were Bulganin and Molotov, both allies of Khrushchev in the post-Stalin factionalism in the Soviet Union.[11] It has been argued[N] that by 1954, Khrushchev and the CPSU did control Soviet foreign policy and the relations with Central Europe, so Khrushchev's absence from the WTO is not necessarily important. What is important is that the WTO, having been created in the face of a specific threat from the West, was virtually moribund for several years, and was not really used in Soviet foreign policy for several years.[12]

In the second half of the 1950s the USSR continued to pursue its own disarmament initiatives in the UN, and its own negotiations with the West and the USA. The foreign policy strand that led to the creation of the WTO was just another aspect of this world-wide foreign policy – military, diplomatic, and ideological. It was another tool in the Soviets' overall system.

3 The Structural Development of the WTO

BASIC HISTORY

Prior to the signing of the Warsaw Treaty as a multilateral political-military alliance, the signatory states were linked by a series of bilateral Friendship, Co-operation, and Mutual Assistance treaties, which have been maintained throughout the existence of the Warsaw Treaty. The two methods of alliance must, however, be seen as fulfilling different functions, and therefore have complementary rôles.

The main direct benefit of the Warsaw Treaty was to link all the states of the European socialist community within a multilateral alliance that had a definite inter-state structure with specific rôles and activities. Signed by the leaders of the governments of the eight founding states, this inter-governmental alliance seemed to give precedence to military over political co-operation. Of the two articles of the Treaty that deal with the organizational structure, article 5 permitted the setting up of a joint command of the states' armed forces and Article 6 established a political consultative committee.

A separate document was issued with the Treaty, announcing the 'Formation of a Joint Command of the Armed Forces of the State-participants to the Treaty of Friendship, Co-operation and Mutual Assistance' (*Pravda*, 15 May 1955). Naming Marshal of the Soviet Union I. S. Konev as the first Commander-in-Chief (C-in-C), it announced that the 'Ministers of Defence and other military leaders' of the participating states were to command the national armed forces 'allotted to the joint armed forces', and to act as the C-in-C's 'assistants'. The document also announced that a Staff of the Joint Armed Forces, to be based in Moscow and including 'permanent representatives of the general staffs' of the member-states, was being established. Overall control of the Joint Command would lie elsewhere:

> This decision envisages that general questions pertaining to the strengthening of the defence capacity and to the organization of the joint armed forces of the state-participants of the treaty will be examined by the Political Consultative Committee, which will take appropriate decisions. (Ibid.)

This seemed to give the political structure precedence over the military, even though the military structure was given precedence in the Treaty itself.

In fact, the formation of the Political Consultative Committee (PCC) was not announced until 20 January 1956, when a communique from Warsaw announced that the PCC had been created and would convene its first session in Prague on 27 January 'with a view to examining the problems and the measures to be taken in common for application of the Warsaw Treaty' (*Pravda*, 20 January 1956). So, even though the Treaty had been in force from 4 June of the previous year, it did not properly go into operation for over six months.

The Prague PCC meeting 'approved' the Statute of the Joint Command as proposed by Marshal Konev, 'and settled organizational matters connected with the activities of the Joint Armed Forces of the states signatories of the Warsaw Treaty' (*Pravda*, 29 January 1956). After agreeing that the German Democratic Republic's proposed national army, and its Minister of National Defence, should be fully and equally integrated into the structure of the Warsaw Treaty, two 'auxiliary agencies' were announced, which were 'to be set up under the Political Consultative Committee' and be based in Moscow. These were described as: 'A standing commission charged with the elaboration of recommendations on foreign policy questions; A joint secretariat to be formed of representatives of all the signatories of the Warsaw Treaty' (ibid.).

Thus, at the start of 1956, the declared structure of the Warsaw Treaty Organization was as indicated in Figure 1. In formal terms, this is how the structure remained until the Budapest Reforms of 1969. In practical terms various changes took place over the intervening sixteen years.

The final paragraph of the document announcing the formation of the Joint Command declared that the 'Distribution of the joint armed forces on the territories' of the member states 'will be carried out in accordance with the requirements of the mutual defence in agreement among the states' (*Pravda*, 15 May 1955). In effect, the Soviet forces that were already stationed in the GDR, Poland, Hungary, and Romania, were given a new raison d'être in relation to the Warsaw Treaty. These Soviet troops were to be considered as stationed temporarily by individual agreements between the Soviet forces and the host nation. According to Tyushkevich *et al.* (1985?, pp. 410–11) beyond the agreement to station these troops, 'there was also a formal signing of agreements on the number of Soviet soldiers and the conditions of their stay on the territories of friendly countries'.

In the midst of the crisis over Hungary in 1956, the Soviet Union issued a 'Declaration of the Government of the Soviet Union on the Principles

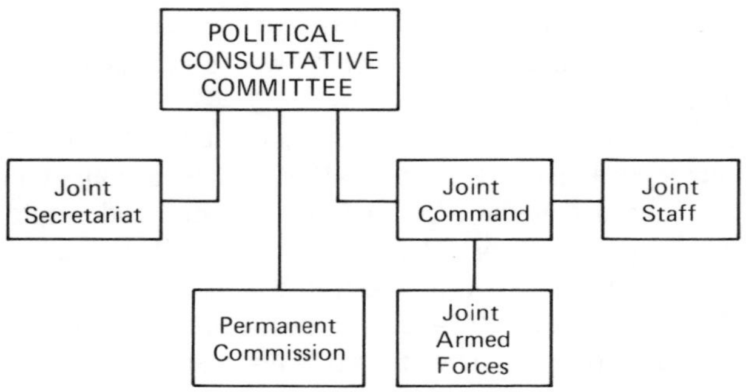

SOURCE Treaty text; document forming Joint Command; PCC Communique, 28 January 1956

FIGURE 1 *WTO formal structure, January 1956*

for Further Developing and Strengthening Friendship and Co-operation Between the Soviet Union and Other Socialist Countries' (*Pravda*, 31 October 1956). This Declaration, in its analysis of the economic and political relationships within the Soviet bloc, offered to re-examine the question of Soviet military units on Central European territory (ibid.). In the aftermath of the Hungarian crisis, status of forces agreements were signed with Poland (17 December 1956), the GDR (27 March 1957), Rumania (15 April 1957),[1] and Hungary (27 May 1957).[2]

During 27–28 April 1959, the foreign ministers of the Warsaw Treaty member states met in Warsaw. (A Chinese representative was also present.) Although this was not officially recognized within the formal structure of the Warsaw Treaty, some Soviet commentators argue that this was the beginning of the practical work carried out by the foreign ministers who were later formally convened in the Committee of Ministers of Foreign Affairs (see, for instance, Menzhinskii *et al.*, 1980, p. 36). In fact, the foreign ministers did not meet again publicly until 1966, and it was this meeting that was the first of the regular meetings of the foreign ministers. (From 26–27 February 1968, the deputy foreign ministers also began to have regular consultations.)

The Warsaw Treaty defence ministers held the first of what became regular meetings on 8–9 September 1961. (The national Chiefs of Staff have also attended these meetings.) This first meeting was probably timed to coincide with the first multilateral exercises, held in the following month.

The question of the rôle of Albania within the WTO is not officially discussed in any detail. Prior to the Warsaw Treaty, Albania had only a bilateral treaty with Bulgaria to tie it in to the general Soviet bloc (excluding the wider and weaker ties of the CMEA). The Warsaw Treaty thus was the first real link Albania had politically and militarily with the rest of the socialist community. As part of the machinations of the Sino-Soviet schism in which Albania sided with the Chinese, Albania was excluded from the PCC meeting held in Moscow on 7 June 1962. The Albanians waited until 13 September 1968, and the pretext of the invasion of Czechoslovakia, to pass a law formally withdrawing from the WTO. Arguably, Albania was only an active member during the initial period when the WTO was generally moribund and the Organization could not really be considered as an important international body.

While the series of multilateral exercises (beginning in 1961), can be seen to mark the beginning of the WTO's claim as a force to be noted, the structural reforms that were agreed on at the PCC meeting in Budapest on 17 March 1969 (the 'Budapest Reforms') mark the most important changes in this process. New Statutes on the Joint Command and the Joint Armed Forces were agreed, along with the creation of a Military Council and a Technical Committee.

The Communique of that meeting (*Pravda*, 18 March 1969) says that these changes were based on 'a report from the Commander-in-Chief of the Joint Armed Forces on measures worked out by the Ministers of Defence with the approval of the respective governments'. Though these changes have been referred to by successive Soviet and Central European commentators, the Communique carries on to say that 'other documents designed to bring about a further improvement in the structure and bodies of administration of the defence organization of the Warsaw Treaty (ibid.) were likewise 'unanimously endorsed' by the PCC. As with the wording of the Statutes revised at this meeting, these other documents have never been revealed, and it is unclear whether they refer to the Military Council and Technical Committee, or to something covert. (The wording of the Legal Convention adopted in 1973 referred in its preamble to the states' 'taking into account the Decision of the state-participants of the Warsaw Treaty' taken by the PCC in 1969.)

After the Budapest Reforms, the known formal structure of the Warsaw Treaty Organization was as depicted in Figure 2.

The PCC meeting in 1972 announced for the first time that its activities were aided by a 'Secretary-General to the PCC' (Communique, *Pravda*, 27 January 1972). The activities of this person have nonetheless remained obscure. Other than the founding documents and the Protocol of extension the only formal document that has been published is the 'Convention concerning the legal status, privileges, and immunities of the Staff and other

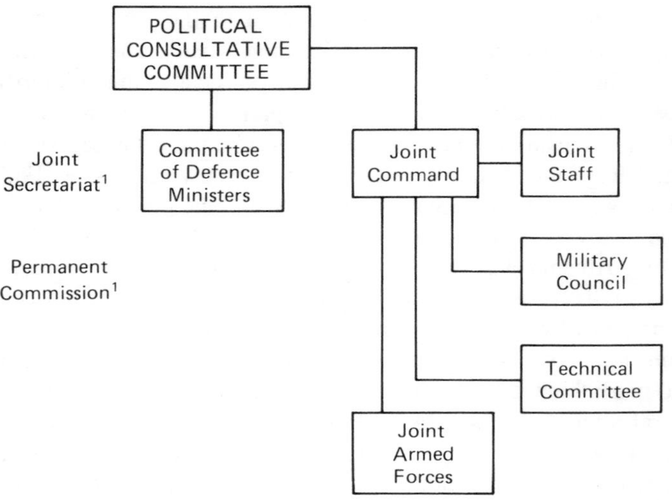

SOURCES As in Figure 1; PPC Communique, 17 March 1969

[1]The Joint Secretariat and the Permanent Commission had carried out no public functions.

FIGURE 2 *WTO formal structure, March 1969*

administrative bodies of the Joint Armed Forces of the state-participants to the Warsaw Treaty'. This appeared in *Krasnaya Zvezda* on 27 April 1973, and was dated 24 April. Menzhinskii writes that it came into force on 21 November of the same year (though the event does not appear to have been reported in *Krasnaya Zvezda*, *Pravda*, or *Izvestiya*) when the final state deposited its ratification papers in Moscow (Menzhinskii *et al.*, 1980, footnote, p. 39). The second round of structural changes that took place, this time to the political side of the Organization, was adopted by the PCC at its meeting in Bucharest, in 1976. These changes were:

> In view of the further improvement of the machinery of political co-operation within the framework of the Treaty, the decision was taken to create a Committee of Ministers of Foreign Affairs and a joint secretariat as bodies of the Political Consultative Committee. (*Pravda*, 27 November 1976)

The formal structure of the WTO thus became as is illustrated in Figure 3. In conjunction with the PCC meeting, a Declaration 'For fresh advances in international relaxation, the strengthening of security and the development of co-operation' was issued by the WTO (ibid.). It must be seen as more than just the standard statement on various issues of the contemporary international situation, since section four of the Declaration appears to include a post Helsinki Final Act statement on how the Warsaw Treaty member-states proposed to broaden their public international face, both within the socialist community and by implication in wider terms. After reiterating their ideological basis as a socialist community, they declare:

> To continue to expand effective co-operation in the strengthening of peace in Europe and universal peace . . . ;
>
> To deepen the political contacts of the fraternal peoples, including the practice of holding consultative meetings of Parliamentarians and also representatives of the public for the discussion of topical problems of international affairs; to expand mutual information and the exchange of experience of socialist and communist construction and to promote the development of contacts between states and public organizations and labour collectives;
>
> To develop bilateral and multilateral co-operation in all spheres of the economy, in the application of the achievements of scientific and technological progress for the further rise in the material and spiritual well-being of their peoples, to promote together with other countries which are members of the Council for Mutual Economic Assistance, the ever fuller implementation of the Comprehensive Programme and the fulfilment of the decisions of the 30th session of the Council for

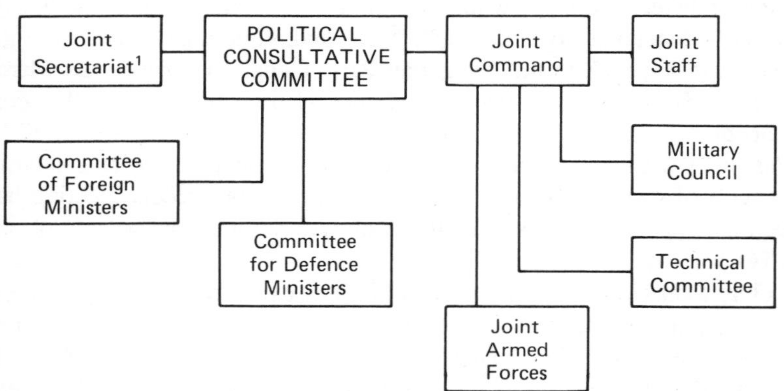

SOURCES As in Figure 2; PCC Communique, 26 November 1976
[1]As established in 1976.

FIGURE 3 *WTO formal structure, November 1976*

> Mutual Economic Assistance concerning the joint working out and implementation of long-term special programmes. The joint flights of cosmonauts from socialist countries in Soviet spaceships and stations planned for 1978–1983 will be a striking manifestation of the high level of co-operation in science and technology; To cement cultural co-operation, exchanges of literary and artistic values, contacts between professional unions, twin regions and cities and to encourage broader tourist contacts and communications between individuals. (Ibid.)

The section was concluded with a resolution to strengthen friendship and co-operation within the world socialist community.

This section of the Declaration was singled out for particular stress when the Political Bureau of the CPSU Central Committee, the Presidium of the USSR Supreme Soviet, and the USSR Council of Ministers issued a joint statement approving the WTO Declaration (*Pravda*, 4 December 1976).

Some time after this Declaration, and presumably in conformity with its proposals on improved relations within the bloc, the first meeting of Chairmen of the Parliaments of Warsaw Treaty states was held in Leningrad (5–8 July 1977), though it limited itself to reinforcing the established proposals of the PCC and other common policy lines.

The original Treaty would formally have expired on 4 June 1985. However, the BBC Radio 4 news at 08:00 hours on 7 March 1985 announced, without naming a source, that Hungary had intimated that the Treaty would be extended. *The Guardian* of March 8, quoting the then Hungarian Foreign Minister Péter Várkonyi, who was visiting London, said that the Treaty would be extended 'for another 20 years, and without any changes to the text'. In his speech to the Hungarian Party Congress (*Pravda*, 26 March 1985, p. 5), Kádár only stated that there had been 'Recently in Moscow a meeting of the main party-State delegates of the state-participants of the Warsaw Treaty . . . ' which had unanimously endorsed the extension of the term of operation of the Treaty. The only known recent meeting had been held at Chernenko's funeral, which was not a formal session of any WTO body.

Only weeks before the Treaty was formally extended, the Western press, quoting unpublished sources, reported continued resistance to the terms of the extension. It was stated that the Soviets were wanting formally to link the anniversary of the Treaty with the anniversary of the end of the Second World War in Europe (*The Observer*, 14 April 1985, p. 10). While resisting such a move Romania also intimated that it wanted the Treaty renewed for 'only ten or even five years' and had Hungarian and GDR support for this line, though it was apparently

Romania that had been first 'to agree in principle to the renewal of the pact' (ibid.).

On 26 April 1985, only 18 days before the 30th Anniversary of the signing of the Treaty, a meeting of 'the highest party leaders and statesmen of the state-participants of the Warsaw Treaty' was held, which signed a Protocol of just two Articles 'On prolonging the period of validity of the Treaty of Friendship, Co-operation, and Mutual Assistance, signed in Warsaw on May 14, 1955' (*Pravda*, 27 April 1985).

Certainly, in view of the state of East–West relations and the continuing existence of NATO (which has an indefinite period of validity), such a move was to be expected, but it seems unusual that the Preamble to the original Treaty, so explicit of the fear of a remilitarized West Germany being included in the new military alliance of the Western European Union and in NATO, was not rewritten, since it is such an obvious anachronism. Of most significance is that it was not the PCC which signed the Protocol, but an extraordinary meeting of 'Warsaw Treaty member states'. The signatories of the Protocol were all the party leaders; with the exception of Gorbachev for the USSR and Kádár for Hungary, the other signatories also signed in their concurrent State capacities. The original inter-state Treaty was being treated as an inter-party agreement with state aspects, which is a very unusual scheme of things, particularly when the formal structure of the Organization is taken into account.

In the keynote address on the 30th Anniversary, CPSU Secretary Konstantin Viktorovich Rusakov said of the Warsaw meeting (the meeting that signed the Protocol):

> It demonstrated with renewed strength the determination of the allied socialist countries' parties and peoples to continue to strengthen their unity and cohesion, jointly defend socialism's positions, act in a co-ordinated manner in international affairs, and strive for lasting peace on Earth. (*Izvestiya*, 15 May 1985)

In such an analysis the allied governments really had no part at all, and if they had any rôle in an inter-state treaty it must have been as a front for the parties. However, Rusakov later stated that the use of the Protocol as the form of extension was 'an expression of the continuity of the socialist states' policy and the immutability of the objectives for whose sake they considered it necessary to form a relationship of alliance 30 years ago' (ibid.). This suggests that it is the states who decide WTO policy. (But as this and following chapters discuss, there is no clear indication from the original sources as to where policy is decided, or whether the parties or the governments are officially in control.)

INTRODUCTION

> An international organization was formed on the basis of the Warsaw Treaty. The organization is equipped with suitable organs operating on the basis of the Treaty itself and their own statutes . . . [I]t is a regional *allied organization of collective self defence*. It has come to be called the Warsaw Treaty Organization.
>
> The importance of the Warsaw Treaty Organization goes, however, far beyond the framework of preparation for a joint defence in case of an armed attack. The organization constitutes a forum for adopting a common political line, common attitude of its member States towards the most important problems of international politics. It is one of the organizational forms of the community of socialist states. (Tyranowski, 1973, p. 118; italics in original)

The structure of the WTO, and perhaps even more importantly the structural development of the Organization, illustrates the paradoxical nature of the alliance. Under the overall general policy-making control of the Political Consultative Committee, two quite separate formal structures have developed, the military and the political, each with its own goals and perspectives and with virtually no interaction between the two. (The *informal* structure is discussed separately, at the end of this chapter.)

While arguing since its formation that the Organization was a response to the aggressive militarism of the United States and its NATO allies (for example in the first PCC Declaration, 28 January 1956), that in fact this military confrontation has continued (see, for example, Alexandrov, 1980, p. 23; Kozlov, 1977, p. 212; Stepaniuk, 1972) even to the present day (as claimed in the Protocol of extension), the signatory states continue to have military links outwith the WTO, in the form of the bilateral treaties, which are specific to military co-operation, and other military and political relations on bilateral terms. Indeed in defence terms, the structures of the WTO could be disbanded with little or no disruption to the states' defence co-operation and capabilities. So what function is the WTO intended to have?

A catch-phrase from statements about the WTO is that the 'unity and cohesion' of the members is being cemented and developed through their participation in the multilateral alliance. This is in fact mainly in *political* relations. Despite the early stress on military activities, with the creation of the Joint Command in 1955 to the inauguration of regular multinational military exercises in 1961, an equal if not predominant role of the Organization has always been to indicate a co-ordination of the foreign-policy activities of the members (see, for example, Stepaniuk). The PCC is the only formal institution which regularly gathers the leading representatives from both party and state machineries from all the active members of the European socialist community. Including Romania the meetings agree on a formal document.[3] These people can be called together on an ad hoc basis, for example at the Chernenko funeral or in the Crimea. But if only to give the impression of equal sovereignty and voice, a formal political body, such as the PCC, is necessary to show a co-ordinated international position for the socialist community.

With due regard to the claim that the PCC merely co-ordinates East-bloc support for an independently-generated Soviet foreign policy (e.g. Kobal, 1974, p. 191), and the writers who decry any multilateral non-Soviet Warsaw Treaty role in any prospective European conflicts,[4] it would seem that the prime function of the WTO is political, in both intra-bloc and external terms. It presents an image of being a war-fighting, war-winning military alliance (at least to NATO, the US Department of Defense, and the majority of the West's politicians and opinion-leaders), while internally it is the political functions which have become dominant.

Arguably, the WTO has almost from the beginning had a function as a force for bloc integration. Meissner (1966, p. 238) argues that the original bilateral treaties were part of Stalin's scheme for Soviet dominance of post-war Central Europe. He notes the twin aims of bloc security and also a means to effecting the political loyalty of the new socialist commonwealth to a hegemonic USSR (ibid., p. 240). Officially, the establishment of the WTO was the second stage in the development of the socialist combat community, the internationalist solidarity that was 'characterized by a more active participation of each socialist state in the strengthening the common defensive might of the fraternal alliance' (Grechko, 1977, p. 332.). In broader terms the WTO as a whole was generally moribund until the 1960s. Khrushchev, who had overseen the founding of the WTO, used it to argue the scope for a general reduction in Soviet ground forces (as part of his internal Soviet political debate), but relied more on the CMEA as a multilateral means to encourage integration. Although the first PCC session was attended solely by governmental representatives, all the subsequent ones have included at least Party First Secretaries (from the third PCC session in 1960 the party leaders have also been the 'heads of delegation' to the PCC), indicating that the WTO has a distinct inter-party role. The dates 3–5 August 1961 saw the first meeting solely of party representatives as opposed to a formal PCC meeting, and a foreign-policy Communique was issued. Although this meeting is mentioned by E. S. Shevchenko (1971, p. 315) to the exclusion of the August 13 Berlin Declaration that led to the building of the Berlin Wall, it is only the latter document that is included in the official volumes of documents and materials. However, Kobal (1974, p. 249) sees the Moscow meeting as being the beginning of a more overtly political role for the Organization. Both these meetings were, it must be remembered, outwith the formal structure.

The Communique covering the Budapest Reforms (*Pravda*, 18 March 1969), specified that the changes were designed to improve the structure and administration of the *defence* aspects of the WTO. It was not until the Bucharest Reforms of 1976 that an officially-constituted (as opposed to a limited ad hoc), *political* structure took shape. This indicates a specific (if delayed) response to the changing status of the Warsaw Treaty Organization in bloc politics. Over the same period the corresponding public statements surrounding the WTO also changed from those bringing the military mechanisms and activities to the fore (e.g. Stepaniuk, in a 17th anniversary article), to those that give precedence to the political mechanisms and activities (e.g. Menzhinskii *et al.*, 1980 and Savinov, 1980 – see also Chapter 4). Over its first thirty years, the WTO in general shifted from being an overt defence pact issuing statements on foreign policy to being the main centre for the co-ordination of the fraternal countries' foreign policy activities. Military policy is of course an aspect of foreign policy. (This is not to ignore any role that individual countries or politicians may have at various times used the WTO to play in their internal or intra-bloc politics, or any role ascribed to the WTO or its members in broader international relations, for example with the Third World, which are not directly covered by the WTO's European focus.)

Thus although the bulk of the official bodies within the structure of the WTO are military, the activities of the Organization seem to belie this. The WTO must be seen in the context of being an aspect of bloc, and in particular Soviet, politics, within the 'structure of world socialism' (Alexandrov, 1980, p. 25), in which the direct European confrontation plays its part.[5]

THE BODIES OF THE WTO

The Political Consultative Committee

The PCC is repeatedly described as 'the highest body of the WTO' (e.g. Menzhinskii *et al.*, 1980, p. 34; see also Savinov, 1980, p. 15, and Alexandrov, 1980, p. 21). Article 6 of the Treaty states that 'each state-participant of the Treaty will be represented [in the PCC] by a member of the government or another specially appointed representative'. The first session of this body was attended by Chairmen or First Vice-Chairmen of the Councils of Ministers, and the Ministers of Defence. (The USSR and Czechoslovakia also sent their Ministers of Foreign Affairs – *Pravda*, Communique, 29 January 1956.) Delegations of later meetings soon became swelled by the First or General Secretaries of the national parties, and the Foreign Ministers (see also Savinov, 1980, p. 16). Since the March 1961 session the Commander-in-Chief (C-in-C) of the Joint Armed Forces has generally been reported as having attended the PCC sessions. Later still the Chief of Staff of the WTO was known to attend, and from 1972 to 1980 inclusive, meetings of the PCC were attended by a 'General Secretary' (see separate entry below). Shtemenko (1976, pp. 168a, b) states that 'other party and state leaders' are 'invited' to the PCC, while Menzhinskii states that the size of delegations is not limited, and that 'other leaders of high rank' can attend (p. 34). After the formation of the Committee of Ministers of Defence in 1969, the Defence Ministers did not attend sessions of the PCC until the sessions from 1983 onwards (though at the session in 1980 all the states except Bulgaria sent their Defence Ministers).[6] However, photographs of sessions of the PCC in, for example, Kulikov (1980) and Shkarovskii show that behind the formal delegations there are what must be advisers to each delegation, who have never been listed in the communiques or otherwise referred to as attending.

The Treaty is very vague in its reference to the PCC. Article 6 explains that it is being formed to facilitate 'the consultations provided for' by the Treaty, but that it will also be 'considering problems arising in connexion with the implementation' of the Treaty. The consultations are by implication to be for the securing of arms control (Article 2), and on important international issues (Article 3).[7] In broad terms the Treaty was signed to ensure peace and stability in Europe and around the world, so in theory issues covered by the PCC should have this in mind.

In practice, the PCC 'discusses', or carries out an 'exchange of views' on, a broad range of the international problems of the day (as it is described in the communiques), about which it issues a range of documents from brief communiques to draft international treaties. Menzhinskii *et al.* (1980, p. 35) explains that these documents show the common position of its members.[8] The meetings also discuss reports from the C-in-C on matters covering the activities of the Joint Armed Forces (ibid.), and thus the common defence. However, in an article covering the 30th Anniversary, it was stated that the PCC was 'set up for *consultations* and for reviewing the Warsaw Treaty activity' (Nezhinsky, 1985, p. 63; my italics), which seems to be vaguer than the wording in the Treaty.

Article 6 of the Treaty also states that the PCC can 'form auxiliary bodies for which the need may arise'. The first two of these were the Permanent Commission on foreign policy and a Joint Secretariat, established by the PCC in 1956. (But see the specific discussion of these two bodies below.) The *Spravochnik Politrabotnika*, in describing the WTO's structure, said that the Committee of Ministers of Foreign Affairs, and the Joint Secretariat, were bodies of the PCC (p. 214). The *Bol'shaya Sovetskaya Entsiklopediya's Ezhegodniks* for 1983, 1984, and 1985 state that the PCC's bodies were the Committee of Ministers of Foreign Affairs, the Committee of Ministers of Defence, and the Joint Secretariat; they then go on to discuss the Joint Armed Forces and its structure. Further confusion about what the PCC actually controls is added by Kulikov (1985, p. 75), who claimed in an article from the 30th Anniversary that the PCC was fundamental to the military development plans; this is despite the fact that there is virtually no direct reference to military plans in the PCC's documents. Even if the *Ezhegodniks* are correct, there is no obvious means by which the PCC can organize the military structure of the WTO; all that can be seen publicly is that the PCC's Communiques occasionally refer to a report having been delivered at the session by the Commander-in-Chief of the Joint Armed Forces.

According to Zamyatin, the PCC is a co-ordinating body to ensure the fraternal co-operation of its members. The question arises of just how much control the PCC does exert. If it is accepted that the body 'examines general political problems [and] international issues . . . including defence' (Grechko, 1977, p. 325) then it could in practice be considered as just a rubber-stamping authority. The Communique covering the Budapest Reforms stated that, 'The Political Consultative Committee heard a report from the Commander-in-Chief of the Joint Armed Forces on measures worked out by the Ministers of Defence with the approval of the respective governments' (*Pravda*, 18 March 1969). This amounts to saying that an ad hoc meeting of the defence ministers told the PCC to convene the defence ministers as an official body of the WTO. Meissner takes this further and claims that the PCC proposals for the strengthening of the WTO's defence capabilities are actually drafted by the Committee of Ministers of Defence (1983, p. 361b).[9] Tyranowski states that the PCC examines problems concerning the Joint Command 'on the motion of the Commander-in-Chief' (p. 109). Other writers have claimed that the C-in-C only 'takes part' (Menzhinskii *et al.*, 1980, p. 35) in the proceedings, and the C-in-C has not been listed as an official member of the PCC; in fact a study of the attendees (see footnote 6) reveals that the C-in-C has not been listed as attending every session of the PCC.

If the PCC can be seen as issuing general policy (see Chapter 4), whether or not it is independently generated, Alexandrov explains that these ideas and proposals 'are further defined and developed in other Warsaw Treaty Organization bodies, especially those at ministerial level' (p. 22). For example, the PCC Communique of 1983 states that 'It was agreed that at its next meeting the Committee of Ministers of Foreign Affairs of the state-participants of the Warsaw Treaty is to study the question of further steps directed at the implementation of this initiative' (*Pravda*, 6 January 1983). The Communique of 1986 also stated that the PCC 'positively evaluated the work of the Committee of Ministers of Foreign Affairs and the Committee of Ministers of Defence over the period that has passed since the previous meeting of the Political Consultative Committee, and determined their further tasks' (*Pravda*, 12 June 1986). In 1969, however, the PCC instructed the C-in-C to ensure the practical implementation of the military policy, though this may have just referred to the formation of the Committee of Ministers of Defence (*Pravda*, 18 March 1969).

The Communique of the first session of the PCC stated that it had been decided to meet 'as necessity arises, but not less than twice a year' (*Pravda*, 29 January 1956). Tyranowski (1973, p. 106) repeats this, but argues that, 'The Committee meets in principle once a year . . . '. Even this is an overstatement, since the PCC had not met at all in 1957, 1959, 1964, 1967, and 1971, the year Tyranowski was writing. From 1970 to 1983 inclusive, the PCC in fact met biennially, mainly issuing declarations on wider foreign-policy themes. Such activity of the PCC underlines that its control of the activites of the WTO can only be of a general nature, and emphasizes its role as a *political* body, one that issues statements on political rather than practical military matters.

Since each document from the PCC is intended to bear the signature of each state's chief delegate it can be assumed that the PCC, like the CMEA, operates on the principle of unanimity, implying that PCC documents are evidence of at least a minimum consensus. Despite Menzhinskii *et al.* writing (1980, p. 34; also *Völkerrecht*, 1982, p. 87a) that each delegation had only one vote, a leading Central European specialist[N] stated that, in his understanding, there was seldom any formal voting in the PCC. Therefore the non-Soviet states cannot really be said to have a veto of any sort, but can carry out 'obstruction' to the attainment of consensus. Several Central Europeans[N] also spoke of a semi-formalized expression of 'non-participation' by the Central Europeans, again affecting the ultimate decisions.[10] What are described[N] as informal talks also take place in meetings outwith the PCC where, for example, the Soviets are asked what they will give through, say, CMEA aid, to compensate for, say, the non-Soviets having to accept WTO agreements in foreign policy that could damage national trading patterns. The Central Europeans have also asked for trade compensation when the WTO agreed on increased military spending during times of national economic stringency.[N]

This explains why PCC documents are almost invariably of a more-conciliatory tone than the independent statements from the Soviet Union. It also indicates that the WTO, the only formal multinational political body of the Soviet bloc, is not of paramount importance or significance. The most striking example of both these points is that there was no PCC meeting between January 1983 and well after the 30th Anniversary. A regular meeting of the PCC was scheduled for January 1985, but was postponed, presumably due to Chernenko's ill-health. During this period the decision was taken to extend the WTO's period of operation, so the negotiations for such an important action must have been taken outwith the PCC, and so outwith the formal structure of the WTO.

Despite such obvious limits to the WTO's main body, the official propaganda still describes the PCC as 'one of the most important forms of co-operation between the leaders of the fraternal parties and countries' (*SWB* SU/5375/A2/1, 27 November 1976).

Official writers on the WTO repeatedly describe it as an organization of sovereign nations. Grechko, for example, explains that 'The principle of the sovereignty of states . . . is clearly expressed in the composition, powers and procedures of the Political Consultative Committee of the Warsaw Treaty Organization and the organizational structure of the Command of the Joint Armed Forces' (1977, p. 321). As has been shown in this discussion, such an assessment would be hard to justify from other official descriptions of the PCC. Research (see footenote 6) shows that the composition of the delegations of the PCC is not uniform, either between the nations participating or in a national delegation at different meetings; the powers of the PCC are obscure; the procedures have not been officially described. It has been explained in this book that unofficially the Central European states can influence the proceedings of the PCC, but only through extra-procedural means, though this cannot have been the national sovereignty Grechko meant. Chapter 4 concludes that the influence of the WTO on national and internal policies is limited, but again this cannot have been what Grechko meant. His claim seems to be one of intent, or propaganda, rather than official practice.

The Permanent Commission and the Joint Secretariat

The Political Consultative Committee concluded its first Communique (in 1956) by stating that it was setting up a foreign policy commission and a joint secretariat (*Pravda*, 29 January 1956). These were presumably to be seen as the political counterparts of the military structure set up with the Treaty. Nothing has ever been heard of these bodies, in that they have never issued any public communiques or other documents, and no meetings have ever been recorded as having been held. The 1957 *Ezhegodnik* of the *Bol'shaya Sovetskaya Entsiklopediya*, in its analysis of the 1956 session of the PCC, did not refer to these two bodies having been set up, while later issues also did not refer to them when discussing the WTO's structure.

Tyranowski (1973, p. 110) did refer to their being formed by the PCC , but said no more about them; Menzhinskii *et al.* (1980, p. 37) referred to them, in a single sentence, adding that they 'work on a continual basis' , but did not explain what this work was. Kobal, as a Western source writing in 1974, said that 'the Secretariat . . . has been responsible for administering the internal goals of the WTO, specifically in the co-ordination of the armed forces supplied to WTO by member states' (p. 230), but he does not cite any original source for this.

In a footnote, Savinov (1980, p 16) contradicts all this, by writing, that 'to all intents and purposes these bodies were not operative. Questions which had to be studied were examined in the meetings of the ministers of foreign affairs and their deputies'. Even this does not quite resolve the problem. Menzhinskii says that the foreign ministers had met from 1959 and their deputies from 1968 (p. 26), though there were no meetings of the foreign ministers attributed to WTO business between 1960 and 1965 inclusive. In political terms the WTO was doing very little in these early years, so even if Savinov is giving the correct account of the structure, the foreign ministers either had very little to do or were not meeting at an overt multilateral level.

Perhaps the most telling point is that at the Bucharest PCC session in 1976, when the political structure was reorganized, the Communique explicitly stated that 'the decision was taken to *create* . . . a joint secretariat' (*Pravda*, 27 November 1976 – my italics), indicating that this was a completely new part of the structure, and not just a tinkering with an existing body. (See also the specific discussion below on the Joint Secretariat of 1976.)

The Joint Command of the Joint Armed Forces

The Warsaw Treaty created the socialist community's first permanent and multilateral military institution. While the bilateral treaties linked the states with the obligation of a common defence, the Warsaw Treaty promised 'concerted measures necessary for the strengthening of their defensive capacity' (Article 5), the focus of which would be 'the establishment of a joint command for their armed forces, which shall be placed, by agreement among these parties, under this command, which shall function on the basis of jointly defined principles' (ibid.). A separate document anouncing the establishment of this Joint Command was signed and issued at the same time as the Treaty. Menzhinskii *et al.* (1980, p. 38) described the Joint Command as 'working on a permanent basis'.

The document forming the Joint Command explained that it would be headed by a Commander-in-Chief (C-in-C) of the Joint Armed Forces (JAFs), with 'assistants' who would be 'the Ministers of Defence and other military leaders of the state-participants to the treaty'.[11] In his 30th Anniversary article, Smorigo (1985) described the Joint Command as comprising the Commander-in-Chief and his deputies (p. 31). The Legal Convention states that the Joint Command has its own Statutes (which have never been published).

Neither the Treaty nor the resolution creating the Joint Command[12] state how the Commander-in-Chief is to be appointed. The resolution on the Joint Command merely records the appointment of Marshal of the Soviet Union I. S. Konev (a member of the Soviet delegation to the Warsaw Conference) as the first C-in-C, but the Treaty was the result of a second extraordinary Conference of European States for Safeguarding Peace and Security in Europe. Menzhinskii *et al.* (1980, p. 38) states that the Commander-in-Chief is 'appointed by the PCC', though in this initial case the PCC was not formed until the following January. Savinov is more explicit, saying that 'The Commander-in-Chief of the [JAFs] is appointed . . . by the joint decision of the governments of all the members of the Warsaw Treaty Organization' (p. 17).[13] Since the PCC includes both state *and* party leaders, it might be assumed that the PCC must ratify a decision taken elsewhere. In fact, there have been no PCC sessions remotely corresponding to the dates of the appointments of the various Commanders-in-Chief, with the exception of the 1976 PCC (which was more concerned with political matters), which occurred four days prior to the death of Marshal Yakubovskii, and more than a month before the press notification of the appointment of Marshal Kulikov as his successor.

The post of the WTO's Commander-in-Chief does not seem to be a full-time one. *Krasnaya Zvezda* for 1 June 1966 carried an article on its front page, 'Meeting of voters with A. A. Grechko', explaining that Grechko and other deputy Ministers of Defence of the Soviet Union had been in attendance. Despite Grechko's having been the WTO's C-in-C for six years, this post was not referred to in the article. Similarly, *Pravda* for 9 April 1977 carried a page two article describing a meeting held on Air Defence Forces Day. Kulikov was listed as an attendee, but he was designated 'deputy Minister of Defence of the USSR, Marshal of the Soviet Union' – he was not referred to as Commander-in-Chief of the WTO, a post he had been given in January of that year. The most glaring example of such an ommission was during the 30th Anniversary celebrations, where Kulikov was at one point described as a 'Marshal of the Soviet Union', and not even as a deputy defence minister, let alone the WTO Commander-in-Chief (*Izvestiya*, 15 May 1985).

According to Shtemenko (1976, p. 189a), the Joint Command has 'definite powers to carry out [its] functions', which are the co-ordination and direction of the Joint Armed Forces, from the headquarters in Moscow. E. S. Shevchenko puts it more broadly when he says that the Joint Command aims to 'secure the co-operation of the military forces and the strengthening of the defence potential of the country-participants of the Warsaw Treaty'.

Meissner (1983, p. 361b) explains that the PCC's resolutions 'in the military sphere' are turned by the Committee of Ministers of Defence into recommendations for implementation by the Joint Command. (This is consistent with Alexandrov's description of ministerial elaboration – see above under the PCC.) PCC Communiques usually contain a paragraph explaining that a report on the 'practical work' of the Joint Command has been heard. These presumably include the co-ordinated training programmes, and the regular joint military or staff exercises, though these are more the purview of the Joint Staff, which Meissner describes as the C-in-C's 'executive organ' (ibid., p. 362a).[14] Writing on the WTO in 1980, Kulikov stated that the C-in-C actually reports on the activities of the Joint Command both to the Political Consultative Committee *and* to the Committee of Ministers of Defence (1980b, p. 166). Elsewhere, he also described the Staff as the C-in-C's 'body of administration' and the 'working body' of the Committee of Ministers of Defence (1980a, p. 26).

This raises the question of just what role the Joint Armed Forces, under the WTO Joint Command, can ever play. Since the PCC was never convened to discuss the threat posed to the alliance by Hungary in 1956, Czechoslovakia in 1968, or even Poland in 1980–81; and since the military intervention of Hungary was carried out by the USSR alone while the Czechoslovak intervention was not the work of all the members of the WTO,[15] we can discount these sole examples of the member armies in action in Europe.[16]

There is speculation in the West about the peacetime nature of the Joint Command. Condoleezza Rice (1984b, p. 140) quotes one Václav Prchlík, 'the highest member of Czechoslovakia's political-military elite', as having said in 1968 at 'a nationwide press conference':

> Relations within this coalition [the WTO] . . . should be improved . . . in such a way as to emphasize the real equality of individual members of the coalition . . .
>
> The problem is that the 'joint command' is a command formed by marshals, generals, and officers of the Soviet army, and other member armies have only a few representatives who have so far held no responsibilities, nor had any hand in making decisions. They play, rather, a role of liaisons. (Ibid., p. 141)

Certainly, despite claims that the posts of Commander-in-Chief and Chief of Staff could be filled by any of the WTO nationalities (e.g. Savinov, 1980, p. 17) these posts, plus the senior deputy command and staff officers, have all continued to be filled by Soviets. It can therefore be argued that the non-Soviet Deputy Commanders-in-Chief and Deputy Chiefs of Staff are just token appointments. There may not have been any significant changes for the Central Europeans since Prchlík was speaking in 1968.

Quite apart from this, the C-in-C has representatives posted throughout the allied armed forces (though presumably only the non-Soviet allies) and the allied military establishments, ostensibly to liaise between the Joint Command and the national militaries on issues such as 'the training of the troops appointed to the structure of the joint armed forces' (Savinov, 1980, p. 18). (Shtemenko, 1976, is more general and speaks of the national forces' 'preparation' – p. 189a.) A further function of these representatives is to 'ensure constant contact between the national command and the Commander-in-Chief of the [JAFs]' (ibid.), though Savinov (1980, p. 18) is more particular and refers to liaison between 'the Deputy commanders of the [JAFs] and the commanders of the national military forces', which amounts to helping liaison within the national ministries of defence, since even within the Joint Armed Forces the national commanders retain control of their own forces. (See below, under the 'Joint Armed Forces'.) According to Mackintosh (1974, p. 124a), 'Each mission is headed by a two- or three-star General with a considerable staff, on which the Soviet Army, Navy, and Air Force are normally represented' though he does not give a source for this information.

A Central European expert[N] specified that the WTO representation in the national military structures is quite independent of other, Soviet, bilateral representatives; the two are separate, covering different subjects and remits of concern. This again shows that the Soviets seem to have a military relationship with their allies quite distinct from the putative rôle of the WTO to this end. The Central Europeans themselves have representatives in each others' military structures, on behalf of the Joint Armed Forces (*SWB*, EE/7952/C/18–19), but the role of these is unclear.

In purely military terms, the role of the multinational Joint Command seems to be minimized. This would be consistent with the conclusions of footnote 4 in this chapter, as regards the military activities of the Joint Armed Forces under that Joint Command.

The Joint Armed Forces

According to Article 5 of the Treaty, the Joint Command was created by the signatories 'for their armed forces, which shall be placed . . . under this command'. This implies that the JAFs cover all the military forces of each member state. The resolution forming the Joint Command said that it would cover 'The armed forces . . . allotted to the joint armed forces', which suggests that the JAFs are more limited in scope. Menzhinskii *et al.* (1980, p. 38) talks of troops that are 'apportioned in the composition of the Joint Armed Forces' while Alexandrov (1980, p. 24) is even more limited when he writes that 'the Joint Armed Forces consist of contingents of troops'. Shtemenko (1976, p. 168b) makes this 'a definite contingent' (p. 168b), but adds that 'their composition, organization, and equipment are determined by the governments of each country, noting the recommendations of the PCC and the Commander-in-Chief' (pp. 168–9).[17]

The national contingents are not led by the C-in-C directly, since each is commanded by its own deputy defence minister, acting as a deputy c-in-c of the Joint Armed Forces (Alexandrov, 1980, p. 24). (Prior to the Budapest Reforms and the creation of the Committee of Ministers of Defence, the deputy c's-in-c were the non-Soviet defence ministers.) The document forming the Joint Command in fact states that the Commander-in-Chief's assistants include 'other military leaders of the states . . . who are vested with the command of the armed forces of each state . . . allotted to the joint armed forces'. While this seems to emphasize the lack of multinational direction of the forces, such a broad description does not seem to have been repeated in later official discussions of the WTO.

Shtemenko (1976, p. 169a) adds that the JAF contingents 'are regulated by the laws, statutes, and military regulations of their countries'. This was repeated by Gribkov in his 30th Anniversary article in *Izvestiya* (14 May 1985), and he concluded that this ensured that national equality was guaranteed. Unlike earlier writers, he specified that within the national contingents, 'The Joint Armed Forces include formations and units of the land forces, forces of the Anti-Aircraft Defences, Air Forces, and Navy' (ibid.). This is obviously not an efficient state of affairs for the running of a multinational army, and raises the question of how the JAFs would be co-ordinated in wartime (if they would be used at all), again calling into question the rôle of the WTO as a military rather than political body.

Even during the 30th Anniversary the disparate nature of the JAFs was being emphasized. In an address to a meeting, Commander-in-Chief Kulikov spoke of the JAFs in terms of national armies (*Krasnaya Zvezda* 14 May 1985). In another Anniversary article he explained that the JAFs consisted of the 'best-trained contingents' who had the best equipment (Kulikov, 1985, p. 75). Katrich (1985, p. 56) specified that the national armies were 'predominant' within the JAFs. To Lt.-Gen. Morocz Lajos, Hungarian State Secretary of Defence, in an Anniversary article in the Hungarian party daily *Népszabadság*:

> The Warsaw Treaty is not a transnational organization, the basis of the alliance is the unity of interests of equal states. The units of the [Joint] Armed Forces are under national authorities and they are developed and trained under mutually co-ordinated plans. (MTI *Daily Bulletin* vol. 20/135, 15 May 1985)

As these descriptions show, even after thirty years the WTO's military functions were not being organized under a single leadership. This does not mean that they would not function together, just that in war, as described in footnote 4 of this chapter, the WTO would not be operative and any military co-ordination and action would take place outwith the WTO structure.

The Staff of the Joint Armed Forces

The Joint Staff operates under the Commander-in-Chief, co-ordinating all the bodies that make up the Joint Command, which Menzhinskii *et al* (1980, p. 38) explains leads to the Staff being 'made up of corresponding departments and administrations'. The Legal Convention states that the Staff is covered by 'documents accepted' by the member states. In practice according to Menzhinskii, the Staff solves the problems encountered in running the Joint Armed Forces, their improvement and development, and carries out the tasks that will strengthen 'all-round co-operation and ties between the fraternal armies' (p. 39). Savinov (1980, p. 18) puts this in more detail when he says that the Staff 'plans combined measures, manoeuvres, exercises, and generalizes experience of the training of the armies and navies and works out recommendations from its utilization'. E. S. Shevchenko (1971) merely states that the Staff, with the Joint Command, is to 'secure the co-operation of the military forces . . . of the country-participants of the Warsaw Treaty'. This is explained by Stepaniuk as being 'In everyday work and training [it] develops and strengthens the business-like international friendship elaborated in the staff [for] the service of the generals, admirals, and officers of the allied armies.' In other words, the Staff, being a permanent body, ensures the day-to-day functions and general planning of the military alliance.

The *Voennyi entsiklopedicheskii slovar* (1983), in its entry for the Staff of the Joint Armed Forces, goes into much greater detail:

> [It] keeps an eye on the military-political conditions, military preparations, and other measures [pertaining] in the system of the aggressive bloc NATO, works out corresponding proposals and informs the general (main) staffs of the armies of the countries of the [WTO]. [It] provides preparations, the carrying out of the meetings of the [CDM], the Military Council of the [JAFs] and realizes their decisions and recommendations. [It] works out proposals for the development of troops (forces), apportioned to the structure of the [JAFs], raises their military and mobilization readiness, the convergence of the organizational structure, equipment [of the Theatres of Military Operations] and the accumulation of reserves of material means. It plans annually and in the perspective of combined measures for the operational, military readiness of the [JAFs], other questions of their activities (training, military games, conferences, meetings, courses of instruction), realizes their preparation, carrying out, generalization of experience and takes it to the [JAFs]. It works in close mutual activity with the corresponding general (main) staffs.

But even this modern analysis presents some problems. After saying at the beginning and end that it 'informs' and works closely with the national military structures, it speaks in the middle as if it is only responsible for the apportioned units of the JAFs, and still talks as if the national military structures are not fully 'converged' for joint activities. The reference to the theatres of military operations ('TVD') is highly irregular and perhaps quite spurious. It could be explained by the fact that the Dictionary was produced by a main editorial committee under N. V. Ogarkov, whose view of the military rôle and structure of Central Europe is very individual. (See, for example, Erickson, 1985, and Radio Free Europe RL 325/85, 27 September 1985.) However, even this description of the Staff seems mainly administrative, so the references to an operational rôle need not supersede the analysis of a limited military role for the JAFs discussed above.

The Staff is headed by a Chief of Staff of the Joint Armed Forces who, according to Savinov (1980, p. 18), is simultaneously 'the first deputy of the Commander-in-Chief and a member of the Committee of Ministers of Defence', 'appointed by the governments of the members of the Warsaw Treaty, by mutual agreement, from the staff of the military forces of any member of the WTO'.[18] Under the Chief of Staff are deputies from the other member-states (ibid.), though Yakubovskii (1975b, p. 145), said that there were deputies including from each of the allied armies. (Mackintosh describes them as being 'of Major-General or Rear-Admiral rank' – 1974, p. 123b – but again without quoting any source.) The Staff in general comprises representatives of all the General Staffs of the members (Menzhinskii *et al.*, 1980, p. 38), whom Savinov (1980, p. 19) describes as 'generals and officials from all seven allied armies'.

In analysing the Joint Staff, Mackintosh (1974, p. 123a) points out that the functions of the Staff are really quite limited, since it does not appear to have any 'operations, signals, transportation or supply services', nor does it seem to be responsible for air defence.[19] Mackintosh explains that all these areas would be needed for the WTO to have an independent wartime function (ibid.). Writing in an anniversary article in 1975, WTO C-in-C Yakubovskii (1975a, p. 23) refers to the plan of the Joint Command being carried out through 'training and other joint measures' in the preparation of the WTO's air defences, ground forces, allied naval fleets, 'forces of communication, bodies of the rear, etc.'. Apart from this being one of the few such references to the 'rear services' in the official literature, it places them along with troops who are specifically under national command, and in fact only talks of 'joint measures' rather than a specific WTO body or function. Rather than disprove Mackintosh's analysis, this further underlines the limited military rôle of the WTO.

In discussing the Soviet General Staff, Rice (1985b, p. 18) explains that it has a Foreign Military Directorate 'which co-ordinates the General Staffs of the Warsaw Pact nations . . . [T]he boundaries between the Warsaw Pact staff and the General Staff are unclear'. The Soviet General Staff also has a Deputy Chief of the General Staff for WTO affairs (ibid.). This would imply that the WTO Joint Staff must have severely restricted duties, or even no independence at all, throwing even more doubt on the WTO's military activities and rôles; the USSR has once again duplicated through bilateral relations what is supposed to be co-ordinated on a multilateral basis through the WTO. Rice concludes that 'Since there is no apparent conflict between coalition doctrine and Soviet theatre doctrine, one might surmise that the Warsaw Pact's staff would be called on primarily to report on the state of affairs in Eastern Europe (ibid.). This would amount to the WTO's Joint Command in its entirety being a glorified watchdog. This would imply that its direct military activities, such as joint exercises, are for public relations or propaganda purposes only,[20] which is how Mackintosh (1974, p. 122b) describes them. Nonetheless, at the end of the first exercises in 1961, it was claimed that the direct co-operation of the armed forces would be intensified under the Joint Command, and that the 'socialist military coalition' would be raised to 'a higher level' (ADN in German, *SWB* EE/787, 6 November 1961).

Further evidence of the lack of any real military purpose for the Joint Staff is that, despite its having permanent representatives from the national military structures, the first meeting of the defence ministers (September 1961) issued instructions to the Chiefs of the General Staffs, in other words directly to the national military structures, circumventing the putative multilateral relations in which the defence ministers were participating. (Such wording has continued intermittently throughout the documents.) This might have been because there was in 1961 no full-time Joint Staff. However, the Chiefs of the General Staffs also met after the Budapest Reforms (12–16 May 1969), and again in 1971, implying that the Reforms had not gone far enough towards total multilateral co-ordination.

There is some confusion over the location of the Joint Staff. The document forming the Joint Command states that the Staff will be based in Moscow, which is where it was placed in the discussion of the WTO in the *Bol'shaya Sovetskaya Entsiklopediya*'s 1957 *Ezhegodnik*. The Legal Convention of 1973 also specifies that the Staff is in Moscow. However, writing in 1974, Mackintosh (1974, p. 125a) stated that 'There were also Western reports in 1973 that a forward administrative HQ of the Pact had been set up at Lvov in the Western Ukraine – this would be a logical development for an organization responsible for improving the co-ordination and control of the East European forces'. And a year later, this had become the probable reference source for the claim that there was a 'Permanent WTO headquarters in Lvov, USSR' (Caldwell, 1975, p. 8). Even in 1981, Wiener (1981, p. 14) was insisting that the Joint Command was 'relocated' in Lvov in 1972.

Yakubovskii (1975b), did not seem to give a location for the Joint

Staff, though the 1975 *Bol'shaya Sovetskaya Entsiklopediya Ezhegodnik* did again specify Moscow. (From the 1976 *Ezhegodnik* the format of the articles changed, and the location of the WTO's Staff was no longer mentioned.) Kulikov (1980b) did not state where the Staff was located, but a photograph (facing p. 161) pictured Staff workers at the Lenin Mausoleum in Moscow. For the 30th Anniversary, Shkarovskii (1985) printed a photograph of the Staff Building, and placed it in Moscow (p. 37). A GDR source (*Völkerrecht*, 1982, p. 88a) also places the Staff in Moscow.

The only public use of Lvov in the structure of the WTO has been for the holding of a meeting of the Military Council (26–29 October 1983). While unusual, this is not unique, since the Military Council has also met in Varna, Bulgaria (27–30 October 1970), Minsk (17–20 October 1972), and Kiev (25–27 May 1976). Thus the possibility of an alternative location for the Joint Staff must remain unresolved.

The Committee of Ministers of Defence

The CDM is described by Menzhinskii *et al.* (1980, p. 37) as 'the highest military body of the WTO', a sentiment also expressed by, for example, Katrich, in the course of the 30th Anniversary (1985, p. 55). It was officially created as part of the Budapest Reforms, on the direct recommendation of the defence ministers themselves, who had been meeting on an ad hoc basis and issuing reports from 1961. The second time they met, they resolved to get the next session of the PCC to 'endorse' their decisions (*Pravda*, 2 February 1962). This took place four months later, indicating the slow progress for such decisions. Meissner (1983, p. 316b) describes the CDM as being 'the link between the political and military organs of the Warsaw Pact and the national forces . . . '.

The Committee comprises all the national ministers of defence, plus the Commander-in-Chief and the Chief of Staff of the Joint Armed Forces, who 'also enter in its affairs' (Menzhinskii *et al.*, 1980, p. 37). Tyranowski (1973, p. 111) explains that the debates of the CDM are 'presided over as a rule by the Commander-in-Chief of the armed forces'. Savinov (1980, p. 18) adds that the CDM meetings are prepared and also supervised by the Joint Staff. This shows that the C-in-C and the Chief of Staff have a much higher profile in the CDM than in the PCC.

Shtemenko (1976, p. 189a) writes that the CDM discusses 'All the most important questions on the strengthening of the defensive capacity of the allied states' and the Joint Armed Forces. Savinov, stating that the CDM was created specifically 'For the implementation of the directions of the Joint

Armed Forces', says that it also 'resolves' the issues of defence potential and the development and improvement of the Joint Armed Forces (1980, p. 17). (This would seem to reduce the rôle of the PCC on these matters.) The practical effect of the CDM is that 'the joint recommendations and proposals concerning the defence of the members of the Warsaw Treaty, and about other military questions requiring mutual agreement, enter into force' (ibid.). Rice (1984b, p. 194), quoting no apparent source, says that the CDM's decisions 'had to be approved by the national governments before they could be adopted'. As noted above concerning the PCC, this is because the CDM, as a ministerial committee, elaborates PCC recommendations (Alexandrov, 1980, p. 24). In fact, Meissner (1983, p. 361b) goes so far as to state that the CDM prepares the PCC's military proposals arguing that the CDM's 'main task' is to co-ordinate the allies' defence policies (ibid.).

The Military Council of the Joint Armed Forces

After the Staff and the Committee of Ministers of Defence, the third institutional arm of the Joint Command is the Military Council (MC). Like the CDM, it was created in 1969 under the Budapest Reforms.

The Military Council is more broadly based than the CDM, in that it includes the Commander-in-Chief, his deputies (ie the national deputy defence ministers and the C-in-C's deputies for specific military functions), the Chief of Staff, and representatives of the allied high commands (Menzhinskii, p. 38). Savinov (1980, p. 18) refers only to the deputy c's-in-c as sitting on the MC.[21] The MC meeting of October 1972 announced that 'military leaders' also took part (*Pravda*, 21 October 1972). Virtually every session since then has been attended by the official members of the MC 'and their delegations', the latter being otherwise unspecified, though the report of the May 1975 session referred to 'representatives of the separate national armies' (*Pravda*, 22 May 1975).

Again like the CDM, the MC is concerned with the practice and development of the Joint Armed Forces' administration and troops (Menzhinskii *et al.*, 1980, p. 38; Savinov, 1980, p. 18; Shtemenko, 1976), though this is often restricted to 'current questions' of these subjects (Savinov, 1980, p. 18) or 'Questions on the current activity' (Shtemenko), which implies that it does not concern itself with more long-term issues. The reports issued by the autumn meetings of the MC generally refer to an assessment of the concluding year's activities of the JAFs and the setting of tasks for the next year. Another function of the Military Council is apparently to render 'effective aid to the command' (Yakubovskii, 1971, p. 30).

While Menzhinskii *et al.* (1980, p. 38) says that the MC meets annually, Savinov (1980, p. 18) says it meets 'as a rule, twice a year' which is how it is reported in the Soviet press. According to Savinov, the Staff of the Joint Armed Forces prepares and supervises MC meetings, and also ensures its resolutions and recommendations are carried out (ibid., pp. 18–19), though this would question the supervisory role of both the CDM and the PCC over the Military Council's affairs.

Even taking into account the confusion surrounding the relationship between the PCC and the CDM on matters of who is ultimately behind policy recommendations, the rôle of the MC must add further confusion. Meissner describes it as 'an advisory organ to the Joint Command' (1983, p. 362a) on what amount to day-to-day operational matters, but given the broader remit quoted by Soviet sources it could be seen as the originator of some of the CDM's policies. Mackintosh goes so far as to say that the MC decisions are reviewed and approved by the CDM (1974, p. 123a) which would not give the CDM much part in what it passes on to the PCC, while Rice (1984b, p. 194) argues that 'It is apparently a consultative organ for the very senior officers of the Warsaw Pact', though none of these Western writers offers a source for such information. In fact Mackintosh (1974, p. 123b) concludes that the MC is at the root of the Budapest Reforms as a concession to the non-Soviet Warsaw Treaty states' having a greater access to WTO policy '(if not decision-making)'. This, however, would mean that what amounts to political-military policy would lie in the hands of a majority decision by professional soldiers rather than politicians or party leaders, which is surely an overstatement. Even allowing for the politicians of the CDM to add breadth and a political dimension to the policy aspects of the MC's deliberations, this analysis adds more doubt to the full military role of the alliance.

The Technical Committee of the Joint Armed Forces

One other 'further improvement in the structure and bodies of administration of the defence organizations of the Warsaw Treaty' (Communique, *Pravda*, 18 March 1969) but not mentioned then by name was the formation of a Technical Committee for Military-Scientific Technical Advice (Menzhinskii *et al.*, 1980, p. 39), which 'mainly' oversees and co-ordinates military-related research and development in the member-states (Savinov, 1980, p. 19). According to Savinov, this covers weapons, 'techniques', and 'the design-experience of works of a defensive character' (ibid.). Rice (1984a, p. 68) attributes this Committee to a Czech proposal for greater non-Soviet input to weapons research etc. No meetings of this body are reported in the Soviet press, and some Soviet writers do not even refer to it (e.g. Zhilin *et al.*, 1984, pp. 22–3, discussing details of technical co-operation). (See also under 'Economic Co-operation and the CMEA' in the section below on 'Extra-structural Factors in the WTO'.)

* * *

The Budapest Reforms

The above completes the known structure of the WTO up to and including 1969 (as in Figure 2). However, Vladimir and Teplov (1980, p. 31) list these structural additions and then specify 'and other bodies of the Warsaw Treaty Organization'.

Writing in 1971, and discussing the Budapest Reforms, Yakubovskii (1971, p. 26) stated that there had been agreement on new Statutes for the Joint Armed Forces and Joint Command, on Statutes for the Committee of Ministers of Defence, 'and other documents, having the aim of the improvement of the structure and bodies of administration of this organization'. Later on, he refers to the Military Council in this context (ibid., p. 30). Considering that such oblique references occur again and again in official writings, while mention of the Permanent Commission and Joint Secretariat of 1956 does not recur, it seems likely that a further obscure but official structure does exist. However, since even on the 30th Anniversary it was explained that, 'The practical co-ordination of the military measures are realized by the . . . military bodies: the Committee of Ministers of Defence, the Joint Command, the Military Council, Staff, and Technical Committee of the Joint Armed Forces . . . ' (Gribkov, *Izvestiya*, 14 May 1985), all of which were under the guidance of the PCC (ibid.), it is hard to imagine what additional bodies might be needed for 'administration', even within the very limited amount of multilateral co-ordination that goes on. (But see, 'Other Bodies of the WTO' in the section below on 'Extra-Structural Factors in the WTO'.)

The Budapest Reforms must not be seen as a spontaneous reaction to the events in Czechoslovakia of 1968, or as a Soviet rearguard reaction to the obvious shortcomings of its policies in Central Europe.[22] Johnson (1978, p. 254) claims that changes in the WTO's military structure 'had been broached as early as 1966', and that 'detailed planning was evidently carried out in the fall of 1968' (in other words, in the immediate aftermath of the Prague Spring).

But this does not go back far enough. In a speech to the plenary meeting of the CPSU Central Committee (29 September 1965) Brezhnev reported on the foreign relations of the USSR, and stated that 'In short, the substance of our foreign policy is to strengthen the international socialist community in every way . . . ' (*Pravda*, 30 September 1965). Only after expressing satisfaction with the series of bilateral talks between the USSR and the Central European states (plus other members of the CMEA), did he go on to say that:

> Great attention has been paid to co-ordinating the foreign policy of the socialist countries, in particular to co-ordinating our actions in the United Nations and its specialized bodies.
>
> We have discussed the question of improving the work of the Warsaw Treaty Organization and the need to set up a permanent and prompt machinery for considering pressing problems within the framework of the Treaty. (Ibid.)

In other words, notwithstanding claims that the WTO played a central role in co-ordinating the allies' foreign policies, he seems to have been saying that in its first ten years there was no adequate institutional multilateral co-ordination of foreign policy or even, presumably, miltiary policy 'within the framework of the Treaty'. The PCC was, according to Brezhnev's analysis, ineffective in its declared role of 'considering problems arising in connexion with the implementation of this treaty' (Article 6 of the Treaty). (It also reinforces the analysis that the Permanent Commission and Joint Secretariat mentioned in 1956 were not in operation.)

What Brezhnev wanted was presumably some form of 'supranational permanent political committee to provide overall guidance' and linking the member-states together much more closely than before, which Kobal (1974, p. 203) claims was discussed at the PCC meeting in Sofia in 1968.[23] By that time the proposals for a broad restructuring must have been rejected, indicating some ability of the Central European members to influence the USSR at that time. The defence ministers met in Moscow on 29–30 October 1968 and 'discussed the strengthening of the WTO' (*Pravda*, 31 October 1968). The PCC the following March endorsed the defence ministers' recommendations, but there was no meeting of the foreign ministers and no recommendations for political reforms.[24]

The overt reason for the PCC session in 1969 was not for carrying out institutional reform. Radio Moscow broadcasting in Albanian[25] claimed that it was due to 'the complicated international situation caused by the dangerous and frequent provocations of the forces of imperialism in the centre of Europe, in the Near East, and in Asia . . . ' (*SWB*

SU/3028/A2/2, 19 March 1969), which was presumably referring to the Budapest Declaration's call for an all-European conference.

The documents that the PCC agreed to in Budapest, both the political Declaration and the institutional reforms, must have been drawn up at least in draft form prior to the session. The meeting, which officially lasted one day, in fact began at 14:00 hours on March 17 (ibid.). A report by Tanjug, the Yugoslav Press Agency, dated March 17 (the day of the session), claimed that: 'The delegations were waiting for their Assistant Foreign and Defence Ministers to add finishing touches to draft documents so that the summit meeting itself could start from positions which had been made as uniform as possible' (ibid., EE/3027/i, 18 March 1968). The full accuracy of the Yugoslav report is perhaps open to question, since an abstract of reports claimed that the meeting had been 'postponed by five hours because preliminary consultations were still in progress between some delegations according to unofficial reports' (ibid.). (Moreover, not every delegation included deputy foreign and defence ministers – see footnote 6 of this chapter.) The report later added that:

> According to a telephone dispatch from Budapest, the short duration of the meeting can be explained by the fact that one delegation preferred bilateral talks during which various topics were discussed, and the communique and the appeal to all European countries were jointly formulated and approved. (ibid., C1/2)[26]

It is perhaps significant that, whatever their effect and however they were formulated, the 1969 reorganistion of the WTO's military structure has not since been publicly amended. Furthermore, no *political* reforms took place for another seven and a half years, and these were not of the scope that Brezhnev had apparently originally wanted.

* * *

After the Budapest Reforms, two other organizational developments took place before the Bucharest Reforms of 1976.

The General Secretary of the Political Consultative Committee

The post of the General Secretary is obscure, and may perhaps be no more than a name attending the PCC. Menzhinskii *et al.* (1980, p. 35), for example, lists the post with the Commander-in-Chief, who 'take part in the sessions of the PCC' (p. 35), which is also how Savinov (1980,

p. 16) describes him. It is reported[N] that the post of 'Deputy Secretary' was mentioned by the Albanian party daily newspaper in May 1965 as being held by Nikolai P. Firyubin, who on 5 May 1968 was described as 'Secretary-General' by the Bulgarian News Agency (ibid.) (this was the day before a PCC session in Sofia). The Communique from the first day of the 1956 PCC session specifically reports that 'General A. I. Antonov, secretary-general of the Political Consultative Committee' gave a report on 'organizational questions' (*Pravda* 28 January 1956). Antonov, however, has without exception been described elsewhere as the Chief of Staff of the WTO. The next time that *Pravda* mentioned the post was in the Communique of the 1972 PCC session, and Firyubin was for the first time acknowledged by the Soviets in that capacity.

Tyranowski, writing in 1971, did not mention the post. The last time that Firyubin was mentioned as attending a PCC session was in 1980, in Warsaw, at the 25th anniversary of the WTO (Communique, *Pravda*, 16 May 1980). At the PCC session in Prague in 1983, in the absence of Firyubin, 'Dusan Spacil, Deputy Foreign Affairs Minister of Czechoslovakia, acted at the meeting as general secretary of the Political Consultative Committee' (Communique, *Pravda*, 6 January 1983). Firyubin, in fact, died the following month (*Pravda*, 16 February 1983).

The post does not seem to be prestigious, nor do the WTO members seem to want to replace Firyubin with a full-time post, since the Communique of the 1986 PCC concluded by noting that 'Herbert Krolikowski, representative of the GDR, State Secretary and First Deputy Minister of Foreign Affairs, was appointed the PCC General Secretary for the subsequent term' (*Pravda*, 12 June 1986). It seems that whatever the functions of the post, they can be carried out between session of the PCC by the deputy foreign minister of the state hosting the next session. (Krolikowski was not listed as an attendee of the 1986 session.)

A GDR text from 1981 (*Völkerrecht*) did not refer to the post. Meissner (1983, p. 361a), without quoting a source, claims that the General Secretary heads the Joint Secretariat.

The Legal Convention

On 27 April 1973, *Krasnaya Zvezda* published the text of a 'Convention on the legal status, privileges and immunities of the staff and other bodies of administration of the Joint Armed Forces of the state-participants of the Warsaw Treaty', which had been signed in Moscow on 24 April. The signatories were named, but no designation given to them (see Appendix 1). (By comparison, *Pravda* had briefly noted the signing of the Convention, but did not supply the text – 25 April 1973.) It was not until Yakubovskii's book in 1975 that it was stated (p. 292) that 'The deputy ministers of foreign affairs of the country-participants of the Warsaw Treaty signed in Moscow a Convention . . . ' in April 1973, a wording repeated verbatim by Kulikov (1980).

This is a very strange state of affairs, since it gives minor state representatives authority over senior military representatives. Since the Committee of Ministers of Defence is a 'body of administration' of the WTO, the precedence in theory (but not in intent, judging by the wording), is given for the deputy foreign ministers meeting outwith the formal WTO structure to predominate over the Ministers of Defence. All this happened prior to the extension of the formal political structure of the WTO (which still does not include a committee of deputy foreign ministers).

The Legal Convention is the only additional document that appears to have been published, even though all the bodies within the structure of the WTO are said to be governed by individual statutes (see, for example, the preamble of the Legal Convention; Kozlov, writing in 1971, said that the Soviet forces in Central Europe were governed by 'Legal statutes between the Soviet forces and the state bodies in the allied countries' – p. 213).

The Legal Convention in general gives the administrative staff of the Joint Armed Forces, of whatever nationality and wherever situated, what amounts to diplomatic status.[27]

* * *

Further structural changes were agreed on at the Bucharest session of the PCC, 25–26 November 1976, when a Committee of Ministers of Foreign Affairs (CFM), and a Joint Secretariat, were set up as 'bodies of the Political Consultative Committee' for 'the further improvement of the machinery of political co-operation within the framework of the Warsaw Treaty' (Communique, *Pravda*, 27 November 1976).

The Committee of Ministers of Foreign Affairs

'Practical work' had been carried out by meetings of foreign ministers, beginning in 1959 (though no such meetings were announced as taking place between 1960–65 inclusive), and the deputy foreign ministers (from 1968) (see Menzhinskii *et al.* 1980, p. 36 – see also Appendix 2). According to Tyranowski (1973, p. 111), these pre-1976 meetings should not be seen as 'organs of the Warsaw Treaty' but their decisions 'may be treated as directives of a political nature by which the governments of the Treaty member states and their organs should be guided'. Addressing the attendees of the first session of the CFM, Brezhnev declared that the Committee would improve co-operation 'in international affairs, to the successful fulfilment of the foreign policy tasks of the fraternal parties' (*Pravda*, 27 May 1977).

The CFM works 'by taking into account' PCC foreign policy resolutions and recommendations, which are seen as the 'common positions' of the member-states, and then the Committee 'bring[s] about in actual forms the co-ordination of their foreign policy activities' (Menzhinskii *et al.*, 1980, p. 37). Menzhinskii adds that CFM Communiques should be seen as having a role analogous to PCC Declarations (ibid.). He explains that CFM communiques are thus also to be seen as a co-ordinated evaluation of the international situation, and therefore a policy statement of the members on these issues but which, more than a PCC Declaration, offer 'concrete suggestions' for peace and security – which leads Menzhinskii to argue that 'A communique of the Committee is a document of great political significance' (ibid.).

For practical purposes, the CFM is intended to improve the co-ordination of foreign-policy activities (Savinov, 1980, p. 17), which would mean that it does not just endorse and apply PCC positions but is actually the place where debate takes place as to what that position should be. Alexandrov, in fact, cites the CFM and the meetings of its deputies as being 'the most important part' of the mechanism for foreign policy co-operation (p. 22), which would seem to place it above the PCC on these matters in all but general terms. By comparison Gribkov, on the 30th Anniversary, described the CFM only as 'An important link in the mechanism of the co-operation and co-ordination of the activities in international affairs . . . ' (*Izvestiya*, 14 May 1985).

A further rôle for the CFM, according to Alexandrov, is for it to propose the full agendas, schedules, and working documents, for the international meetings proposed in outline by the PCC, and then carry out the work to implement the decisions of that meeting (p. 22). However, the example given by Alexandrov was the process surrounding the Helsinki Conference on Security and Co-operation in Europe which, being concluded in 1975, took place before there was an official WTO body within which the foreign ministers could operate.

The Deputy Foreign Ministers

The rôle of the meetings of the deputy foreign ministers is obscure. Bloed (1980) gives them the status of a full 'Conference' (p. 36), but gives no source for this description. Zamyatin links 'periodic meetings' of the deputy foreign ministers with the co-operation of socialist delegates at the UN and other international fora, in helping to work out 'joint positions on actual problems'. In general, though, the original sources do not discuss the work of the deputy foreign ministers within the WTO.

Various Central European sources[N] have given the activities of the deputy foreign ministers much greater status than official Soviet or Central European published sources. One expert[N] stated that the deputy foreign ministers were the consulting body for WTO-CMEA ties, another[N] that they set the agendas for the bigger meetings.

What setting the agenda might mean in practice is the carrying-out of the active inter-bloc diplomacy that the formal structure is too institutionalized to cope with. A third expert[N] furthermore equated meetings of the deputy foreign ministers under WTO auspices with the CMEA's Executive Committee.

The Joint Secretariat

Prior to 1976, a 'Joint Secretariat' was not referred to in the official literature. Despite their both writing four years after the Bucharest Reforms, neither Menzhinskii nor Savinov (1980) referred to the joint secretariat as mentioned in the 1976 Communique. Meissner, referring to what he calls 'the reorganized Joint Secretariat' (personal communication, 17 March 1985), claims that it is of 'particular importance', since it prepares PCC meetings, conducts the PCC's day-to-day business, and constantly liaises with the CMEA (1983, p. 361a), and that it also carries out 'technical preparations' for CFM meetings (ibid.). One of Meissner's sources (personal communucation, op. cit.) turns out to be a legal handbook (*Völkerrech*) from the GDR, which states that the Joint Secretariat is a full-time body that 'prepares the sittings of the Political Consultative Committee, attends to its current business and maintains a constant link to CMEA' (p. 87b), but does not seem to mention its work with the foreign ministers or the post of the General Secretary, whom Meissner says heads the Joint Secretariat (1983, p. 381a). Meissner's insistence that he is referring to the post-1976 affairs is confusing, since in the same article he writes that 'at the beginning of the 1970s' the General Secretary took over from the Chief of Staff as heading the 'Joint Secretariat' (ibid.). This pre-1976 Secretariat, as discussed above (under the Permanent Commission and Joint Secretariat of 1956), was referred to as 'not operative' by Savinov (1980, footnote, p. 16). That the 1976 Joint Secretariat was new rather than reorganized would seem to be borne out by the Bucharest Communique's use of the term 'to create' in reference to it (*Pravda*, 27 November 1976) and by, for example, the reference to the Committee of Ministers of Foreign Affairs and 'a Joint Secretariat' being 'set up' by a decision adopted at Bucharest (*SWB* SU/5377/A2/1).

(A Central European specialist[N] was insistent that the WTO's Joint Secretariat is not on a par with the CMEA Secretariat because the Central Europeans had consistently rejected Soviet proposals to make the WTO's structure similar to that of the CMEA.)

* * *

Judging by the BBC Monitoring Service, in the month preceding the Bucharest session of the PCC in 1976 there were several radio commentaries, often linked to newspaper articles, stressing the improving unity, cohesion, and joint foreign policy positions of the WTO member states, saying that this unity would be used by the PCC meeting to work for detente and arms control. As in the post-session commentaries, it was mainly the Bucharest Declaration which was stressed as significant. Despite the new political mechanisms set up, one of the commentaries stated that both multilateral and bilateral co-operation in all spheres were to be developed (*SWB*, SU/5377/A2/1). Further, the Soviet 'Party-Government Statement on the Warsaw Treaty Meeting in Bucharest', issued by TASS in both Russian and English for abroad on December 4 referred to both the institutional changes announced in the Communique and the various ad hoc proposals contained in the Declaration, as being important 'for broadening effective interaction in international affairs' (*SWB*, SU/5383/A2/1–2, 7 December 1976) – thus circumventing the intended rôle of the official structure of the WTO in intra-bloc affairs and its place in the international relations of the bloc.

EXTRA-STRUCTURAL FACTORS IN THE WTO

Other Bodies of the WTO

Some actual or potential extra-structural bodies of the WTO have been referred to in Western sources. For example, during the 30th Anniversary, the BBC's *Summary of World Broadcasts* reported that the Warsaw Home Service referred to 'the annual meeting of the member states' institutes of military history' (EE/7952/C/19, 16 May 1985). Such a regular gathering has not been mentioned in any of the other Soviet or Central European materials consulted.

Jones (1986, pp. 137–8, p. 143, p. 161) discusses a variety of extra-structural bodies, which he takes from 'available evidence' or 'clear evidence', but for which he cites no sources, either Soviet or Central European. The one exception is where he points out (ibid., p. 143) that Kulikov referred both to a 'Technical Committee' and to a 'Military-Scientific Technical Council' in discussion of other bodies of the Joint Armed Forces (Kulikov, 1980, p. 168). From this Jones argues, again without quoting a source, that 'Romania probably refused to participate in the work of the Technical Committee' (1986, p. 143). The latter of Jones's two titles is, however, virtually the same as that used by Menzhinskii in 1980 (p. 39) when apparently otherwise discussing the Technical Committee (see above under 'Technical Committee of the Joint Armed Forces' section).

The bodies that Jones (1986, p. 138) describes as operating under the aegis of the WTO would co-ordinate 'national agencies for military doctrine, officer education, political administration, paramilitary youth training, border troops, and perhaps other internal security forces as well' and for co-ordinating 'the corresponding bureaucracies of the paramilitary youth training and sports organizations' (ibid., p. 161). Jones argues that these agencies 'lack participation by the Romanians' which 'probably accounts for the Warsaw pact policy of not publicly acknowledging their existence' (ibid., p. 138).

Economic Co-operation and the CMEA

Notwithstanding Article 9 of the Treaty, claiming that other states can accede to it, it is also claimed that one of the WTO's strengths is that its members have a 'similarity of social and state system, common political goals, and the identical Marxist–Leninist ideology of their peoples' (Lototskii *et al.*, 1971, p. 347). Within this similarity, it is also claimed that the members' 'powerful economic base' is effected by conforming to 'the single-type planned national economy' (Alexandrov, 1980, p. 24). The Council for Mutual Economic Assistance is said to hold 'great importance' in creating economic unity (Shtemenko, 1976, p. 189a). Tyushkevich *et al.* (1985?, p. 446) singled out as especially significant the adoption by the CMEA in 1971 of the Comprehensive Programme for Economic Co-operation, which was reaffirmed in the Bucharest Declaration of 1976 (*Pravda*, 27 November 1976) and again in 1980 (Savinov, 1980, p. 23). Claiming that the CMEA's trade policies, including with the West, were a 'guarantor of peace', one Yurii Popov commented that 'integration of the CMEA member countries effectively helps the dynamic economic development of every single member country' (Moscow in Slovak, 14 November 1976 – *SWB* SU/5367/A1/4, 18 November 1976).[28] The same analysis was presented during the 30th Anniversary (Skorodenko, 1985, p. 62), when it was also claimed that extending economic co-operation 'in the framework of the Council for Mutual Economic Assistance' was part of the joint measures for maintaining the defence potential of the WTO (Shkarovskii, 1985, p. 158a).

Zhilin, however, in discussing how the extension of the states' material base through economic co-operation aided defence, considered that the CMEA played 'a great rôle' rather than an overwhelming or paramount rôle. The CMEA Secretariat's division on arms industries has a sub-division on WTO co-ordination.[N]

Outwith the immediate purview of the CMEA, Yakubovskii (1976) lists 'the mutual supplies of all the more basic parts and weapons', the co-ordination of research and development, and the moving towards the unification of weapons, all being included in the states' military and technical co-operation. All these come into the remit of the Technical Committee, which Yakubovskii does not refer to in this context. Kozlov (1977, p. 214) gives the Soviet Union pre-eminence with its 'continuous and unselfish assistance' towards the improvement of all the states' weapons and equipment. Such a positive view of both the weapons and the intra-bloc defence trade might not stand up to a rigorous analysis (see, for example, Rice, 1985, and other contributors to that volume; see also the section on 'Military Co-operation').

Military Co-operation

Military co-operation in the framework of the Warsaw Treaty is not restricted to the formal institutional processes of the Joint Command. Menzhinskii *et al.* (1980, p. 38) lists 'consultative meetings' of 'the top generals of the (main) staffs' as having taken place since May 1969 (since after the Budapest military Reforms) and regular planned meetings since 1967 (before the Reforms) of 'generals and officers of the Main Political Administrations' plus 'gatherings of cadres of the armies of the allied states'. Meanwhile, Shtemenko (1976, p. 169b) refers to co-operation of all the allied armies in a broad range of military training, military-theory and political education studies, plus top-level conferences on a variety of topics, and 'joint instruction in military schools'.

Writing on the 17th anniversary, Yakubovskii described exchanges and gatherings of military personnel, covering issues such as new weapons and training, 'and of information concerning the ideological and political education of military personnel' (*Pravda*, 14 May 1969). Strangely, though, despite his article being published just two months after the Budapest Reforms, he made no mention of them, and his discussion of such military co-operation seemed to lie outwith the formal WTO structure. He also gave as the only example of this co-operation the extra-structural meeting of military leaders that took place between 26–29 November 1968.

The object of the formal and informal concerted moves is, according to Yakubovskii, 'assisting the attainment of unified opinions in the basic problems of training the army and navy', building patriotism, and unifying opinions on 'the character and methods of the conduct of wars on the basis of Marxist-Leninist methodology', the latter aim being 'one of the most important sectors of socialist military co-operation' (1976). The broad designation of military and political co-operation at all levels and in all frameworks is the building of the comradeship-in-arms of the armies of the fraternal states (Lototskii *et al.*, 1971, p. 349). Within the formal military exchanges and training, the rôle of the Soviet 'higher military establishments' in training Central European officers is seen as preponderant (ibid., pp. 349–50), while the Soviet Union also sends specialists in military training to the military education establishments of its allies (Grechko, 1977, p. 335). The reason for this leading role is seen to be because the USSR is 'the most powerful country in the socialist world' (Tyushkevich *et al.*, 1985?, p. 446; see also p. 411). Even prior to the first multilateral exercises, it was claimed that, 'The exchange of experience in the training and education of troops, training commands, and literature, is widely practised between the fraternal armies . . . An important part is played by the exchange visits between vessels and the exchange of delegations' (*SWB*, SU/764/A2/1, 10 October 1961).

Tyushkevich also sees as important the co-operation in 'the co-ordination of military technical policy' in the supplies of the allies' weapons (p. 446). Here again, apart from joint consultations and research, the Soviet Union has a dominant rôle in supplying weapons, military hardware, and licences or documentation for Central European production of Soviet designs (Grechko, 1977, p. 335).

It seems debatable whether or not to include the joint exercises carried out in the name of the WTO in a discussion of extra-structural military co-operation. Yakubovskii described them as 'an important aspect of military co-operation' (*Pravda*, 14 May 1969), and this is typical of such descriptions throughout the history of the WTO. However, in the context of the 30th Anniversary, Rusakov's address did not specifically refer to joint exercises when explaining how military co-operation was developing and improving (*Izvestiya*, 15 May 1985). Also from the 30th Anniversary, it was stated that:

> The highest forms of collective preparation of the armies of the state-participants of the Warsaw Treaty for the repulse of imperialist aggression are the holding of periodic joint exercises, unilateral and bilateral, with the involvement of the staff and troops of the Joint Armed Forces. (Shkarovskii, 1985, p. 158a)

Since, as explained above, the Joint Armed Forces officially comprise only selected units from the national armies, Shkarovskii seems to be arguing that these selected troops then exercise with the national armies (which are not part of the WTO). (But see also the 'Political Co-operation' section below.) Since he did not specifically mention *multi*lateral exercises, Shkarovskii implies that they have nothing to do with the WTO. A further question arises when the way in which the joint exercises are officially described is taken into account. In his chronology, Kulikov (1980b) uses the term Joint Armed Forces only eight times when listing exercises, and most of these references are to do with the Joint Staff. The rest of the time the joint exercises listed are described as involving the forces of the national armies. This once again emphasizes the problems involved in establishing the formal military co-operation, either bilaterally or within the WTO, that actually takes place.

It is not the purpose of this work to argue the military merits or demerits of the WTO, or whatever structure actually exists. Nor is it intended to engage in an analysis of the minutiae of the joint exercises and the weapons or doctrines involved. Such discussions must be pursued elsewhere.

As with the discussion above on economic co-operation, it is possible to question the rosy platitudes about the military co-operation of the allied states. It would lead to an analysis of the political and economic relationships within the Soviet bloc, and the indigenous political, social, economic, military, etc., needs of the non-Soviet Warsaw Treaty member states. Such an analysis is also beyond the scope of this book.

One factor of military co-operation that is not discussed by the original sources is that of the KGB or national military intelligence bodies. Any role that they play in maintaining the unity of the Joint Armed Forces, or in reporting back to the Soviet leadership on military cohesion, would obviously occur outwith the formal structure of the WTO.

Political Co-operation

The political education of the troops referred to above as part of the military co-operation is given very prominant attention within the overall relationships of the allied armies. A correct political understanding is considered to be essential for 'instilling in servicemen devotion to their country, faithfulness to their international duty, and constant combat readiness' (Kozlov, 1977, p. 215). This is intricately bound up in socialist patriotism and proletarian internationalism (Lototskii *et al.*, 1971, p. 349; Tyushkevich *et al.*, 1985, p. 433; and e.g. *SWB* SU/746/A2/1, 10 October 1961).

The paramount importance given to political training is explained by Shtemenko (1976, 189b) when he says that, 'The brotherly communist parties realize that the main force in war has always been man' (p. 189b). He goes on to say that military specialists trained in and devoted to socialism must be 'capable of leading troops ably, of seeing that battle machinery is constantly ready for action, of carrying out, on a scientific basis, the ideological and political education of personnel and creating in them high moral and military qualities' (ibid.). The Soviet military experience would seem to confirm that properly-motivated troops can prevail against an otherwise militarily-superior enemy.

As with direct military matters, there is a constant exchange and gathering of political representatives in conferences, meetings, and direct training (ibid.; Yakubovskii, 1976). One Central European source[N] did, however, state that WTO co-operation between 'political representatives' was at a bilateral level, the WTO negotiating individually with each state. Also included in the overall process are direct contacts of military journalists and sporting events of allied troops, and 'youth-army camps' (Yakubovskii, 1976). These activities are not just for raising the political awareness of the allies, but also to increase the unity and cohesion of the combat community (ibid.).

In discussing the political aspects of the joint exercises, Shkarovskii (1985, p. 158b) explained that 'Commanders, political workers, party and youth bodies, in the period of preparation and in the course of training are in charge of purposeful ideological and political-educational work with individual staff of the participating forces'. There were also joint seminars and exchanges of experience. During the exercises, the joint production of a multinational newspaper was prominent within the political co-operation: 'This newspaper is one of the important means of up-to-date informational and propaganda work.' above all creating joint editorial processes in the field (ibid.). Shkarovskii also stressed the rôle of press-centres during the joint exercises for all the allied armies (ibid.). It might seem that fostering political unity took precedence over combat efficiency during practical military training under the aegis of the WTO.

Like the stress placed on the allies' having similar economic and social systems, Shtemenko (1976, p. 189b) refers to the allied military structure having theoretical military views based on 'the Marxist-Leninist teaching on war and the army . . . on Leninist principles of party leadership of the armed forces'. This has led to the co-ordination of party-political work within the military structures (Tyushkevich *et al.*, 1985, p. 433). Such co-ordination is carried out by the Main Political Administrations referred to by Menzhinskii *et al.*(1980, p. 38), which Jones (1984, p. 67) describes as 'the agencies officially designated by the WTO states to secure the political reliability . . . of the allied armies, and thereby to promote reliable performance in hostile circumstances'. According to Jones, all the non-Soviet Warsaw Treaty military structures, with the exception of Romania,[29] have MPA structures that are 'virtually identical' to the Soviet MPAs (ibid., p. 68). He describes the two primary objectives of such work to be to minimize the spread of anti-Russian sentiments from the Central European militaries to the non-Russian soldiers of the Soviet army, and to 'acculturize' all non-Russian and European soldiers to the Soviet military ethos (ibid.).

While Jones describes the *multi*lateral MPA activities of joint meetings, exchanges, co-ordination of publications, touring political lecturers, and so on (ibid., pp. 69, 70), he also states that the bilateral ties between the Soviet MPA and the individual Central European militaries are more extensive and of greater importance (ibid., p. 72, p. 67). Once again, as with the formal political and direct military ties, the USSR seems to be trying to circumvent the multilateral structures associated with the WTO, and to minimize their significance in intra-bloc relations. This again raises doubts as to the active rôle of the WTO in Soviet and Central European affairs.

The Parliamentarians

Individual ad hoc conferences of representatives of the Parliaments of the Warsaw Treaty states began in 1975, with a meeting to mark the 20th anniversary of the WTO.

The Declaration issued by the PCC in 1976 (*Pravda*, 27 November 1976) singled out meetings of the Parliamentarians as one of the means by which there was to be greater political co-operation of the allies. Explaining this, Savinov (1980, p. 22) quoted that the PCC had decided 'to extend the political connexions of the fraternal people, including to practice and further the carrying-out of consultative meetings of parliamentarians, and also representatives of the communal organizations for the discussion of current problems of international life . . . '. Later, Tolkunov (1986) highly appraised the work of the Parliamentarians to this end.

In discussing such work, but without mentioning the WTO meetings of Parliamentarians, Savinov also wrote that 'the Parliaments and Governments' of the states were working to reduce the threat of nuclear war, end the arms race (especially nuclear arms), on Earth and in the cosmos, and were working for disarmament, détente, and co-operation in international relations (1986, p. 249). Such a list of activities, or perhaps of intentions, is nothing new, since it is virtually the same peace policy contained in WTO documents and in descriptions of national foreign policies (cf. Bulgarian Academy of Sciences, pp. 883ff).

The documents issued by Parliamentarians, including that of their 30th Anniversary meeting, are nonetheless quite lacklustre, generally reiterating and supporting issues and policies raised in the most recent PCC documents. In this manner, these meetings seem to follow, rather than lead, 'the discussion of current problems of international life'.

The Party and State Leaders

There have been meetings of party chiefs, or the party First Secretaries and the heads of the governments, at various intervals throughout the history of the WTO. With one major exception, these meetings were careful not to usurp the official status of the PCC. The meeting in 1983 of 'leading party and state leaders' in Moscow, for example, issued a Joint Statement which 'confirmed the evaluations and conclusions of the Prague Political Declaration [of the PCC in January 1983]' (*Pravda*, 29 June 1983). The next session of the CFM, however, reaffirmed both the PCC Political Declaration and the Joint Statement of June (ibid., 15 October 1983). Tyranowski (1973, pp. 110, 111) is adamant that these ad hoc metings are not part of the WTO structure, but only have a capacity to advise the WTO members.

The one exception to this attempt not to over-ride the formal WTO processes was the 'meeting of the highest Party leaders and statesmen of the state-participants of the Warsaw Treaty' which signed the Protocol extending the WTO. The PCC, the WTO's highest body, was not considered suitable for this purpose.

The Communist Parties

A number of Soviet writers have given individual attention to the rôle of the communist and workers' parties in the work of the WTO and the national armies. All their comments underlined the understandable concern that the parties should have a leading rôle in the defence affairs of their states and of the socialist community. For example, Stepaniuk, writing as a 'General-lieutenant-engineer' in an article commemorating the 17th anniversary of the Treaty, stated unequivocally that the leading Marxist–Leninist parties 'determined first and foremost' the joint foreign policies and military co-operation (including economic, ideological, and doctrinal affairs) of the 'indestructable fraternity of arms'. Kozlov (1977, p. 212) gave a leading position to the CPSU in the move to strengthen the WTO against imperialist military aggression, as did Grechko (1977, p. 318), even giving to the parties the rôle of determining 'the forms of [military] alliance of the fraternal armies' and the WTO, as just one part of the 'decisive role' in maintaining the parties' 'socialist social system' (ibid., p. 324). Tyushkevich *et al.* (1985?, pp. 446–7) stated that the whole structure of the Joint Command (mentioning every body from the Committee of Ministers of Defence down to the Technical Committee) was under the constant attention of the 'fraternal communist and workers' parties', which he put behind every proposal and recommendation of a military nature.

The stress on the rôle of the parties was explained by Tyushkevich (ibid.):

> The ultimate basis on which the armies of the Warsaw Pact were built is Lenin's principle on the direction of the Army by the communist and workers' parties. Creating and indoctrinating the armed forces of the socialist countries, the parties depend on Marxist–Leninist teaching on war and the army. (p. 411)

Such outspokenness on the rôle of the parties on the work of the WTO presents us with a problem, or perhaps a solution to the ultimate workings of the Organization. As it was originally formulated and signed, the Warsaw Treaty was an alliance of states, and was signed by members of governments without mentioning any positions they may have held in their respective national parties. As described in this chapter, the whole structure of the WTO is geared towards inter-state relations, with only the PCC allowing a significant formal input from party representatives. In any case each delegation has only one vote (Menzhinskii *et al.*, 1980, p. 34), so party and state members of delegations would have to confer and agree. (Even so, the above analysis of the PCC shows that it cannot be seen as a very active and significant body.)

In fact, hidden within the WTO's documents, there are several references to the parties, which could be interpreted to signify that, as Rice (1984, p. 132) expressed in a slightly different context, the party ties 'transcend national boundaries and are links of a socialist world order', thus superceding any inter-state relations.

Within the text of the Treaty, Article 6 stated that the PCC would be formed 'in which each state-participant to this treaty shall be represented by a member of the government, or any other specially appointed representative'. This did not specify that there should be party delegates. In practice, the 1956 PCC listed the attendees only by their state designations, the 1958 PCC had attendees with party designations but not as the chief delegates, but from the 1960 PCC onwards the chief delegate from each state was the First or General Secretary of the party (see footnote 6 of this chapter).

The rôle the parties were playing in the WTO was specified by the then Commander-in-Chief Yakubovskii (1971, pp. 24–5):

> For the development and strengthening of the military alliance of the countries of socialism it has paramount importance that the leadership of all the affairs of the defence of the countries of socialism are accomplished by the communist and workers' parties.
>
> . . . Of extraordinary importance in the activities of the Organization of the Warsaw Treaty is this, that the communist and workers' parties and the governments of the country-participants go forward in a united front on the international arena . . .

Only then did Yakubovskii discuss the rôle of the PCC (ibid., p. 25). Also writing in 1971, Bakhov spelt out the importance of the parties as an extra-structural factor, when he explained that:

> The leading role of the communist and workers' parties in the country-participants of the Treaty guarantees for the unity and cohesion of these countries, and the strict [implementation] of the basic peace policies. (p. 6)

In other words, even though the WTO worked as an inter-state body, it was taken as read that the parties had a leading, albeit extra-structural, rôle.

In 1977, Brezhnev, addressing a reception following the first session of the CFM, argued that this new (inter-state) body would help fulfil 'the foreign-policy tasks of the fraternal parties' (*Pravda*, 27 May 1977). Again in 1977, a regular meeting of the WTO's Military Council sent a message to Brezhnev, as Chairman of the Presidium of the CPSU, and the Soviet Government, but principally to the CPSU, on the 60th anniversary of the Great October Socialist Revolution 'in which was conveyed profound acknowledgement for the tireless work concerning the increasing of the defensive might of the state-participants of the Warsaw Treaty' (*Pravda*, 21 October 1977). Not only were the parties to have a leading rôle but, as noted in the section above on military co-operation, the rôle of the Soviet Union (or CPSU) was to be seen to be fundamental. In other words, it was being stated that the main bodies putting into practice the foreign and military policies of the PCC were in fact carrying out the tasks of a higher, but generally unacknowledged, authority.

Even the PCC acknowledges this higher authority. In the Communique of the 1978 session it is stated that the participants, the leaders of both the parties and the states, were in the accompanying joint documents being true to the foreign policy course worked out by the congresses of the members' leading parties (*Pravda*, 24 November 1978). This rôle for the party congresses was repeated in the 1986 PCC Communique (*Pravda*, 12 June 1986). Thus, taking into account that the PCC was the leading body of the joint action of the WTO members, Savinov (1980, p. 24) was still able to explain that the foreign-policy co-operation of the WTO, 'as in all other spheres of joint action, has at its heart the inter-party ties at the highest level'.

In the same vein, the 30th Anniversary analysis of the WTO repeated the paramount rôle of the parties. Katrich, for example, stated that 'The first principle for the successful activity of the Organization of the Warsaw Treaty as a reliable shield of the socialist community' was the leadership of the parties within the member countries (p. 55). On purely military grounds, Chief of Staff Gribkov (1985b, p. 96) stated that, 'The greater place in the life and activities of the allied armies is occupied by the co-operation of the political bodies, which are accomplished on the basis of the decisions of the communist and workers parties'. This latter statement would imply either that the WTO military structure detailed above is irrelevant to 'the activities of the allied armies', or that these bodies are in fact a front for the 'decisions of the parties'. Or, as Gorbachev said at a plenary meeting of the CPSU Central Committee, since the 1986 PCC occurred so soon after a number of party congresses, 'the foreign-policy guidelines of the supreme party fora became, naturally, the focus of collective discussion' (*Pravda*, 17 June 1986).

As this chapter has shown, the formal structure of the WTO does not include any formal mechanism for inter-party ties; in fact, since the basis of inter-party relations is bilateral, there could be no formal mechanism for bringing the rôle of the parties into the WTO other than through participation in the PCC, which is no more than a forum for irregular guidance of general policy.

Central European sources[N] informed me that, bearing in mind that the party foreign-policy structures are superior to the state foreign ministries, the rôle of state mechanisms is to transfer to the WTO's PCC and Joint Secretariat, policy or information worked out by the parties. Thus the real originators of WTO policy are the national party Politbureaux, where the highest decisions are made . . . except that their decisions are taken on the basis of information worked out by their International sections, through meetings (or even 'phone-calls),[N] generally on a bilateral level, developing policy compromises.

But even this is not quite the case. The WTO Joint Secretariat has no more than a consultative rôle as a group of 'experts and co-ordinators' with a special understanding of how the parties and states inter-relate, and how best to co-ordinate the national policies.[N] The WTO Secretariat does not have a commanding rôle. The CPSU controls both the Joint Secretariat and military matters, so it is in fact the CPSU International Department which effectively writes WTO documents, taking into account the advice of both the Joint Secretariat and the non-Soviet bilateral representatives to the CPSU.[N] The level of this Central European input can, at times, be no more than to point out that if the CPSU commits the WTO to a certain policy, it will affect the Central Europeans economically in such a way that the USSR will have to support its allies economically to ameliorate the consequences of the foreign or military policy (ibid.).

The statements on the rôle of the parties seem to indicate that the whole structure of the WTO, as an inter-state body, is either irrelevant or just a front. Given the prominent rôle of the national parties in all other aspects of their countries' lives, it would be improbable to discount their equal rôle in the multilateral defence of their community, far beyond their admitted role of whipping up proletarian enthusiasm in the military conscripts and officers. So just what is the status of the WTO in the international affairs of the socialist community?

CONCLUSIONS ON THE WTO STRUCTURE

At the end of the day, both the official statements and the unofficial analysis of the rôle of the parties shows that the WTO as an inter-state body has

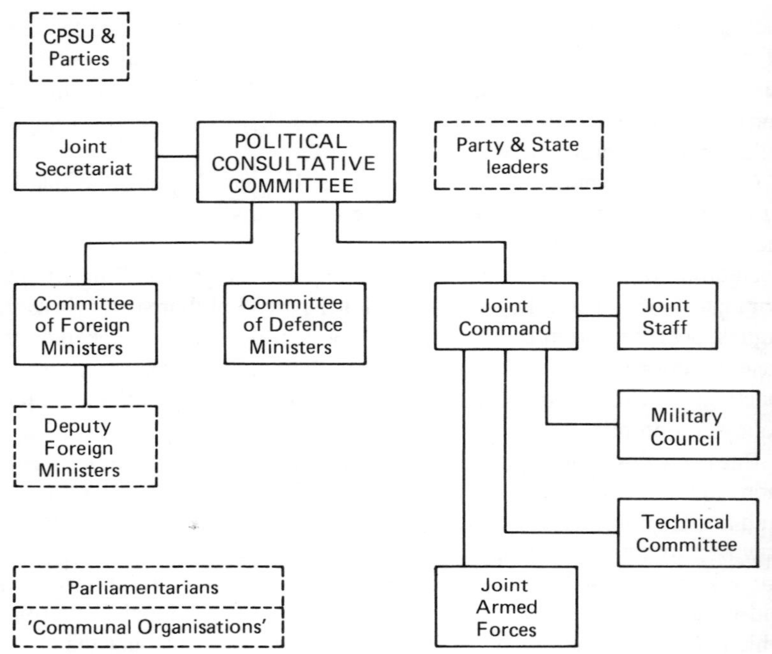

SOURCES As in Figure 3; Bucharest Declaration, 26 November 1976

—— denotes bodies within the formal structure

– – – denotes bodies within the informal structure

FIGURE 4 *WTO formal and informal structure, 1985*

little independence either in determining the national foreign and defence policies of its members, or in multilateral policy. Chapter 4 assesses just what the WTO says in its documents, and makes conclusions as to the rôle of the WTO in the joint foreign policy that is expressed by those documents.

Taking into account all the extra-structural factors to the WTO, Figure 4 shows a truer picture of the WTO, as it existed in 1985 at the time of the Treaty's prolongation. It shows both the formal and informal mechanisms, and suggests how they might interrelate. (The national armed forces do not appear, since they are not part of the formal or informal structures.) Chapter 4 goes on to discuss the formal documents issued by this structure, and discusses what further conclusions can be drawn on the place of the WTO in the multilateral relations of its members.

4 Analysis of the Documents and Materials, 1955–85

PART A – THE DOCUMENTS AND MATERIALS

The documents issued in the name of the Warsaw Treaty Organization display the breadth and continuity of the WTI's formal and informal structure. They can be divided broadly into two categories: those which give a brief notification that a meeting took place, with a very general explanation of the subjects discussed; and those which give a fuller account of the issues and proposals raised in the meeting. The former documents cover the meetings of the military structure of the WTO, from the Defence Ministers down, plus the meetings of the deputy foreign ministers; the latter, with one or two exceptions, cover the meetings of the political structure (Menzhinskii *et al.*, 1980, pp. 35–6, discusses the variety of PCC documents – see footnote 8, Chapter 3.)

DOCUMENTS OF NOTIFICATION

The meetings of the military bodies of the WTO have been almost exclusively concerned with such issues as 'the enhancement of the preparedness of the Warsaw Treaty' (defence ministers, *Pravda*, 10 September 1961) and examining 'current questions concerning the strengthening of the Joint Armed Forces' (defence ministers, *Pravda*, 2 February 1962). Very little explanation of how these improvements are to be effected, or indeed what concrete decisions have been taken, is evident from the documents issued by the meetings. A report of a meeting of the defence ministers and military leaders (*Pravda*, 19 May 1965) explained that 'Tactical exercises demonstrating new specimens of arms and military equipment were carried out . . . '. Many of the earlier reports of meetings of the defence ministers mention that the Ministers observed exercises of the national army of the country in which the meeting took place. By the third meeting of the defence ministers (*Krasnaya Zvezda*, 1 March 1963) it is explained that questions of the co-ordination of the training of the states' armies were being discussed.

These are the issues referred to throughout the thirty years and more of the WTO, by all levels of the military structure. The meeting of leaders of army cadres (*Pravda*, 19 November 1967) also stated that tasks for the next year were set, a function taken over by the Military Council in its autumn meetings, after that body's formation in 1969 (see, for example, *Pravda*, 31 October 1970). In fact, prior to the Budapest Reforms, meetings of the (then informal) military structure were somewhat ad hoc. This was exemplified in the second meeting of the defence ministers who reported that 'It was decided to ask the governments of the Warsaw Treaty countries to endorse the decisions [of the defence ministers] at the next meeting of the Political Consultative Committee' (*Pravda*, 2 February 1962).

The one major exception to the documents of the military structure prior to the 30th Anniversary is that of the only 'extraordinary' meeting of the Committee of Ministers of Defence. This meeting discussed 'the development of the military-political situation in Europe' (a topic normally the prerogative of the political structure), referred to the peace proposals of the political structure (again unprecedented), and made a statement against the NATO medium-range nuclear force developments (once again a topic normally limited to the political structure). The document concluded by stating that 'The Committee of Ministers of Defence adopted a corresponding decision on the question discussed' (*Pravda*, 22 October 1983). This seems to have referred to the fact that, three days later, the Defence Ministry of the USSR announced bilateral arrangements with Czechoslovakia and the GDR for the prospective stationing of 'operational-tactical' nuclear missiles in those two countries (*Pravda*, 25 October 1983). This specifically-Soviet announcement did not refer to the Warsaw Treaty Organization, except to state that the Soviet measures were 'directed at maintaining the equilibrium in the nuclear systems between the Warsaw Treaty and NATO'.

THE FOREIGN MINISTERS

The earliest meeting of the foreign ministers reported that the meeting 'examined questions connected with the forthcoming Geneva negotiations, regarding Germany, the signing of a peace treaty with Germany, and the question of the elimination of the occupation regime in West Berlin' (*Pravda*, 29 April 1959). This illustrates both its ad hoc nature and the need to delegate foreign policy discussion down from the PCC.

The Bucharest PCC session (1966) was seen as the start of the campaign for an all-European conference (ultimately the Conference on Security and

Co-operation in Europe). In the WTO's European security campaign it was the meetings of the foreign ministers which carried out the active diplomacy under authorization delegated from the PCC. The documents of these foreign ministers' meetings show that their main concern was with the successful convocation, and then the successful outcome, of the CSCE process.

The Statement issued after the meeting of 30–31 October 1969 spoke on behalf of 'The governments represented at the conference . . . ' (*Pravda*, 1 November 1969). It suggested, 'acting on the instructions of the governments', that certain issues be included on the agenda of the proposed all-European conference. (Namely ensuring the non-use of force in Europe, and extending equal economic relations as the basis for developing equal political co-operation.) The 21–22 June 1970 meeting of the foreign ministers also issued a document on the proposed European meeting, this time a Memorandum, again calling for the same two issues to be discussed but adding that an all-European conference should discuss creating 'a body to deal with questions of security and co-operation in Europe' (*Pravda*, 27 June 1970).

The foreign ministers met again on 18–19 February 1971, but this time announced that they were 'Guided by' the PCC Statement on Europe adopted in Berlin in the preceding December. They repeated that their governments (rather than the PCC), were calling for the speedy convocation of the Conference (*Pravda*, 20 February 1971). Again it was the foreign ministers' carrying out the joint diplomacy by commenting that international tensions were being relaxed and that 'the contributions of other states' had been beneficial to this process. They balanced this by objecting to the militaristic line they perceived in 'The resolutions of the recent session of the NATO Council . . . ', and also commented that the GDR still did not have full diplomatic relations with all states (ibid.). This mixture of optimism tempered by unease at the activities of 'certain forces' was repeated by the foreign ministers' next communique (*Pravda*, 3 December 1971).

The next substantive document issued by the foreign ministers was issued by a meeting following the completion of the CSCE. This Communique (*Pravda*, 17 December 1975) was the first issued by the foreign ministers covering a whole range of foreign-policy issues (CSCE, the Middle East, the UN General Assembly, the Vienna arms talks, and Angola) rather than the single issue of the all-European conference.

Following the formal creation of a Committee of Ministers of Foreign Affairs (CFM) in the Bucharest Reforms of 1976, European foreign policy issues have continued to be the main concern of the communiques issued by the foreign ministers, though also with passing references to broader issues and the proposals of the PCC. No doubt the successful use of the multilateral meetings and documents of the foreign ministers prior to the Helsinki Final Act contributed to the structural developments – in a meeting following the first session of the CFM (25–26 May 1977), Brezhnev expressed the conviction that the Committee would help work towards the further strengthening and improvement of the co-operation of the Warsaw Treaty states 'in international affairs, to the successful fulfilment of the foreign-policy tasks of the fraternal parties' (*Pravda*, 27 May 1977). In formal terms, however, the CFM carries out the decisions of the PCC (see, for example, the Communique dated 15 May 1979).

Meetings of the foreign ministers have been increasingly supplemented by meetings of the deputy foreign ministers. Reports of these extra-structural meetings, though sparse and insubstantial in content, show that the deputy foreign ministers have been taking over the duties of the foreign ministers in co-ordinating their countries' positions in the various European fora such as the Madrid and Stockholm conferences. Most recently the meetings have become the mechanism for a non-Soviet presentation of views on Soviet bilateral East–West foreign policy. The meeting on 1 March 1985 (for example) carried out 'an exchange of views in connexion with the commencing on 12 March of the Soviet–American discussions on nuclear and space weapons' (*Pravda*, 2 March 1985).

THE POLITICAL CONSULTATIVE COMMITTEE

The documents issued from summit-level meetings – the PCC and, to a lesser extent, the extra-structural meetings of party and state leaders – are a history of the basics of WTO joint foreign policy, its issues and principles, over the entire length of the WTO's existence. The Declaration issued by the 25th anniversary session of the PCC was proud to declare that 'the state-participants of the Warsaw Treaty have always displayed, and continue to display, consistency, loyalty to principles . . . ' (*Pravda*, 16 May 1980). An analysis of these documents does indeed show a marked continuity.

The first thirty years of WTO diplomacy can be seen, as indeed the Preamble to the Treaty declared in 1955, as the diplomacy of the struggle for collective security in Europe, as defined by the USSR. The documents from 1955 to the final major declaration before the Treaty's prolongation consistently call for international relations to be conducted through a series of interrelated principles which, it is felt, would ensure collective security and a peaceful European continent. The way would be cleared for economic construction and material advancement. The peace proposals put forward in the name of the WTO also show continuity. It is argued that, having acted under the principles of international relations, the international legal guarantees of collective security in Europe could be codified, and then extended to world-wide peace and security. In this respect the WTO, which is a regional defence alliance, is assuming a global rôle in what is largely the issue of bilateral Soviet–US nuclear relations.

Despite this overall continuity, the documents fall into three rough periods: the Khrushchev years; the pre-Helsinki years; and the post-Helsinki years. The various General Secretaries of the CPSU will be seen to have used the WTO in different ways, though this may not be directly evident from the documents as such. (This would be more a question for the study of Soviet internal policies.)

The Khrushchev Years

Roughly the ten years of the WTO, from the first PCC session in 1956 to the first PCC session under Brezhnev, display an organizational inconsistency. Despite the fact that the 1956 Communique resolved that the body would meet 'not less than twice a year' (*Pravda*, 29 January 1956), such regular consideration of 'matters arising from the implementation of the Warsaw Treaty' (Article 6 of the Treaty) has never taken place. Throughout the Khrushchev period, indeed, WTO top-level meetings were generally held in tandem with top-level CMEA meetings of the same leaders, reportage of which dwarfed the publication of WTO documents in the Soviet press. Khrushchev seems to have been playing down the rôle of the WTO. Indeed, in an article by Khrushchev written for the US magazine *Foreign Affairs* and reprinted as a *Soviet News* pamphlet 'Khrushchev on Peaceful Coexistence' (September 1959), there are repeated references to NATO, but the WTO is never mentioned. Obviously it played no significant part in Khrushchev's foreign policy during its early years.

In terms of the content of the documents, in the earliest years the WTO declarations on foreign policy were indentical to the general Soviet concerns about encirclement, Cold War and NATO rearmament, and so on (*Pravda*, 29 January 1956). The 1956 Declaration was in fact a précis of Molotov's speech to the PCC (ibid.). Likewise the 1958 Declaration was a précis of Khrushchev's much longer speech to the PCC (*Pravda*, 27 May 1958).

In these first-period documents, however, a paradox occurs, since it was only in these earliest years that the PCC carried out anything resembling an active diplomacy. In addition to their paramount interest in the German question, these documents also covered troop levels in Europe. The 1956 PCC session claimed that NATO was rearming despite 'the fact that the peaceloving European countries have already effected a number of measures to cut their armed forces and military budgets' (Declaration, *Pravda*, 29 January 1956). In 1958 the PCC spelt out levels of 'unilateral reductions' in WTO armed forces (Communique, *Pravda*, 27 May 1958). This was repeated by the next session of the PCC (Declaration, *Pravda*, 5 February 1960) and specifically called on NATO, which it again accused of building up its forces, to reciprocate Soviet moves to disarmament. Beginning with the first PCC session under Brezhnev (1965), the documents became limited to the general foreign policy themes.

In the Khrushchev period the biggest issue was the question of the division of Germany in the absence of a formal peace treaty, and to a lesser extent to the Berlin question. (These issues extended into the early Brezhnev period.) In these cases, Khrushchev's inconsistent approach to the rôle of the WTO is more apparent. Despite the inclusion of German issues in PCC documents, extra-structural meetings took place of the 'First Secretaries of the Central Committees of the Communist and Workers' Parties of the Country-Participants of the Warsaw Treaty' (3–5 August 1961) and of 'The Governments of the State-Participants of the Warsaw Treaty' (12–13 August 1961), both of which meetings were specifically concerned with the German questions. The first of the meetings was a conference 'on the questions connected with the preparation for the conclusion of a German peace treaty'. It 'instructed the corresponding competent bodies to prepare all the necessary foreign policy and economic measures, providing for the conclusion of a German peace treaty and the observance of its enactment, including such observance, which applies to West Berlin as a free city'.[1,2] It was argued that such a move was to guard 'the sovereign rights of the German Democratic Republic' (*Pravda*, 6 August 1961).

The second special meeting in August, which issued a document from Berlin dated August 13, was specifically concerned with the Berlin question and in particular what it saw as NATO and the Federal Republic of Germany using West Berlin 'as a centre of subversive activities against the German Democratic Republic and all the other countries in the socialist commonwealth' which it considered were undermining the GDR's economy and affecting 'the interests of other countries of the socialist camp'. The document called on 'the People's Chamber and the government of the German Democratic Republic and all the working people of the German Democratic Republic' to establish a 'regime' on West Berlin's borders 'which will securely bloc the way to the subversive activity against the countries of the socialist camp, so that reliable safeguards and effective control may be established round the whole territory of West Berlin including its border with democratic Berlin' (*Pravda*, 14 August 1961). In other words, this document was calling for the construction of what became the Berlin Wall. At the same time it argued that such a regime would cease to be necessary on the conclusion of a German peace settlement as envisaged in the document issued a few days earlier (ibid.).

Judging from the content of these two documents, they could just as easily have been considered within the PCC rather than through an extra-structural process. The German question was after all the main concern of the Preamble to the Treaty, and the PCC had been established to consider issues of joint concern. Within this first period of its operation, the WTO was obviously not being used for the purpose for which it was intended. This could imply that the Soviet Union was conducting its joint foreign policy more on an ad hoc basis, or that it wished to treat these issues independently rather than place them within the purview of the WTO.

During the later years of the Khrushchev period, summit-level documents became much terser. On the second of two days of a CMEA session (6–7 June 1962), a Declaration was issued, attributed to the WTO, which covered PCC responses to a report to it by Gromyko 'on the talks between the government of the Soviet Union and the government of the United States of America on a German peace settlement. and confirmed the Soviet position at the talks. (This Declaration actually began with a list of PCC attendees, a format previously reserved for a communique; *Pravda*, 10 June 1962.) A year later a meeting of the Party First Secretaries and the Heads of Government of the Warsaw Treaty states issued a Resolution (*Pravda*, 27 July 1963) approving the results of Gromyko's negotiations with the USA and Britain on a nuclear test ban treaty. This extra-structural meeting led directly into a CMEA meeting which was itself followed by a PCC session that issued a Communique which covered only the discussion of a report from the WTO Commander-in-Chief Grechko on 'questions connected with the condition of the armed forces of the state-participants of the Warsaw Treaty'.[3] By the end of his leadership, Khrushchev was using interchangeably all the multilateral mechanisms of the socialist community.

The Pre-Helsinki Years

Brezhnev's accession to power was quickly followed by a meeting of the PCC, which issued a Communique that, while continuing to cover the campaign for a German peace settlement, was dominated by th issue of the moment, NATO's discussions on whether or not to se up a multilateral nuclear force. The PCC claimed that this would giv 'West German militarists' access to nuclear weapons (*Pravda*, 22 Januar 1965). The Communique also included a brief suggestion, in support o 'The initiative of the Polish People's Republic', calling for 'a conferenc of European states to be convened in order to discuss measures ensurin collective security in Europe'.[4]

The Brezhnev years of the WTO, and in particular the pre-Helsinki year (starting with 1966), show a marked use by the PCC of single-issue docu ments (in addition to the Communique), rather than a generic Declaration In this second period there was just one meeting of Party and State leader (4 December 1969 – issuing a Statement on Vietnam), but it also saw th instigation of annual summits held in July or August at the Crimea. Th first three of these Crimea meetings were full multilateral summits issuin joint documents that were originally included in the official *Documents an Materials* volumes despite the fact that the sessions included full partici pation by representatives of the wider socialist community rather than jus the members of the WTO. (Issues discussed were broadly similar to PC documents, but with a greater emphasis on ideological questions.) Th 1966 PCC, which lasted three days, preceded a one-day CMEA session and appears to have been the last such joint conference. (In succeedin documents of both organizations there have been cross-references to th activities or proposals of the other, and the two have been associated withi the general call for closer unity and cohesion of the member states.)

Brezhnev seems from the outset of his leadership to have wanted th WTO to be a well-developed and comprehensive multilateral foreign policy organization. In effect, as can be seen in the documents, the Sovie leadership in joint foreign policy moved from the active European diplo macy of the Khrushchev years to the broad declaration of commentary o the world issues of the moment. While under Khrushchev the preponderan concern over Germany was accompanied by declarations of general interes in other issues, in the pre-Helsinki years there was not just the campaig for European collective security but a pronounced interest in out-of-are problems and the full development of the thesis that 'peace is indivisible (see Tyranowski, 1973, p. 116). In other words global superpower relation had a direct bearing on the level of confrontation in Europe, a solution t the military confrontation in Europe could lead to a wider world peace and vice versa.

The Communique of the PCC session of August 1970, for example commented that 'The main attention was devoted to the present situatio in Europe which, in the general opinion, exerts major influence on the world situation as a whole' (*Pravda*, 21 August 1970). This direct linkage concisely expresses the earlier general assertions that, for example, a USA involved in the Vietnam war could not at the same time be truly interested in disarmament (PCC Statement on Vietnam, *Pravda*, 8 July 1966). Thus what remains a purely European defence alliance was claiming a direct involvement in world issues, and the right to assert a multilateral global political perspective. By the PCC session of 1974, the Communique argued that 'the easing of tensions must cover all parts of the world' and was the concern of all states and everyone (*Pravda*, 19 April 1974). Such a global linkage continues in the documents to the present day.

The 1966 PCC session tried to involve the WTO directly in the world arena, by stating that the governments represented 'declare their readiness, if the government of the Democratic Republic of Vietnam requests it, to allow their volunteers to go to Vietnam in order to help the Vietnamese people in their struggle against the American aggressors' (Statement, *Pravda*, 8 July 1966). The offer was repeated in the 1968 Declaration on Vietnam (*Pravda*, 9 March 1968). This seems to be the only such extra-European threat of involvement. Throughout the whole WTO period the documents have included broad and unspecific declarations of support – apparently only moral support – for national liberation movements around the world.[5]

The 1966 Declaration on Strengthening Peace and Security in Europe marked a high point in the WTO's tirades against the USA as an imperialist aggressor, and an attempt to decouple Western Europe from the USA:

> There can be no doubt that the aims of the United States policy in Europe have nothing in common with the vital interests of the European peoples and the aim of European security.
>
> American ruling circles would like to impose their will on their allies in Western Europe and make Western Europe an instrument of the United States global policy . . . (*Pravda*, 9 July 1966)

The rest of the Declaration was directed towards 'all European states' in the hope of establishing a mutual European security system in place of bloc confrontation. However, as the European security campaign developed, the anti-US diatribe subsided rapidly.

The pre-Helsinki period is exemplified by the extension of a general WTO voice in wider world affairs, and the European security campaign, both of which were directed through the issuing of individual documents in the name of the PCC. Despite the fact that the rest of the political structure of the alliance was undeveloped and operating only on an ad hoc basis, the WTO was maturing as the world voice of the socialist states. The aims of the WTO had not changed, and their proposals for establishing world peace were still the same. But their presentation was seeming more unified and polished.

There was only one minor crack in the cohesion, and that was in 1968 with the Statement on nuclear non-proliferation (dated March 7 and issued with the PCC documents – *Pravda*, 9 March 1968). This statement began in the customary fashion by listing the names of the Warsaw Treaty states and stating that they 'in the spirit of complete unanimity, outline the following position on nuclear non-proliferation'. However, the Socialist Republic of Romania was not listed, and the Statement had to engage in tortuous and unusual wording by referring to 'The above-mentioned states . . . ' rather than 'The state-participants of the Warsaw Treaty'. With the exception of Albania in 1961, this was the first time that complete unanimity had *not* in fact been reached. Rather than avoid it the subject was seen to be important enough to issue an unofficial document on the matter. (This document has been included in the official *Documents and Materials* volumes.) In fact all the document covered was to say that a non-proliferation treaty would lead to 'favourable conditions' for the end to the arms race and an end to nuclear weapons, and that the states had examined a draft treaty (that was not published) which it was thought 'corresponds to the above-mentioned task'. The 'above-mentioned states' declared their support for the draft treaty and called for the conclusion of a non-proliferation treaty. A further indication of the importance given to this issue was that the Statement was published on page 1 of *Pravda* beside the Communique and Declaration issued in the name of the Warsaw Treaty.

The PCC session in 1974 expressed the view that peaceful coexistence and the principles of international relations that would be the basis of this coexistence were being ever more widely established. This relaxation of international tensions was seen to have been 'decisive in the transition to the political sphere' of the confrontation problems around the world, (mainly in named South-East Asian countries), 'and it creates favourable conditions for the struggle of the peoples for freedom, independence, democracy, and progress' (Communique, *Pravda*, 19 April 1974). The 'constructive activity of the USSR, plus its socialist partners' was seen to be the main cause of this relaxation, as was to be seen in the convocation of the all-European conference (ibid.). The PCC called on the CSCE 'to turn Europe into a region of truly equal co-operation among all states' and in general establish principles and measures of international relations that would ensure security in

Europe, and thus the conditions for economic and cultural co-operation (ibid.).

After the extremely negative and aggressive language of the documents from the PCC in 1966, what really was the cause of the 'relaxation of tensions' which the PCC perceived in 1974? In Europe there had been some measure of rapprochement between the Federal Republic of Germany and the socialist states (and in particular the German Democratic Republic). On the world arena there had been a Soviet–US rapprochement, including a partial test-ban treaty, the Anti Ballistic Missile Treaty, and SALT-I. But none of these was the outcome of WTO diplomacy or were multilateral East–West accords.

In fact, the 1974 Communique continued to see cause for concern: 'Militaristic circles are trying to intensify the activities of NATO. They are continuing to increase the military budgets of this closed imperialist bloc' (ibid.). These were sentiments similar to those expressed from the founding of the WTO and before. The Communique saw positive trends towards peace, but such a perception was not new to PCC documents. In European terms, the only success the WTO had achieved was to see the convocation of an all-European conference, which had not had a chance to reach any substantive agreement on the principles or policies which the PCC already considered were becoming the norm in inter-state activities. It would seem likely that the growth of what became known as détente was, in WTO terms, merely a change of emphasis, or a change of tone, in the documents of its joint foreign policy.

The Post-Helsinki Years

The year 1975 saw a new type of extra-structural WTO meeting, with two special conferences. The first was a gathering of 'representatives of the parliaments of the state-participants of the Warsaw Treaty', on the 20th anniversary of the WTO; the second was of 'representatives of communal organizations of the state-participants of the Warsaw Treaty' (3–4 June). Both sessions supported the results of the CSCE process and called for its extension, despite the Parliamentarians noting that 'the forces of the "cold war" strive to put the brakes on the process of detente' (*Pravda*, 17 May 1975). The communal organizations claimed that NATO 'continues to expand its military potential' (Report, *Pravda*, 7 June 1975). Both documents called for wider contacts between East and West at all levels.

The PCC, as the supreme body of the WTO, meeting for the first time after the conclusion of the CSCE, tried in 1976 to create a framework for the extension of the Helsinki process. In its Declaration it proposed not just the broadening of political contacts, but also the extension of the peace process into 'military détente'.[6] To this end, the 1976 Declaration proposed a variety of arms-control agreements, and in particular issued a Proposal (and a draft treaty on that Proposal) for the CSCE states to promise not to be the first to use nuclear weapons. (This was the same Declaration, discussed in Chapter 3, on the WTO's structural development, that took the unusual step of spelling out how the member states of the WTO would continue and expand their political and economic intra-bloc relations.)

The Declaration began in a very optimistic mood; it noted that

> essential favourable changes have taken place in international relations in recent years; a process of relaxation of international tensions has begun and peaceful coexistence between states, irrespective of their social system, is being established . . .
>
> Major problems which were outstanding after the Second World War have been peacefully solved in Europe and relations between European states are increasingly being switched over to a firm foundation of equal co-operation. (*Pravda*, 27 November 1976)

The successful change in the international climate was seen as being directly attributable to WTO diplomacy.

More than this, the Declaration indicated that the Warsaw Treaty party and state leaders anticipated that the Final Act promised that détente would be continuous and increasingly comprehensive (ibid.), that it had 'confirmed the territorial and political realities that have taken shape on the continent as a result of the victory of the peoples in the anti-fascist war and of post-war developments' (ibid.). Lastly, the Final Act was seen to have promised that international relations would be conducted with adherence to the principles that WTO documents had always been listing (ibid.).

In other words, it would seem that after 20 years of existence, the WTO had achieved its primary aim of peaceful coexistence, and could get down to the business of developing economic and cultural ties for the peaceful advancement of its peoples' well-being. What was not suggested was either that Germany could be reunited or that the two military alliances would do more than scale down their military operations, though the WTO's willingness for mutual dissolution was repeated. The PCC thus did not consider the CSCE to have created a mutual security system in Europe, which would have implied a change in the WTO's basic reason for existence.

Once again, the 1976 Declaration perceived that 'There are still forces of reaction, militarism, and revanchism . . . ' trying to distort the Final

Act (ibid.), which suggests that even in that year the WTO was unsure of the stability of the international situation, and could only conclude that all peoples struggle 'to abolish completely the hangovers of the cold war and to strengthen peace and develop international co-operation' (ibid.).

After 1976, the post-Helsinki euphoria quickly disintegrated. While seeing some benefit from the CSCE process, such as an increased frequency of meetings between state leaders (PCC Declaration, *Pravda*, 24 November 1978) and stronger political contacts in general (most of which were on a bilateral basis) (ibid.), the PCC noted that there was a move to reverse détente and increase the military confrontation, in opposition to 'the generally-recognized principles governing relations between states' (ibid.). No real move to increase economic co-operation was perceived. Political detente was not seen as being effective (ibid.). On top of this, the PCC saw no end to the arms race, and no move to military détente (ibid.). Above all, NATO was seen to be taking decisions on the level of its military budgets 'entirely contrary to the provisions of the Helsinki Final Act and they create new obstacles in the way of mutual understanding and peaceful co-operation among the states and peoples of Europe' (ibid.).

The Helsinki Final Act opened the way for a greater emphasis of the principles being enunciated by the PCC, and broadened the range of the WTO's specific proposals. The general consistency of the documents remained. The WTO, however, still had to resort to the forum of Parliamentarians (for example in 1979) to appeal over the heads of the West's state leaders on such issues as Euromissiles, and to note (as in July 1977, only nine months after the 1976 PCC) that things were not going well for the Helsinki process.

The Warsaw Treaty states interpreted and discussed the provisions of the Helsinki Final Act according to their own needs. The WTO documents thus do not consider human rights despite the importance attached to this in the West. Once again it can be seen that the WTO was not used as a major campaigning tool for its members. (Under Gorbachev, 'humanitarian' issues began to be talked about, though this was mainly outwith the documents of the WTO.)

On the occasion of the WTO's 25th anniversary the PCC held a commemorative session in Warsaw to sum up the achievements of the Organization and to set the tone for its future activities. The PCC assessed that, singly and together, the members had 'confidently and effectively been accomplishing vitally important tasks' towards peace, and in general that their activities had shown the correctness of their political line towards détente (Declaration, *Pravda*, 16 May 1980). The whole tone of the Declaration was that the WTO had been and still was a diplomatic success story in the move towards peaceful international relations, despite also noting the attempts by militarists and imperialists to destabilize the general trend towards detente (see section 2 of the Declaration). It once again issued a comprehensive list of proposals, including a call for a multilateral East–West summit.

The PCC met in 1983, for what turned out to be the last time before the Treaty's prolongation and the 30th Anniversary celebrations. The unitary Political Declaration reaffirmed the assessment of the 1978 and 1980 PCC documents that the forces of aggression were still threatening world peace, with a particular downturn from the détente of the 1970s (*Pravda*, 7 January 1983). The PCC, however, was still lobbying for the Helsinki process both to be implemented and extended. The Political Declaration concluded with a reiteration of various arms-control proposals (in its section 6). Within this list, the Communique that accompanied the Political Declaration drew special attention to 'the major new peace proposal to conclude a treaty on the mutual non-use of armed force, and the maintenance of relations of peace' with NATO but open to all states, and 'It was agreed that at its next meeting the Committee of Ministers of Foreign Affairs is to study the question of further steps directed at the implementation of this initiative' (*Pravda*, 6 January 1983). Meeting in April, the CFM resolved, however, for the states to pursue the proposal at a bilateral level with the West (*Pravda*, 8 April 1983).[7]

Such diplomacy did not go well, and 1983 saw an extra-structural meeting in June of leading party and state leaders to continue lobbying for the PCC's proposals and to express alarm at the lack of progress in the various East–West talks going on in Europe (Joint Statement, *Pravda*, 29 June 1983). Even more unusual was that 1984 saw three documents issued in the name of the WTO, a Proposal (11 January), another Proposal (6 March), and then an Appeal (7 May). No meetings took place to issue these documents, which seem to have been agreed internally. Only the third was on the proposal for a non-aggression treaty. The first was on the issue of chemical-weapons-free zones, and the second on the non-increase of military budgets – issues that were also covered by the 1983 Political Declaration but had not been singled out for particular attention. These documents imply that by 1984 the WTO was interpreting the progress of international relations in the 1980s, but in general since 1976, as a catastrophic failure of the CSCE process, and as evidence that its 30-year diplomacy and joint foreign policy had in fact failed, in contradistinction to the tone of its 25th anniversary back-slapping.

A session of the PCC was scheduled to take place in January 1985, but was postponed 'until a later date which is to be agreed' (*Pravda*, 15

January 1985), presumably due to Chernenko's ill-health. It would have been interesting to see what sort of documents were to have been issued. In the event the Treaty was extended and the 30th Anniversary celebrated (without any gala PCC session as 1980 had seen), and by the time the PCC session did take place (in October 1985) a new leadership in the USSR seemed to be taking the WTO in a new direction.

IDEOLOGICAL CONFRONTATION

As some of the quotations from WTO documents have perhaps indicated, the socialist states see themselves in ideological confrontation with the West in general, NATO, and the USA in particular. The documents, in lobbying for the WTO's concept of détente and peaceful coexistence, did not completely refrain from presenting a picture of their military opponents as inherently aggressive, and the WTO as the bulkwark of a peace-loving public. In an article on the 13th anniversary of the WTO, the then Commander-in-Chief wrote:

> The military alliance of the fraternal socialist states restrains the aggressive ambitions of imperialism in Europe and securely bars the way to expansion against the socialist countries and their friends; it is a powerful factor for world peace and security. (*Pravda*, 14 May 1968)

Such sentiments were repeated by Brezhnev in 1980, at a reception after a PCC session (*Pravda*, 16 May 1980).

The documents differentiate between the political and (in particular) military leaderships of the West, and the Western public. They claim the latter group is in favour of peaceful relations with the socialist states. For example, the 1958 PCC Declaration argued that:

> Peace is also supported by the masses of the people and influential public circles, by many parties and trades unions that heed the demands of the workers, by scientists and workers in the cultural field, by clergymen, by people of different political outlooks in the countries of Western Europe, America, and other continents. (*Pravda*, 27 May 1958)

In the 1983 PCC Political Declaration this differentiation was still being made, as 'an increasingly persevering and firm resolve of all peoples' was observed countering a preceding list of actions by 'aggressive forces' that were undermining world peace and security (*Pravda*, 7 January 1983). Intervening PCC documents consistently identified an increase in the size and influence of the forces of peace throughout the world.

What the documents seldom do is to name names. The 'aggressive forces' are never clearly defined, and the only country that is named as a principal opponent of the WTO peace policy is the USA. In other areas the WTO proposals and peace demands are set beside certain NATO decisions, such as the multilateral nuclear force proposal (see the PCC Communique, *Pravda*, 22 January 1965), or the perceived militarism of West Germany (see the PCC Declaration, *Pravda*, 27 May 1958) and the right-wing bias of its military leaders (see the PCC Declaration, *Pravda*, 5 February 1960).

WTO peace policy seems to be aimed towards conducting relations between East and West, after having accepted the post-war political balance in Europe. Socialism and capitalism would be allowed to develop their economies and thus replace military confrontation with a political and economic confrontation. Political détente would operate, meaning a greater understanding and acceptance by each side of the ideological confrontation. This would be a corollary to the WTO policy of diverting military investment to peaceful construction.

In the PCC Political Declaration of 1983, it was stated that:

> the socialist countries strictly separate in their policies ideological issues from problems of state-to-state relations, they build their relations with capitalist states on the basis of peaceful coexistence . . . (*Pravda*, 7 January 1983)

It was concluded that there was a need for the co-operation of all social systems in economic matters. Such co-operation would presumably be carried out within the wider principles of state-to-state relations, which would necessarily exclude from ideological confrontation any question of the post-war borders or political systems of Europe.

If peaceful coexistence is to be strong enough to allow an unrestrained exchange of political invective, the WTO documents would also have to take a softer line on capitalist imperialism in international politics and the excoriation of communism as the West's ideological nemesis.

INTERNAL SECURITY

Although it may seem surprising in the West, WTO documents do not address themselves to the Central European political events of 1956, 1968, or 1980–81. In fact, the only reference to the WTO as a means to internal security is in an article by the then Chief of Staff Shtemenko (1976).

In official terms, the Treaty (Article 3) obliges the signatory states only to 'take counsel among themselves' on common international questions or if they are under attack. Article 4 of the Treaty, in referring to Article 51 of the UN Charter, obviously does not cover an internal conflict. In other words, the WTO is *not* designed to cover civil war, or any other aspect of what, to the internal events in question, are political or ideological issues (see Tyranowski, 1973, p. 107; and footnote 7, Chapter 3 in this volume).

As the chronology of meetings indicates, each of these three internal crises was in fact preceded by a regular summit-level meeting, a level which was not reconvened when the crises took shape. The Hungarian crisis was followed by a PCC session only in 1958, at a time when the organizational structure of the WTO was in any case minimal.

During the Czechoslovak crisis, extra-structural military-level meetings took place, but the documents of these meetings suggest that they covered only regular issues – 'questions of strengthening the Warsaw Treaty Organization' (Defence ministers, *Pravda*, 31 October 1968), and 'the military preparedness of the troops' (military leaders, *Pravda*, 30 November 1968) – and in standard documentary parlance. The 1969 PCC session, rather than analysing the past, was looking to the future. This meeting was in any case attended by Dubcek who signed the PCC's documents.

The Polish crisis of 1980 and after was also concurrent with several WTO meetings, but again these were not geared to covering internal issues. The deputy foreign ministers (9 July 1980) discussed European arms control and the Madrid conference in the CSCE process; the Military Council (17 October 1980) discussed the 'current activities of the Joint Armed Forces'; the Committee of Ministers of Foreign Affairs (20 October 1980) also discussed the European conferences, and the issues raised in the PCC's 1980 Declaration issues; the Committee of Ministers of Defence (3 December 1980) continued the discussion of the JAFs.

Where the Polish crisis was treated differently was in an extra-structural meeting of party and state leaders. After a conventional communique covering the current international issues the concluding two paragraphs did refer to Poland:

> Representatives of the Polish United Workers' Party informed the participants about the development of the situation in the Polish People's Republic . . . The participants in the meeting expressed confidence that the communists, the working class, and the working people of fraternal

> Poland will be able to overcome the present difficulties and will ensure the country's development along the socialist path.
>
> It was reiterated that socialist Poland, the Polish workers' party, and the Polish people can firmly count on the fraternal solidarity of the country-participants of the Warsaw Treaty. Representatives of the Polish United Workers' Party stressed that Poland has been, is, and will remain a socialist state, a firm link in the common family of the countries of socialism. (*Pravda*, 6 December 1980)

Despite the circumspection of the wording, and even allowing for the fact that the formal structure was not invoked to hold a meeting that was not exclusively devoted to the Polish crisis, the most important fact is that the WTO was never formally invoked during the entire Polish August. In WTO terms life carried on regardless. No document covered the Polish issue during 1981, over the declaration of Martial Law, or during 1982. Poland was next mentioned, very briefly, in the 1983 Political Declaration (paragraph 66), where 'western economic "sanctions"' were touched on in relation to 'Polish internal affairs'. The single paragraph on this concluded that 'Socialist Poland can always count on the moral, political, and economic support of the fraternal socialist countries' (*Pravda*, 7 January 1983). (In any case the paragraph must be seen in relation to the surrounding discussion of peaceful coexistence and the need for mutually-beneficial European political and economic contacts.)[8]

What this lack of coverage of internal issues indicates is not that the crises were irrelevant to the WTO, but that they were seen and dealt with outwith the context of the WTO. In each case the WTO was not an overriding issue in the development of the crisis, and was never the sole argument for Soviet action in settling the crisis. The WTO member states were indeed very concerned with the Polish question, but the WTO was only a small factor in their overall view of what was an ideological, not a military, issue.

All three crises were not crises in the WTO, which is a state body, but crises in the fundamental issue of the leading rôle of the party, and the USSR's overriding concern with maintaining the ideological cohesion of its socialist community. It is not surprising that in practical terms the WTO did not cover these issues, for ideological security is not a military or a joint foreign policy issue, but is covered by inter-party relations, which are wholly outwith the WTO official structure. This need not mean that such internal issues and problems are not discussed by those attending WTO meetings. It means that if and when they are discussed, they are not covered by the agenda which leads to the published document.

The formal operation of the WTO's structure cannot be used in these circumstances.

PART B – THE JOINT FOREIGN POLICY

In practice, through the analysis of its documents, the WTO has to be seen not, as implied in the Treaty, as the basis of a general pan-European collective security system, but as an Organization which, despite its original putatively open form (Article 9) is an alliance of socialist countries. To this end, the Treaty creates the basis for joint action on the foreign policy of its signatories. The first paragraph of the Preamble calls for 'a system of collective security in Europe . . . which would make it possible to combine their efforts in the interests of securing peace in Europe'. Paragraph 5 of the Preamble establishes the first principle of this joint action, by claiming that 'In the interests of further strengthening and promoting friendship, co-operation, and mutual assistance' the states will act 'in accordance with the principles of respect for independence and sovereignty of states, and also with the principle of non-interference in their internal affairs . . . ' (ibid.).

The Treaty commits the signatories to the non-use of force and the peaceful settlement of disputes in their mutual relations (Article 1), and affirms the desire of the signatories to work for comprehensive disarmament (Article 2). To these ends, the basis of foreign policy, Article 3 promises that 'The contracting parties shall take council among themselves on all important international questions relating to their common interests . . . ' The Political Consultative Committee was established in Article 6 of the Treaty to be the forum for these consultations.

As the discussion of the structure of the WTO has shown, the joint foreign policy is enunciated by the PCC and put into practice at ministerial level (and since 1976 through the Committee of Ministers of Foreign Affairs), with the deputy foreign ministers also having a rôle.

SOCIALIST FOREIGN POLICY

But what, ideologically speaking, is a specifically socialist foreign policy? one that would be practised by a socialist political-military alliance? The *Bol'shaya Sovetskaya Entsiklopediya* (vol. 24–2) explains at great length the foreign policy of the USSR. Unlike Soviet and Central European discussion of WTO foreign policy, the *Bol'shaya Sovetskaya Entsiklopediya* makes it very clear that it is the party, not the state, which organizes Soviet foreign policy:

> Guided by the principles of Soviet foreign policy established by V. I. Lenin, the Communist Party takes into account specific international circumstances and establishes, primarily at its congresses, the basic outlines of foreign policy. The foreign policy of the workers' state sets as its goal the establishment of favourable, peaceful conditions for socialist and communist construction.

The CPSU Programme was said to recognize peaceful coexistence, as Lenin's view of 'a long historical period during which the coexistence of two different socio-political systems is inevitable.' Therefore peaceful coexistence with the West was to ensure 'favourable conditions in the international arena' for the struggle to take place between the two ideologies.

As part of its overall foreign policy, the USSR also pursued a specifically Leninist foreign policy 'jointly with the fraternal socialist countries'. Within these particularly socialist relations, the CMEA and the WTO played specific rôles working for a closer alliance and the joint building of communism. Such an analysis of foreign policy has also been presented by the Central European countries. Bulgaria, for example, argues that its foreign policy 'is the realization of the external functions of the Bulgarian Socialist State; it is the activity through which the PRB expresses its attitude to the phenomena and events in international life, defends its national and international interests, and guides and directs relations with other states and nations' (Bulgarian Academy of Sciences, 1985, p. 883). Once again the rôle of the party was stressed, the defence of socialist gains given priority, and faith to Marxist–Leninist theory and obligations emphasized (ibid.). Socialist internationalism and peaceful coexistence towards 'relations of mutually-advantageous and equitable co-operation' were given a special mention (ibid.). Once again, the rôle of the CMEA and WTO were mentioned, but not given a commanding significance.

In the Northern Tier of the alliance, a Czechoslovak discussion of the WTO explained that the foreign policy of the alliance was 'based on the principles of socialist internationalism' and that it provided 'the opportunity for effectively linking the common interests of defending Socialism with the national interests and requirements of the countries of the socialist community' (Urban, 1977, p. 61). Yet again the rôle of the party in the country's foreign policy was emphasized, with the WTO and the CMEA seen as contributing to an overall socialist community (ibid., pp. 61–2). 'All-round co-operation' with the USSR was justified by seeing it as the leading force in socialism and communism (ibid., p. 63).

WTO FOREIGN POLICY

In writing specifically on the WTO, the issue of joint foreign policy is repeatedly mentioned. For example, in an anniversary article in 1968, the then Commander-in-Chief Yakubovskii wrote that the WTO 'is a powerful instrument of political and defensive co-operation among the countries of socialism' (*Pravda*, 14 May 1968). In 1976, Sanakoyev described the WTO, through the PCC, as the 'main organizational centre' for the co-ordination of the foreign policy of the socialist countries, with the 1976 PCC session in Bucharest issuing an 'all-embracing programme' to this end (p. 22).

Such a partisan political bias for the WTO was made explicit by the then Hungarian Foreign Minister István Roska, in an interview with *Magyar Hirlap* for the 25th anniversary:

> The aim of the Warsaw Treaty is to ensure reassuring and peaceful external conditions for building socialism and, if necessary, to defend the achievements of socialism in the face of any aggressor. (MTI *Daily Bulletin*, vol. 15/136, 15 May 1980)

However, it is difficult actually to define what this joint action or joint policy is, even from the WTO documents themselves, apart from the broad calls for peace and international unity. Over the years, beginning with the Treaty itself, the documents have called for international relations to be carried out under certain principles, which have remained consistent though have been gradually extended and developed. In one of the enunciations of these principles it was stated that the aim of such principles was the desire to transform the relations of the European states in order to 'overcome the division of the continent into military groupings', and that the pursuit of international relations should lead to a 'system of commitments' covering these principles between states (Foreign Ministers' Communique, *Pravda*, 3 December 1971).[9] The ultimate aim of such a policy, the Communique argued, was for the expansion of all-European co-operation in economic, scientific, technological, and cultural affairs.

Such aims and principles, when they were covered by the first session of the PCC in 1956, indicated that the ultimate purpose of this policy was to ensure the reconstruction of the signatory states' post-war economies. This was 'for economic and cultural development, improvement of the people's welfare, of the all-round development of economy and culture, making it possible to put at mankind's service the latest achievements of science and engineering' (Declaration, *Pravda*, 29 January 1956). While placing economic considerations so strongly to the fore in the question of foreign policy, the Declaration argued that these conditions could only be achieved through an all-European collective security system. The specific policies suggested by the PCC were for East–West agreements on these issues, and for zones in Europe where armaments would be limited and controlled.

In his speech to the 1956 PCC session, Molotov, while spelling out the foreign policy issues and principles which were to be covered in the Declaration, argued another point excluded from the joint document: that the WTO states were 'consistently upholding the Leninist principle of the peaceful coexistence of all states' (*Pravda*, 29 January 1956). While the call for peaceful coexistence did work its way into WTO documents, these documents are not so adamant that such policies are Leninist or even socialist. The Warsaw Treaty states are careful in such public pronouncements to appear politically universal rather than partisan in their joint foreign policy statements.

Thus there is a paradox in WTO foreign policy, whether it is to be seen as socialist, or as international in some other way. In a 1977 article in *Külpolitika*, the then Hungarian Foreign Minister Frigyes Puja argued that socialist foreign policy rested on two principles, proletarian internationalism and peaceful coexistence. He further claimed that 'These principles follow from the very nature of the socialist system' (MTI *Daily Bulletin* vol. 12/134, 14 May 1977). The principles of international relations as stated in Warsaw Treaty documents are obviously worded to sound universally applicable; peaceful coexistence is just one of these principles, and is not mentioned in the founding Treaty – it is not, in fact, mentioned in every document.

By comparison, in a book about the WTO, Kirichenko specifically discussed socialist foreign policy. It is useful to quote this at length, to show the differences between the principles considered.

> The correctness of the principles of proletarian, socialist internationalism is displayed: in the application by every socialist country of the maximum effort for the carrying out of its most important internationalist duty – the construction of socialism and communism;
> – in the carrying out of such policies within their countries and in

> the international arena, which promote the strengthening of the world socialist system as the main factor of contemporary revolutionary development;
> – in the establishment of friendly ties between the socialist countries;
> – in the solidarity with the working classes of the capitalist countries and its Marxist–Leninist vanguard, in support of their struggles;
> – in the rendering of assistance to the peoples, struggling for national liberty and independence;
> – in the strengthening of the unity of the international communist movement, in the resolute struggle against factionalists and dissenters, revisionists to the right and 'leftists', against nationalism and chauvinism, against imperialist reaction and all of its forms of influence at work;
> – in defence of Marxism–Leninism, as international in its essential doctrine, as the ideological basis of the international communist movement, its strategy and tactics;
> – in the joint effort of the socialist states in the field of defence, mutual aid, and the combined protection of the interests of socialism.
>
> These principles are the unshakeable platform on which are worked out the friendship and co-operation of the socialist community. (Kirichenko, 1975, pp. 66–7)

The significance of such an overtly ideological exposition is not so much that it appeared in an obscure book on the Warsaw Treaty, or even that it ranks joint defence as the final of a number of international principles, but that it shows so clearly the difference between intra-bloc policy and a truly foreign policy. It shows that what is displayed in the joint foreign policy documents of the the WTO is indeed intended to be seen as more that just a partisan declaration of principles and appeals, is indeed to be seen as a move towards socialist peaceful coexistence.

The basic principles of WTO pronouncements, either singly or in a bunch, have been issued in some form or another throughout the 30 years of joint foreign policy statements. In conjunction with these principles of international relations, the WTO itself (or the USSR alone), issues peace proposals, generally calling for treaties or agreements to codify the proposals into international law. But the declaration of principles or the recurrent plea for various treaties seems altogether too broad to amount to a joint foreign policy. So what would a WTO as the 'main centre' of foreign policy co-ordination imply?

In an interview on the Budapest home service for the 30th Anniversary of the Warsaw Treaty, Hungarian deputy foreign minister Roska answered a question on the co-ordination of WTO foreign policy:

> I have a feeling that this question is slightly obsessed with the co-ordinated foreign policy of the Treaty, or to be more precise, its process and method. The member-states of the Treaty do not hold co-ordinating discussions on details, rather they co-ordinate the main political direction. This is then reflected in the foreign policy and diplomatic activities of all member states. In our [Hungarian] foreign policy this means primarily that we strengthen our ties in every area with the USSR and the countries of the socialist community. (*SWB* EE/7952/C/13, 16 May 1985)

WTO political statements could be seen as the lowest common denominator of bloc foreign policy, but as Roska illustrates, this is not quite the point. With the exclusion of the 1968 'Statement on nuclear non-proliferation' and the 1978 'Statement on the Middle East situation' all the documents have been signed by all the active members of the time. Romania's non-signing of these two documents does not indicate a failure of the main political direction. Romania had in fact signed the 1974 Middle East statement without breaking off diplomatic relations with Israel as all the other states had done. In fact, these two issues do not have a direct bearing on the main European focus of the WTO. The signing or non-signing of documents rather indicates how the system, as described by Roska, actually works.

It would seem that Warsaw Treaty states can carry out their national and external policies, in all fields, as they like, so long as they can argue that it fulfils the 'main political direction', which would be towards détente and peaceful coexistence, and in general the principles of international relations. This would mean that the USSR has approved, for whatever reason, with Hungary's economic policies – as a means to strengthening bloc economic security – and to Romanian defence policy – as a means to defending the WTO southern flank. To put it another way, the national foreign policy of a Warsaw Treaty state 'corresponds to the foreign policies of the Soviet Union and the rest of the members of the socialist community, concerning its main direction', but that each state also displays its national interests and characteristic traits (Frigyes Puja, MTI *Daily Bulletin*, vol. 12/134, 14 May 1977).

What the WTO documents illustrate is a bloc foreign policy not of how to act, but of how the international situation is to be interpreted. The list of principles depicts the ethos of the international situation as they would ultimately like it to be. If the object of peaceful coexistence is to ensure a European peace and political stability then in general the WTO policy could be said to have succeeded, though the internal economic policies have not quite created the economic benefits that the 1956 PCC Declaration argued the peace was supposed to permit the construction of.

This state of affairs has also been created without the enactment of any specific WTO proposal, for example for an East–West non-aggression treaty. In its first thirty years the only two WTO successes were the convocation of the Conference on Security and Co-operation in Europe and its follow-up conferences, and the convocation of the Stockholm conference on military detente. The minutiae of WTO proposals are in fact evidence of a policy that has been a resounding failure. This would suggest that perhaps socialist foreign policy should push less for specific agreements or bits of paper, and more for what amounts to bilateral East–West action on economic or cultural relationships that would eventually build up into peaceful coexistence through the back door. This would lead to much more tangible benefits than East–West declarations of accord and principle.

Such an interpretation should not mean that the WTO is to be seen as wholly dissatisfied with the results of its joint foreign policy. In a 1983 anniversary article in *Népszabadság*, the Hungarian state secretary for defence considered that 'as the economic, political, and military strength of the socialist countries increased, more and more achievements were attained in détente: east–west inter-state agreements, the SALT, the arms and troop reduction talks in Vienna, and acceptance of the Helsinki Final Act' (MTI *Daily Bulletin*, vol. 18/134–5–6, 14–15–16 May 1983). In a 1980 anniversary article also in *Népszabadság*, Warsaw Treaty Commander-in-Chief Kulikov argued that Warsaw Treaty co-operation 'served and continues to serve as the efficient means of influencing the most important international events' allowing the individual states 'definitely to defend their positions in the international arena, consistently to enforce the guidelines of assuring peace, of détente and disarmament' (ibid., vol. 15/136, 15 May 1980).

That nothing was seen to be wrong with what the WTO had been achieving was argued by the then Hungarian Prime Minister János Borbandi, in a speech to a 20th anniversary ceremony in Budapest: 'We continue to believe our cause to be just and trust in the power of world opinion struggling for peace and security and in the soberness of the Western politicians who recognize the realities of our age' (ibid., vol. 10/135, 15 May 1975). (As was seen in the section above analysing the documents themselves, not all the claims for WTO successes can actually be sustained.)

THE WTO AND 'MILITANT CAPITALISM'

The WTO seems to have an ambivalent, almost paradoxical, attitude to the West. This can be seen both in the references to an ideological struggle and to what could be called the paradox of militant capitalism. Ponomarev (1985, p. 103), for example, describes what he calls 'Lenin's theory of war and peace', which he interprets as showing that 'War has always been inseparable from capitalism.' Since imperialism is the pinnacle of capitalism, then imperialism is the main enemy of peace; in contrast, socialism, led by the October Revolution, has become the only socio-political force 'capable of assuring a just, democratic, and lasting peace'. Writing earlier, Grechko (1972) had been almost as forthright when he wrote that 'imperialism carries with it the threat of war' (1972).

In the WTO documents themselves, for example the 1980 PCC Declaration, it is explained that the change in the balance of world forces which led to 'the strengthening of the positions and influence of socialism in the world' had meant that the 'necessary conditions' had been created 'so that the purposeful policy of the socialist countries and unity of action by peace-loving states and peoples may lead to important political changes in the whole system of relations between states, to the strengthening of peace and international security' (*Pravda*, 16 May 1980). This would mean that it is up to the WTO, through its joint foreign policy, to lead the world to a better and more peaceful system of international relations.

Quite apart from the fact that none of the WTO's concrete proposals has ever been implemented, a paradox could lie in Ponomarev's assertion that Lenin considered capitalism to be inherently aggressive, a view also presented by Gorbachev in his Political Report to the XXVII Congress of the CPSU (*Materialy* . . .).[10] If this were to be the case, then how can socialism ever succeed? How could a policy of détente or peaceful coexistence bear fruit? Is socialist foreign policy having the wool pulled over its eyes by a wily capitalist-imperialism? Capitalism, if it is inherently aggressive, should inherently be unable to accept the socialist principles of international relations. Ponomarev (1985, p. 99) had, after all, stated that 'the ideological controversy . . . directly arises from the nature of the two different world systems . . . ', but he goes on:

> The competition between the two systems and the clash of ideas is a natural phenomenon rooted in the very fact of the existence of socialism and capitalism. Their historical confrontation must not be allowed to head for curtailment of peaceful co-operation . . . On a plea of ideological incompatibility of capitalism and socialism, efforts are

> being made to undermine the generally accepted norms of international relations, above all, the basic principle to be observed in our epoch, the principle of peaceful coexistence of states regardless of their social systems. (Ibid., pp. 99–100)

On the one hand the WTO argues that capitalism and socialism can and must live together in peace, and even trade and have cultural relations with the other; on the other hand, in ideological terms, it seems to be argued that this can never take place, that only a socialist world can co-operate, as the Warsaw Treaty states are supposed to co-operate, under the principles of international relations as described in the joint documents.

WTO UNITY AND COHESION

Intra-bloc foreign policy, it is claimed, is also aimed at increasing the bloc unity and cohesion, at strengthening the socialist community against the capitalist world. (See the description above – Kirichenko, pp. 66–7.) In other words, the act of participating in this multilateral structure is supposed as such to be of benefit to socialism, and to the members' rôles within the socialist community. Soviet and Central European commentators repeatedly claim that, by acting under the principles stated in the documents, they have created an international organization of a new type. By acting in concert on foreign policy issues of defence, economics, and culture (all mentioned in the Treaty) they are also strengthening the ideological security of socialism by their joint action to strengthen its military and economic security. In fact, the WTO is adamant that this has in fact happened. As the then deputy Prime Minister of Hungary argued, 'The international political, economic, and military alliance of the socialist countries has been realized and further developed through the Warsaw Treaty Organization' (János Borbandi, MTI *Daily Bulletin*, vol. 10/135, 14 May 1975). Hungary's István Roska reaffirmed this ten years later when he stated that, 'In our foreign policy this means primarily that we strengthen our ties in every area with the USSR and the countries of the socialist community' (*SWB* EE/7952/C/13).

So is Hungary, or any of the other member states, doing this? Every Warsaw Treaty political document, and every bilateral communique, includes a reference to increasing ties, usually linking this in with a reference to economic co-operation and the CMEA. But, as one Central European specialist[N] asked, 'so what's new?' Such statements are seen merely as ideological lip-service and conformity. The only state that is significantly increasing its economic ties with the USSR after thirty years of the WTO is Romania, through its oil trade deal of the end of 1985, and other such agreements. Economically, to all the other states, reform of whatever extent generally means going for bilateral trade with the West. Ideologically, this could not be seen as boosting socialist norms, even though it fulfils part of the policy of peaceful coexistence.

National foreign policies, not just in economic terms, are in any case only co-ordinated in their main political direction. As one of Roska's predecessors put it, the national 'specific traits' of foreign policy 'are in the first place manifested not in the strategic but tactical questions, thus they cannot be predominant' (Frigyes Puja, MTI *Daily Bulletin*, vol. 12/134, 14 May 1977). He went on to list a comprehensive set of individual influences on each country's foreign policy: economic needs; national economic resources; historic conditions (such as relations with other states, East or West); and 'the workstyle of our party and state leadership'. He argued that, 'There are situations in which one or another socialist country has greater chances than the rest,' and that these chances should not be ignored: 'If their enforcement is not contrary to the interests of the peoples in the other socialist countries or of the international working class, it is our duty to enforce them.'

This underlines that the individual states, within basic overall limits, see themselves as having a capacity to organize their foreign policies as an extension of their states' national internal policies. (To the Bulgarians, 'Bulgaria's foreign policy corresponds to its internal policy and is its continuation in the sphere of international relations' – Bulgarian Academy of Sciences, p. 883.) So to what extent is their bilateral diplomacy co-ordinated, if at all? Mátyás Szűrős (1985, p. 24) claimed that Hungary's diplomacy was 'co-ordinated with the socialist countries' but went on to place this co-ordination within the bounds of full support for WTO declarations and the preservation of détente. This repeats the analysis that the WTO is not designed to prescribe national policies.

When it comes to disagreements, however, it is obvious that the WTO, if it is used at all to cover national bilateral policies, is not very efficient. Such multilateral fora are stuck to specific agendas and timetables, and their 'co-ordinating discussions'.[N] If one Central European country is unhappy about another's national foreign policy, either in relation to the East or the West, then a Warsaw Treaty conference is not seen as the place to raise the issue other than in shrouded terms of advice that 'we would do it another way'.[N] Such opinions are never expressed at the level of official discussions, but can only be exchanged informally.[N] Critical remarks on, for example, 'worries about deviation from the socialist ideological line', or the converse considerations that economic reforms and trade with the West might be useful, are generally voiced in the national presses, or through such extra-structural fora as meetings of deputy foreign ministers or of party ideologists, where there are no such restrictions on the agenda as at meetings within the formal WTO structure.[N] In the main, diplomacy is thus left to bilateral, not multilateral, links.

This once again underlines that the WTO is limited to general co-ordination and the reaffirmation of the alliance *qua* alliance. Such a state of affairs also gives scope for smaller European countries to have a greater rôle in East–West relations. While bilateral superpower relations collapsed after the Helsinki Final Act, many of the Central European countries carried on the Helsinki process at the bilateral level. At a time when Warsaw Treaty documents were bemoaning the rise in Western militarism and the demise of détente, smaller European powers were quite satisfied with the new era of small-power relations. As one Central European specialist put it, 'We do not regard pan-European relations as an illusion. It has been functioning in practice since the beginning of the 1970s.'[N] The Helsinki Final Act is seen as the existing basis for European security and co-operation. For the smaller powers, this process was not entirely interrupted by Soviet–US tensions over crises either in Europe or the rest of the world.

(It must, however, also be emphasized that, as allies of the USSR, the non-Soviet Warsaw Treaty states do feel some effect of changes in superpower relations, and in many cases could be seen to be governed more by this than by NATO–WTO relations. The point is that they must be seen to have some autonomy to carry out their bilateral relations, and this autonomy does not depend on intra-WTO influences.)

In fact, part of the concept of the rôle of small states is that their influence on superpower relations can increase in times of conflict or lack of détente, as intermediaries. While emphasis has been placed on Romania's rôle in or statement of this,[11] Hungary at least also espouses such ideas. A further comment from Roska was that:

> In the current tense international situation, Hungarian diplomacy endeavours to make use of its possibilities and facilitate East–West dialogue, contribute to an improvement of the international atmosphere, and to the strengthening of confidence among states. (*SWB* EE/7952/C/13, 16 May 1985)

Playing such an intermediary role has been considered in these smaller states' national interest.[N]

Roska then added that 'This direction is in harmony with the main direction co-ordinated within the framework of the [Warsaw] Treaty' (*SWB*, ibid.). Evidence of this rôle was Hungary's ability to visit or be visited by various Western leaders, including US figures, at a time when the superpowers were not themselves directly talking to each other, or Poland's leadership's ability to visit the People's Republic of China. (See also the Wettig study [1985].)

THE WTO'S WORLD RÔLE

But the WTO is not seen only to have a European rôle. Despite its legal limitation to Europe, it claims a world influence, partly through its claim that 'peace is indivisible' (Tyranowski, 1973, p. 116), that tension in further areas of the world will have an impact on relations in Europe. The WTO has from the beginning pronounced on world issues, from objections to encirclement by imperialist military blocs (such as in the speeches to the Warsaw Meeting in 1955, and the 1956 Declaration), to questions of national liberation movements in Africa, and US involvement in, say, South-East Asia. While the PCC has issued numerous single-issue documents concerning non-European issues, these call for specific demands; but on European questions the documents are more vague, calling for the establishment of 'relations of peace' or a 'move to détente', or issuing a call for a meeting to be convened to talk about these European matters.

That the WTO sees a linkage between these concerns can be witnessed in, for example, the PCC's 1974 Communique, where it was stated that 'The states represented at the session have expressed the conviction that the easing of tensions must cover all parts of the world' (*Pravda*, 19 April 1974). Gromyko, in his 20th anniversary speech, claimed even more that 'The impact of the Warsaw Treaty Organization on the international situation goes far beyond Europe, and this has become evident to everyone throughout the world' (*Pravda*, 15 May 1975, p. 4).

Soviet commentators also use this world-focus argument in explaining the WTO's strong concerns with nuclear matters. While Central Europe is directly threatened by theatre and battlefield nuclear weapons, the main WTO statements have been on strategic nuclear matters. It was only under the technological developments of the 1970s–1980s that Eurostrategic weapons came to the fore, prompting the comment that: 'It is only natural, therefore, that the focus of the Soviet programme for improving the situation in Europe is on measures to reduce the danger of nuclear confrontation on the continent' (Silin, 1986, p. 89). This could also be seen as a move to defend the USSR against the criticism by its allies concerning their own defence needs, and the changes in the WTO seen since the 30th Anniversary.[12]

CONCLUSIONS

In the final analysis, the WTO is the only formal multilateral agency involved in the foreign policy of the socialist countries, however limited its co-ordination has turned out to be. It is even more significant that important sectors of this structure, the Joint Secretariat and the Committee of Ministers of Foreign Affairs, have only been formally operating, or in the case of the Secretariat convened, since 1976.

But what is foreign policy anyway? It seems to boil down to rules for the guidance of states' relations with other states, either allies or not. Szűrős (1985, p. 16) (from Hungary) claims that Marx's and Lenin's concept is that 'foreign policy is basically a continuation of domestic policy on the international scene'. This is not really very surprising, since a national political leadership will for its own internal reasons, including its perceptions of its relations with its neighbours, decide on a national socio-economic policy, and must then organize the foreign policy conditions to sustain this. Bulgaria decided to pursue export-orientation industries based on close ties with the USSR; Romania for the autarkic development of heavy industry that necessitated closer ties with the Third World as a market for those goods. As Szűrős (ibid., p. 14) puts it, 'in a small country, definite external conditions must exist for the socialist system of society to be able to put down roots and to grow stronger and taller'. National bilateral diplomacy must have a theoretical framework to put around its policies, and the WTO states claim these to be the principles enunciated in their joint documents. In its first thirty years, the PCC met about every two years, and so it was only in a position to give such vague general guidance anyway.

The foreign ministers seem to have been formally put into a Committee to discuss the wider issues only in recognition of their work leading up to the Helsinki Final Act; the deputy foreign ministers do not just meet outwith the formal WTO structure, but also attend even wider co-ordinating discussions within a forum of UN socialist countries. Beyond this, the minutiae of policy and conflicts, especially intra-bloc conflicts and issues, are carried out on a non-WTO, bilateral, level, not just at state level but also between the ruling parties.

In other words, as Chapter 3 revealed, the WTO minimizes the scope for multilateral relations. In this case, substantive issues of foreign policy and diplomacy are neither covered in documents nor it seems in official multilateral discussion. The main direction, that of basic principles, would in any case be understood as the Leninist foreign policy of peaceful coexistence, so it should not really need periodic meetings to discuss it. What the WTO does in foreign policy is to reinforce the ideological basis of the alliance and its relationship with the rest of the world.

If the WTO does not formally co-ordinate foreign policy or even diplomacy, and is not designed as an efficient military mechanism, then all that is left is the WTO as a vehicle for ideological unity, reinforcing the political basis for the socialist community and giving it a formal character. But ideology is really a matter for the ruling parties, who only became visibly active within the structure from the 1960s, and predominant over the state leadership designations from the signing of the Protocol in 1985. In this way, the PCC has become a legalistic protocol method to indicate where the Party controls the State, and why it is the party leaders rather than the state leaders who take precedence on inter-state visits and occasions, including those involving Western delegations. In converse terms the rest of the WTO structure shows where the State has become the legitimizing front for the Party.

In other words, the member states can formally do what they want economically, and pursue the foreign policy that derives from that policy, so long as there is ideological unity, so long as the national leaderships can argue that they are pursuing the basic principles. The analysis of the first thirty years of foreign policy proposals shows them to be mainly an extension of direct Soviet foreign policy concerns, which were a question of superpower politics. The specifically European dimension of that policy was for peace in Europe against the USA, in other words some form of decoupling; this would leave the specifically bilateral Central/West European links, which amounts to freedom in foreign policy within the ideological constraints of the WTO.

In ideological terms, in Poland the Party has not been usurped, Hungary is still an ally, and Romania is just an extreme of the basic model. Academics from Warsaw Treaty states continually argue[N] that basically, all the member-states are politically part of the same continuum, that the ideological unity is being maintained and is not in question. This confirms the WTO as a mechanism for ideological unity rather than anything else. The same academics also argue that the most important thing to look at is to understand the national and foreign policies of the individual states. Only then can the bilateral Central European and USSR relations or Soviet policy towards its allies be looked at. In the estimation of these academics,[N] in Central Europe the joint foreign policy of the Warsaw Treaty Organization does not figure at all.

OTHER EXTERNAL FACTORS

But to conclude that the WTO, a multilateral body, has little bearing on the foreign policies of its members is not to conclude that there are not other factors which are bilateral, and external to the WTO. Some Central European specialists[N] argued that to study the area one should 'begin in Moscow', but at the same time still claimed a 'national substance' to foreign policy. Szűrős (1985, p. 15) pointed out that the basis of Hungary's foreign policy was that Hungary was a socialist country. He went on:

> Our socialist policy must, in compliance with its meaning, differ as compared to the international policy of the other socialist countries, in compliance with the spirit of Lenin's theory that socialism must be built, in addition to enforcing general features, by taking into consideration the specific circumstances of the given countries. This requirement affects every field of the country's life and activity, including foreign policy. (Ibid., p. 16)

However, unofficially, it has been pointed out that a foreign policy being implemented by Central European countries does not mean that overall goals are set by them.[N] Any such external influences are also external to the WTO. These would include bilateral relations with the USSR, which would generally be carried out through inter-party, rather than inter-state, mechanisms. The individual room for manoeuvre in these affairs would be bound by the individual country's relations with Moscow. It has been suggested, including within Central Europe,[N] that the countries of the WTO's military Northern Tier (Poland, the GDR, and Czechoslovakia), being of greater strategic importance, have less leeway to assert national objectives.[13]

Another specialist[N] argued that Moscow's influence on individual allies need not be by direct intervention. Central Europe's lack of independence in foreign policy was also due to a bureaucratic 'permanent fear of uncertainty'. Was the USSR watching, and if so, how would it react to a country acting in a certain way? This suggests that in carrying out their national policies, Central European party and state officials employ a self-censorship. Soviet reaction to national internal changes has, as this chapter has pointed out, resulted in major intervention only when *ideological* factors, in particular the leading role of the party, have been in doubt. It was pointed out[N] that Hungary has never been denied oil imports from the Soviet Union, and Romania has never been invaded.

In final conclusion, it must be repeated that the WTO has not proved to be a significant factor in socialist foreign policy. Research into foreign policy should therefore be geared not towards the analysis of the application of the Warsaw Treaty, but to these other external factors.

5 The Thirtieth Anniversary

INTRODUCTION

The Politburo of the Central Committee of the Communist Party of the Soviet Union discussed the WTO Anniversary[1] at a regular meeting held on 6 September 1984 (*Pravda*, September 7). The report of this discussion merely stated that the Politburo 'approved measures . . . in connexion with this great political event', and went on to stress the rôle of the WTO for the unity and cohesion of its members, against US and NATO aggression, and for European and world peace (ibid.). That this was apparently the first mention of the impending Anniversary is significant, since the Politburo merely 'approved decisions' which were presumably taken elsewhere in the Party Secretariat. The need to commemorate the Anniversary had therefore been under discussion for some time prior to the September meeting of the Politburo. What is also significant in the preparations for the Anniversary to be commemorated is that the next, and final, paragraph of the Politburo report stated that the meeting also discussed 'other questions' on 'furthering the development of the political and economic co-operation of the fraternal countries of socialism, and of the foreign and international policies of the Communist Party and the Soviet state' (ibid.). Apparently, even the 30th Anniversary of the only multilateral political-military alliance of the European socialist countries was just one part of a wider foreign policy of the CPSU.

In the event the 30th Anniversary celebrations were a remarkably low-key affair. The most important meeting, in terms of its attendees and keynote speech (by CPSU Central Committee Secretary K. V. Rusakov) was a 'solemn gathering' at the Bolshoi Theatre, attended mainly by representatives of Moscow working people and the USSR Armed Forces' (May 14). The most senior multilateral political gathering was of the Parliamentarians – an extra-structural body – (May 13–15) in Budapest. The Communique of this meeting was the only formal document issued to mark the Anniversary. For an organization that prides itself on being a political-military defensive alliance, it seems strange that all the other Anniversary meetings were of a military nature, from a 'solemn gathering' at the Central House of the Soviet Army (May 13) addressed by Commander-in-Chief Kulikov, through a meeting in Warsaw of military historians (May 13), to an 'international scientific conference' held at the

Academy of the Social Sciences, Moscow (May 14–15). It also seems strange that, when such care was taken to have the meeting that extended the Treaty held in Warsaw, there was no significant meeting held there for the 30th Anniversary of the original Warsaw signing.

The Anniversary was, perhaps, notable more for its absences. The most important of these, given the precedent of the 25th anniversary, was that there was no celebratory session of the PCC, in fact no summit-level gathering at all. Also, unlike the PCC documents, which are given full page 1 treatment in *Pravda*, the coverage of Rusakov's keynote Anniversary speech was limited to page 4, the normal site for standard foreign news such as coverage of all the lesser and extra-structural meetings. While the anniversary address by Rusakov was by far the longest and most widely reproduced (all the major Soviet newspapers and more), there is no obvious reason in terms of protocol why a CPSU Secretary who had in Warsaw Treaty terms done no more than attend PCC sessions as a tail-end member of the Soviet delegation should be shown precedence over the WTO Commander-in-Chief, whose address of May 13 was referred to in *Pravda* (14 May 1985) and given a brief summary in *Krasnaya Zvezda* (14 May 1985). Kulikov addressed the same solemn gathering as Rusakov, but he was only mentioned as the first of a variety of speakers from the floor (including 'Hero of Socialist Labour N. M Motova, grinder at the No. 1 state bearing works'). The newspaper text of this meeting stated that 'The floor was given to Marshal of the Soviet Union V. G. Kulikov', which rather obscures his rôle in the Organization being celebrated. Significantly for a multilateral body, no-one from any of the allied countries was reported as having taken the floor after Rusakov This would seem to be a remarkable absence for the principal Anniversary meeting.

Even in the Anniversary articles published in the Soviet journals,[2] a greater rôle was given to Kulikov's First Deputy, the Chief of Staff of the Joint Armed Forces A. I. Gribkov. While Kulikov's name was given to one article (in *Kommunist*), not only did Gribkov have his name given to two journal articles (*Voennyi vestnik* and *Voenno-istoricheskii zhurnal* but he was also credited with the Anniversary article in *Izvestiya* (14 May 1985, p. 3).[3] Gribkov further addressed the first day of the Anniversary 'international scientific conference' (*SWB* SU/7952/C1/4, 16 May 1985).

While the PCC session on the 25th anniversary issued a major foreign policy Statement and Declaration, no opportunity was taken in 1985 to issue to the world a top-level restatement of the WTO's peace policy. Such a policy had not been spelt out for 16 months, since the PCC's Prague Political Declaration of 5 January 1983. The Parliamentarians, contrary to their own precedent, did not issue a full document or even appeal, but merely a communique. Nor did the Parliamentarians take this opportunity to support the WTO's various standing peace proposals, as they had done on other occasions. Instead they offered their support for the Address 'To the Peoples, Parliaments, and Governments of all Countries' issued by the CPSU Central Committee, the Presidium of the Supreme Soviet, and the USSR's Council of Ministers (none of which are officially part of the WTO's structure) to mark the 40th anniversary of the end of the Second World War.

Thus, just when the WTO was secure for the next thirty years, no opportunity was taken to reassert it as a major force either for international relations, inter-state relations, or even specifically as an international peace organization. Judging only from the list of known meetings and of the attendees of those meetings, the WTO was on its 30th Anniversary primarily in the hands of the military. As throughout its preceeding thirty years, despite a preponderance of military meetings, the content of these was not made available beyond the predictable political platitudes, along the lines that the practical activities of the WTO as a defensive alliance were furthering peace and bringing about a relaxation of international tensions – which was, for example, the reported conclusion of Kulikov's address to the May 13 'solemn gathering' (*Pravda*, 14 May 1985).

In their general content, the published speeches and articles were as lacklustre as the run of events. They followed a unitary and predictable line that was little different from the gist of general or anniversary articles of earlier years. Topics covered were: the origins of the WTO, and its defensive nature; the structure and the peace initiatives of that structure; a summary of foreign policy successes attributed to WTO diplomacy; an extended section of anti-imperialist diatribe attributing to NATO, the US in particular, and especially the contemporary US political and military leadership, the most extreme militaristic anti-Sovietism and anti-socialism. The discussions did, however, conclude that the WTO was a useful and efficient way of furthering peace through the joint activities of its members, with the 1985 Protocol on prolonging the Treaty held up as a sign of the WTO's significance and of the members' commitment to furthering the unity and cohesion of the Organization. If it were not that these comments were made in relation to a specific landmark in the WTO's history, they would not have been worth more than a perfunctory glance to ascertain that they did not cover any new ground or analysis. The substance and significance of these speeches and articles could be summarized by Kulikov's description of the WTO:

> The defensive military-political alliance of the fraternal peoples and states – the Warsaw Treaty, created in response to the formation of the NATO bloc, to the intensification of the threat of war in Europe, here now for three decades guaranteeing the security of the socialist countries and maintaining peace in Europe and throughout the world, confidently and effectively resolving the vitally important consequential problems of the present day. (*Krasnaya Zvezda*, 14 May 1985; *Pravda*, 14 May 1985)

So just what was said on these standard topics?

ANALYSIS OF THE SOVIET ARTICLES

The Origins

As Chapter 2 showed, in 1955 the foundation of the WTO was directly attributed to the accession of the Federal Republic of Germany to the the West's military alliance system. The issue of West Germany was bound up with the wider question of post-war Europe and its developing socio-political divisions and confrontations. While the 1955 documents were directly concerned with the FRG, in 1985 this was seen as just one facet of those times. Where the first session of the PCC tied in the current Soviet analysis of its encirclement with the remilitarization of West Germany, in 1985 a much broader analysis was given. To Gribkov (*Izvestiya*, 14 May 1985) the rearmament of West Germany represented only a 'special danger' within the general militarism of the USA and NATO.

Virtually all the Anniversary articles claimed an unexplained significance that the year of the 30th Anniversary of the WTO was also the 40th anniversary of the Victory at the end of the Second World War. The significance was implied in their discussion of the growth of cold war politics. Rusakov, for example, took the origins of the WTO back to the post-war period when the Western powers 'had treacherously jettisoned the fine heritage of the anti-Hitler coalition and had created the NATO bloc aimed primarily against the socialist countries' (*Izvestiya* 15 May 1985). Just why this should require the creation of the WTO in 1955 was explained by Nezhinsky (1985, p. 61), when he wrote that the West's aggressive policy had necessitated the WTO when 'the socialist states had done all they could to prevent the division of the world into ɔpposed military and political alliances'. Katrich (1985, pp. 52–3) even ırgued that Western anti-socialism predated the Victory, by repeating the allegation that Western imperialism had wanted a separate peace with Iitler in order to organize a joint attack on the Soviet Union. To the Soviet Union a post-war world based on inter-state co-operation of the :ind seen in the anti-Hitler coalition would presumably have been the basis of the all-European collective security system called for by the Moscow Conference of 1954, the Warsaw Conference, and the resulting Varsaw Treaty. Finally, Kulikov explained that in the formation of the VTO, 'The most important lesson [of the war] remains, that against war t is necessary constantly and persistently to struggle, it is not permitted o allow it to be unleashed' (*Krasnaya Zvezda*, 14 May). If this was to be he most important correlation between the anniversaries of the end of the var and the formation of the WTO, it would seem strange that it took ten 'ears for the lesson to have been taken by the Soviet Union.

According to Kulikov (1985, p. 68) the year 1945 also revealed the Soviet Union as a new force on the world arena, giving 'socialism and lemocracy' a rôle in international affairs. The USA and Britain were een as imperialist. Kulikov described Truman as wanting the USA to ead the World (ibid.), while Skorodenko argued that the US military nd political leadership wanted to use its nuclear monopoly to bomb the JSSR (1985a, p. 62). Britain's rôle in this new anti-Soviet imperialism vas seen in Churchill's Fulton, Missouri, speech (Kulikov, 1985, p. 68; Katrich, 1985, p. 53).

From this inauspicious start to the post-war years, the 30th Anniversary rticles charted the rise of NATO as an aggressive alliance and what Rusakov considered was the 'threat of a new war' (*Izvestiya* 15 May 985). Gribkov in *Izvestiya* (14 May 1985) referred to the US nuclear ıreat, the US unleashing an arms race and transferring its weapons and nilitary technology to Western Europe, and the creation of a system of nilitary bases close to 'our borders'. The articles saw the conclusion of uch a series of developments to have been the rearmament of West Germany and its inclusion in NATO and the WEU. Nezhinsky (p. 61) saw ıe whole of the 1945–55 period as part of a policy by the US imperialists nd monopoly capitalists to carry out power politics and the roll-back of ɔcialism, manifested in the positions of strength policy that was objected) so much in the origins and early documents of the WTO. As with the ther writers during the 30th Anniversary, Nezhinsky concluded that after en years of such opposition 'the socialist countries were compelled to take ıe necessary measures to ensure their security . . . Thus, the signing of the Varsaw Treaty was an objective necessity brought about by the conditions in which the European socialist countries had to live and act . . . ' (ibid. p. 62). However, unlike the other writers, Yakovlev (1985, p. 16) sough to emphasize certain elements of these conditions. He considered that th need for security had come to require a military basis for the social need of economic and political unity. Such an argument would suggest that th WTO was formed not for any external reasons such as NATO, but merel that its time had come for reasons *internal* to the socialist community.

Ideological Origins

Another aspect of the Anniversary's subtle changing of the foreign-polic position of 1955 is that a number of the Anniversary articles see th founding of the WTO as an example of what they consider to be Lenin' teaching on the principles of socialist co-operation and socialist interna tional solidarity (e.g. Kulikov, 1985, pp. 71, 67) and the necessity of th unity of socialist countries in the face of the aggression of imperialis (Smorigo, p. 27). Svetlov also considered the WTO was designed for th defence of socialist gains (p. 25). This directly contradicts the attem during the WTO's formation to deny any ideological bias in the Treaty c indeed in the wording of its peace initiatives to present a non-ideologica universal, face.

The Defensive Posture

As a corollary to the ideological posture the articles, as througho the history of the WTO, claim that the Organization is only there fc defensive purposes and has no aggressive or expansionist intention Gribkov (*Izvestiya*, 14 May 1985), repeats the assertion that the WT is a new type of alliance, that unlike the capitalist blocs the WTO, bein a socialist alliance, is purely defensive – even that this is somethir inherently socialist. Kulikov places the collective self-defence doctri as being the single military-strategic basis of the alliance of 'the fratern peoples of the socialist countries and their armies' (1985, p. 71). He ti this in with a description of the Organization's ideological basis beir proletarian internationalism and class solidarity (ibid.). By being able place the formation of the WTO at the end of a chronology coverir the formation of NATO and the rearmament of the Federal Republ of Germany, Skorodenko, for example, is able to argue that the WT was a defensive response to 'the aggressive NATO bloc and the oth military-political alliances of imperialism' (1985a, p. 62). In a further effc to portray the WTO as a defensive alliance, Svetlov (1985, p. 30) calls c is readers to compare the 1984 statements from the foreign ministers of both NATO and the WTO, arguing that the NATO foreign ministers evealed aggressive and militaristic aims while the WTO Committee of Ministers of Foreign Affairs were offering peace proposals. In yet another avourable comparison with NATO, Yakovlev (1985, p. 17) argues that he WTO's defensive posture can be seen no further than in its open nembership,[4] which he does not see in NATO.

tructure

o Gribkov (*Izvestiya*, 14 May 1985) the peace-loving character of the VTO could even be seen in the Organization's structure. He, as with the ther articles, combined a potted analysis of the WTO's structure with a istory of its peace initiatives. For Gribkov (ibid.) this defensive nature ould be especially seen in the way the political structure (PCC and CFM), ad been the channel for proposals that found their way into the world's olitical fora.

Even Rusakov, in the keynote address of the whole Anniversary *Izvestiya*, 15 May 1985), saw the need to explain to his audience soldiers, politicians, and other politically-active proletarians) in the 14 May solemn gathering just what bodies the WTO consisted of, how they nterrelated, and what they did. For example that sessions of the PCC formulate large-scale, long-term proposals enjoying broad international upport', while the CFM in 'Its regular activity promotes the effective mplementation of a foreign policy line co-ordinated at the highest level nd the translation of this line into specific co-ordinated steps in favour f peace and international security' (ibid.). As Chapter 3 shows, this is tandard WTO historiography, and it seems ludicrous to have to include in such a time and place. Nezhinsky (1985, p. 63) even felt the need to tress yet again that the WTO was the main centre of its members' foreign olicy co-ordination.

On the question of military co-ordination within the WTO, Gribkov 1985a, p. 13) repeated that it was the rôle of the PCC to be the cornerstone f military co-operation, and tied this in ideologically with Lenin reportedly aying that war depends on various issues, which were seen to be covered y PCC decisions: economy; science and technology; moral-political facrs; and military factors. However, he paid greater attention to the WTO's ilitary structure (he lists only the CDM, Joint Command, Joint Staff, Milirry Council, and Joint Armed Forces) and how they work together to cordinate and improve the military co-operation of the allies. This is in keepg with the way the Anniversary minimized the political side of the WTO.

Political Initiatives

In his Anniversary article, Kulikov (1985, p. 72) considered the thirty years of the WTO to be thirty years of a struggle for peace. The collective decisions and joint initiatives of the PCC, translated by the CFM into a mechanism of co-operation and co-ordination, had, by the 1970s achieved 'the consolidation of the political and territorial realities existing in Europe' (ibid.).

Skorodenko (1985a, p. 63) explained that this achievement, in the Helsinki Final Act, was in fact the result of PCC activities which had led to the recognition of the German Democratic Republic, the treaties with the Federal Republic of Germany of the early 1970s, the 1971 agreement on West Berlin (which he described as a Treaty), the development of bilateral relations with the West, 'and others'. To this impressive list, Svetlov (1985 p. 72) added the post-CSCE fora and the Stockholm Conference, plus the proposals contained in the 1983 PCC Political Declaration. Gribkov (1985b, p.84), who described the Helsinki Final Act as the main success of the WTO, even (1985a, p. 12) included mention of the Soviet–US Genev talks on nuclear and space weapons.

But can such international issues really be considered as foreign polic successes for the WTO? Certainly, as Chapter 4 detailed, the only one o these issues that was covered by WTO documents before the event wa the campaign which led up to the CSCE. (This excludes WTO policy o the German Question that was not backed up by concrete proposals in th manner of the European Security Campaign.) Where the WTO definitel covered these issues was as a post hoc commentary to existing devel opments on the international scene. Even the developments in bilatera relations with the West were the result of national foreign-policy decision and more created the environment in which the WTO operated than vic versa. (The Stockholm Conference, while also being a WTO proposal, wa set up mainly through bilateral diplomacy rather than the persistent publi declarations seen in the earlier European Security Campaign.)

The CSCE was referred to by Svetlov (1985, pp. 30–1), as par of the post-war political consensus, and the recognition of Europe' territorial-political realities, its treaties and agreements, and necessar for the development of East–West relations. Svetlov also refered to th Prague Political Declaration (PCC, January 1983), for its repetition c the WTO call for carrying out international relations under accepte principles. Unlike the other Anniversary articles, he also spelt out i great detail a number of 'major practical steps' in the WTO's programm to strengthen European security, end the arms race, and move toward disarmament (pp. 32–3). However, despite Svetlov's reference to the 1984 CFM statement, the measures he listed do not entirely correspond to what was proposed then.[5]

In a grandiose assessment of the WTO's rôle in world politics, Kulikov asserted that the people of the socialist countries were proud that the WTO 'was and remains the initiator of all the peace initiatives' (*Krasnaya Zvezda*, 14 May 1985). Strangely, this was said to a military rather than a primarily political audience. But certainly it is a rather one-sided analasis. If the WTO's initiatives have not substantially changed over thirty years, then Kulikov's statement is even more ludicrous. Certainly these initiatives have had remarkably little success in foreign policy terms, so they should not really be seen as something to boast about.

Military Structure

In military terms, while all the peace-campaigning had been going on, the military might of the Joint Armed Forces had for thirty years been holding back aggressive imperialism. According to Gribkov (*Izvestiya*, 14 May 1985), the WTO had been strengthening its members' defence-potential, military construction, and military training, through measures formed 'in accordance with the Treaty.' Once again, Gribkov reminded his readers that the military alliance is organized to ensure each country's equal status, and he claimed that this could partly be seen in 'The Joint Armed Forces, in the composition of which each country apportions contingents of its forces and fleet' (ibid.). In other words, Gribkov is revealing that even after thirty years, the JAFs were not a single body fully uniting the socialist forces.

In his article in *Voennyi vestnik*, Gribkov (1985a) reminded his readers of the military structure of the WTO. Like Rusakov he was assuming a high level of ignorance in his audience. He took his readers from the PCC's overall rôle, down through the CDM as the centre of co-ordination and taking important decisions, to the Joint Command resolving crucial problems in its main function of co-ordinating the Joint Armed Forces and realizing the plans for their equipment, with the Military Council making recommendations for the benefit of the military might and the Joint Staff acting as the working body of the military structure (p. 14). However, in his concurrent article in *Voenno-istoricheskii zhurnal*, Gribkov (1985b, p. 88) mentioned that the military co-operation on the basis of PCC decisions was also put into practice by 'the national military bodies'. He did not see any problem of co-ordination or of such decisions overriding national sovereignty or national aims:

> The co-ordinated decisions and recommendations, which are taken b the Committee of Ministers of Defence and the Military Council of th Joint Armed Forces, are carried out by the allied armies, since they ar worked out collectively, by taking into account the interests of the arme forces of each country.

Gribkov continued that the Joint Staff works in close contact with 'na tional General (Main) Staffs' to help put the decisions into practice and that the ultimate aim of such military co-operation was to improv military strength, readiness, structure, and technologies, against the NATC threat (ibid.).

As the section on the military structure in Chapter 3 shows, the structur as officially described, and which was reaffirmed by Gribkov, is no particularly efficient. What Gribkov seemed to be saying was that afte thirty years of its operation the Warsaw Treaty structure did not seen to have a fully prescriptive rôle over the national military structures Even though he argued that the Central European countries participat collectively in the WTO structure, the actual rôle of the non-Soviets in thi structure is in doubt, even without taking into account the unspecified rôl of the party structures, in which the CPSU predominates. In fact Gribkov began by saying that the decisions 'are carried out' by the armies, and only refers to the Joint Staff working closely with the national military structure (ibid.). The actual practice of military co-operation is unclear.

In referring to the national contingents of the Joint Armed Forces Gribkov (1985b, p. 88) specified that the basis of the JAFs are in fact th Soviet forces. Skorodenko (1985a, p. 66) extended this Soviet dominance by specifying that Soviet aid is the basis of the military-economic and scientific-technical potential of the WTO, but since he refered to the rôle of the CMEA Complex Programme as developing economic integratior leading to 'effective measures' on defence, there could be some doubt as to just how much co-operation, albeit dominated by the USSR, there is.

The Rôle of the Party

In contradistinction to most of the earlier writings on the WTO, in the Soviet 30th Anniversary articles a much more open rôle was given to the ruling parties. For example, in his analysis of the development of the military bodies of the WTO, Kulikov (1985, p. 74) was able to write that:

> As a result of the communist and workers' parties and the peoples of the fraternal countries an essential structure was created of the organization

> and structure of the armies and fleets, high quality displayed of their technical equipment, material-technical provision, the level of operational and military preparedness of the commanding staff and forces was promoted, the boldest and most fundamental review in the armed forces of the allied armies.

When addressing the Soviet and Joint Armed Forces representatives Kulikov explained that the parties were not only behind the material level of the forces, but had in fact been working for thirty years on the various forms of military co-operation, and had been furthering the readiness of the Joint Armed Forces and 'of each of the national armies, strengthening their military fraternity' (*Krasnaya Zvezda*, 14 May 1985). According to Rusakov, it was the intervention of the parties that ensured that the JAFs had 'everything necessary to repulse any aggression' (*Izvestiya*, 15 May 1985).

Nezhinsky (1985) limited the rôle of the ruling parties to helping with the constant improvement of the WTO through the participation of their delegates in the work of the Political Consultative Committee. If we accept the official account of how successful the PCC is, despite its limited frequency of convocation, then it would be possible for the parties to influence all aspects of the life of the WTO. But it would be highly irregular for the ruling parties to limit their active participation to the PCC. Katrich (1985, p. 55) though, regarded 'the leadership of the communist and workers' parties of our countries' (and the Marxist–Leninist ideology as the theory behind their policy) as of paramount importance to the successful activity of the WTO.

While not being explicit as to the party direction of the WTO's political activities, Katrich, as a 'Colonel-General of Aviation, Deputy Commander-in-Chief (Air Force)' of the Joint Armed Forces, would perhaps be better placed than Nezhinsky to see at first hand that 'the communist ideology' and 'leadership of the communist and workers' parties', including through the activities of political-workers within the forces (ibid., p. 56), do in fact have a day-to-day rôle within at least part of the WTO.

Both Katrich (ibid.) and Gribkov (1985a, p. 14) stressed the rôle of ideology in the activities of the forces, and in this respect Gribkov also specified that: 'A great place in the life and activities of the allied armies is occupied by the co-operation of the political bodies, which are realized on the basis of the decisions of the communist and workers' parties' (1985b, p. 90). While still not being specific concerning the parties' rôle in non-military affairs, perhaps a general indication of just how explicit this has become can be seen in that unlike all previous documents issued from the PCC or extra-structural summmit-level meetings, the Protocol on the Treaty's prolongation was not signed by both a state and a party representative (some of which would have been the same person), but by all the party First/General Secretaries, only some of whom were able to sign concurrently as having a state position.

Anti-Western Diatribe

A common element in all the Soviet 30th Anniversary presentations is that, having established to their own satisfaction the WTO as a peace-loving and defensive alliance, and having shown a chronology of its initiatives, they then described NATO, 'militarist imperialists', and above all the USA, as being precisely the opposite, the initiator of all the military policies that the socialist countries claimed to be opposing (by both diplomacy and armed preparedness). In summing up the period of the WTO, Yakovlev (1985, p. 18) wrote: 'Today, as also three decades ago, the NATO bloc is unable to offer Europe and the world anything, other than new military plans, new militaristic preparations, new rounds of the arms race'. Rusakov claimed that the whole military expansion of the WTO to the achievement of strategic parity with NATO was necessary 'since what was ultimately at stake was the fate of socialism and the future of human civilization itself' (*Izvestiya*, 15 May 1985). In other words, if it were not for socialism's defensive response to the armed aggression of NATO, there would be no stopping the expansionism and militarism of the West. Rusakov went on to explain socialism's military preparations by claiming that imperialism, 'primarily US imperialism', wished to upset 'the present correlation of forces in the world', in other words the strategic parity between NATO and the WTO (ibid.).

In terms of chronological events, however, the articles generally go from having presented the origins of the WTO as a response to aggression and the ensuing years to be a success for WTO foreign policy (for example with the Helsinki Final Act), straight into arguing that the West, and especially the USA, nonetheless still wanted confrontation rather than co-operation, particularly in the post-CSCE period. (This corresponds to the coverage of international affairs in the documents of the PCC.) The USSR's Anniversary documents therefore ignore military events for the bulk of the WTO's existence, and instead recount how in the post-Helsinki period the USA has, in their view, acted aggressively. The issues of cruise missiles, Pershing-2 missiles, and the size of the US military budget are repeatedly mentioned (e.g. Gribkov, 1985a, p. 13; Svetlov, 1985, p. 28). Gribkov (1985b, p. 86) concluded that the US had turned to a strategy of direct confrontation, and considered this to be seen in its militarization of space and its development of chemical weapons. He also saw (1985a, p. 13) the current West German policy to be once again revanchist and militarist, questioning the post-war borders (which the USSR considers to have been settled by the West German treaties of the early 1970s and by the Helsinki Final Act) and is thus once again a great threat.

On such specific issues, Rusakov argued that the West's Group of Seven had 'recently' presented 'the same policy of strength, de facto encouragement of revanchism and persistent aspiration to interfere in the socialist countries' internal affairs and impose on the peoples ways they have rejected'.[6] He even specified President Reagan's speech on the 40th anniversary of the end of the War, in Bitburg cemetery in West Germany, as 'an act of blasphemy' and evidence of revanchism (*Izvestiya*, 15 May 1985).

One other accusation against the west, but not mentioned earlier in WTO documents, was that several of the writers saw in the west an attempt to wage 'psychological war' against the socialist countries (e.g. Gribkov, 1985b, p. 87; Smorigo, 1985, p. 24; Skorodenko, 1985a, p. 65). Just how this policy manifests itself was not properly explained, though since it was often mentioned in relation to Reagan's crusade against socialism, it could be seen as just part of the ideological confrontation of East and West.

Such an irascible attack on capitalist-imperialist-Western-militarist-revanchist anti-Sovietism is not new, and can only be expected from an Organization that is in opposition to such forces. The strength and vehemence of such attacks changed according to the times. The 30th Anniversary of the WTO occurred towards the end of a peak in hostility, and was followed in November of the same year by the spirit of Geneva which resulted from the Reagan–Gorbachev summit of November 1985.

The Efficacy of the First Thirty Years

The Communique issued by the Anniversary meeting of the Parliamentarians assessed that throughout its period of operation the WTO had 'reliably served the protection of the historic gains of socialism and the development of all-round co-operation among the allied states, and has played an outstanding rôle in the preservation and strengthening of peace in Europe and throughout the world' (*Izvestiya*, 15 May 1985). Once again this was a predictable description, and could equally have been used for any of the Organization's other anniversaries, books, or articles. The only difference is perhaps a tone that a 30th Anniversary requires a slightly greater sense of conviction. But, as was pointed out at the start of this chapter, the rest of the Communique and the other keynote speeches failed to make any particular foreign-policy use of such an Anniversary.

Where some of the Soviet Anniversary documents did go further than earlier documents was in placing the WTO within the broader context of the socialist community. While Menzhinskii (1985, p. 29) had placed the PCC alongside various bilateral and multilateral fora of both the Parties and the states, Smorigo (1980, p. 27) wrote in the context of the Anniversary that: 'The central place in the realization of the joint efforts of the fraternal countries for the defence of the gains of socialism and the prevention of a new world war belongs to the Warsaw Treaty Organization'. While this seems to be one of the most outspoken laudatory assessments of the WTO, it should perhaps be seen in context, as an analysis read on a specific historic occasion rather than in a general treatise on the life of the socialist states. On the occasion of the Treaty's 30th Anniversary, and not quite a month after the extension of the Treaty's operation, it would be necessary to justify the existence of the Treaty in strong terms. However, Nezhinsky (1985, p. 62), also writing for the 30th Anniversary, was just as circumspect as early writers:

> Together with the fraternal socialist countries' [bilateral] treaties of friendship and mutual assistance and their co-operation within the framework of the Council for Mutual Economic Assistance, the Warsaw Treaty was a powerful international legal factor, cementing all the fraternal ties among European socialist countries.

Such an analysis of the WTO's overall significance is consistent with the conclusions of the WTO in context, presented in Chapter 6. Outwith the 30th Anniversary, but also writing in 1985, Ponomarev argued that the cause of building the all-round security and consolidation of the socialist states 'is also effectively served by the Warsaw Treaty Organization' (p. 118).

In a similar vein, but discussing the general integration of the allies, Savinov (1986, pp. 224–5), writing immediately after the 30th Anniversary, argued that the WTO carried out 'a historical contribution' to this integration 'by means of the regular . . . collective and bilateral meetings at the highest level'. (The bilateral meetings are not part of the WTO's formal structure.) It would therefore seem likely that an extraordinary assessment such as Smorigo's is really an aberration.

Kulikov's address to the military gathering argued that the WTO had seen a thirty-year struggle to improve the international situation in favour of peaceful coexistence and the equal-in-rights co-operation of states

(*Krasnaya Zvezda*, 14 May 1985). This is the basic explanation of what the WTO is for, and can be traced back to the wording of the Treaty itself (see Appendix 1). Katrich (1985, p. 54), however, gave it a wider scope, arguing that the WTO was 'not just a military alliance of states, but an all-round mechanism of effective political, economic, ideological, and military co-operation'.

The WTO did not gain its central place overnight. The introduction in *Izvestiya* to Rusakov's address to the solemn gathering of May 14 said only that the WTO 'has *become* a reliable bastion of peace, revolutionary gains, and the people's creative labour' (15 May 1985; my italics). The introduction continued that the member-states 'have been loyally serving the development of the socialist countries, the safeguarding of their sovereignty, security, the inviolability of their borders, and the implementation of a peace-loving foreign policy course' (ibid.). So the WTO, founded in 1955 as a response to the militarisation of West Germany, had grown over the years to cover joint defence, joint foreign policy, co-operation in both these fields and in politics, economics, and ideology, and the general development of the socialist countries.

In arguing for its usefulness, Rusakov even claimed that the very act of belonging to the WTO had 'promoted the consolidation of the political weight and international authority of each state belonging to it'. Moreover, the existence of the WTO had influenced 'our planet's moral-political climate' by acting as a model for national liberation movements in showing a better form of world organisation than the imperialist one (ibid.): a stirring assessment indeed for an Organization with the central place in its members' interrelations.

The WTO in Practice

With the Anniversary assessment of the WTO so favourable, how did its practice measure up? In the analysis of its political initiatives and successes, the Soviet writers were adamant that the WTO had played an effective and leading rôle in East–West relations. Nezhinsky (1985, p. 60) took this further, and argued that since one of the main aims of the WTO was to defend socialist gains, it had successfully acted to 'give a collective rebuff to imperialist intrigues against the cause of peace and democracy'. However, his examples of these successes were unusual. As evidence that the WTO operated to protect socialism he argued that the Organization had pooled its military, economic, and political resources in the defence of Hungary in 1956, Czechoslovakia in 1968, and Poland in the 1980s (ibid., p. 65); as evidence that the socialist countries had given aid against

US imperialism, he referred to Cuba, Vietnam, Korea, Laos, Kampuchea, the movements of national liberation, and Nicaragua (in that order). In strictly historical and documentary terms, the WTO had played no rôle in the defence of Hungary in 1956; the defence of Czechoslovakia in 1968 had been carried out by a group of countries in, but not the entire membership of, the WTO (see footnote 7, Chapter 3); the defence of Poland was carried out without any action by the WTO beyond official and bilateral expressions of concern and support. In terms of aid to other countries, the WTO documents have at various times mentioned the countries Nezhinsky (1985) referred to, but with the exception of offering to send volunteers to Vietnam the documents have only offered moral or ideological support. In the examples cited, this does not deny that the member states took action either through bilateral or extra-WTO collective means. To cite them as successes for the WTO is to ascribe a regional defence body with both an internal-security rôle, and a wider, out of area, rôle. These would seem unusual if not dubious successes to claim for an Organization originally intended as a model for pan-European collective security.[7]

One of the functions of the WTO has been to increase the unity and cohesion of the member-states. Quoting the Politburo report mentioned at the start of this chapter, Nezhinsky (1985, p. 60) argued that the existence of the WTO 'is inseparable from the steady build-up of the unity and cohesion of the socialist countries and their joint action against the aggressive militaristic policy pursued by the USA and its NATO allies . . . '. He also claimed that the Warsaw Treaty meeting of 13 March 1985 (during the Chernenko funeral) reaffirmed the need to increase unity and cohesion, and to work for greater co-ordination (ibid., p. 66), though this is not directly evident from the meeting's report (*Izvestiya*, 15 March 1985) where these issues were referred to but in brief and predictable wording.

Taking into account the analysis of his article (from the origins of the Treaty onwards), Nezhinsky concluded by noting that the Protocol on the Treaty's prolongation was signed on 26 April 1985 (p. 99). He implied that since the WTO was so useful and effective it could not but be extended. The socialist community could not carry on without it. Such an explanation for the significance of the Protocol was also used by Kulikov (1985, p. 67) who stated that the Protocol itself was an indication of the member-states' unity of action on foreign policy, economics, politics, the work of the parties, the work of the military, and the strengthening of their cohesion, in the fight for peace and against the West. Rusakov told his audience that:

> The Warsaw meeting [26 April 1985] confirmed the necessity of the socialist countries' multilateral military-political alliance. It demonstrates

> with renewed strength the determination of the allied socialist countries' fraternal parties and peoples to continue to strengthen their unity and cohesion, jointly defend socialism's positions, act in a co-ordinated manner in international affairs, and strive for lasting peace on earth. (*Izvestiya*, 15 May 1985)

The extension of the WTO seems to have become fundamental to the continued presentation of the socialist community as a multi-national force in world affairs. Writing after the event, Savinov (1986, p. 247) summarized Yakovlev's Anniversary article and said that it concluded that the current international situation – US militarism, West German revanchism, the Anniversary's critique of the West in general – required the continued existence of the WTO and its greater unity. While Savinov's summary is simplistic, it nonetheless captures the basic view of all the Anniversary presentations.

Taking this all into account – the presentation of the work of the WTO, the explanation for why it was prolonged – it might be seen that, after 1985, the WTO exists because it existed. Given that whatever the unspoken justification, its stated workings and effects do not really amount to much beyond a show of ideological unity. The socialist states could not get away with allowing the Treaty to lapse. Even given its limited practical rôle, international events in the 1980s could not be seen to be carried out with the system of bilateral ties that existed in the early 1950s. The Anniversary presentations did not, and presumably could not, admit this. Therefore they ignored the question by focusing on why the Treaty was formed, how it was structured, and just how effective and useful it was.

CENTRAL EUROPEAN ASSESSMENT

The 30th Anniversary of the signing of the Warsaw Treaty did not go unnoticed in Central Europe. The *Summary of World Broadcasts* covered a wide range of speeches and newspaper articles for the occasion (EE/7952/C). (See also the Anniversary bibliography at the end of this chapter.) To a very great extent, the scope of the treatment was the same as that in the Soviet Union.

While not going into the historical roots so much, the origins of the WTO were again analysed as a response to the West, as 'an inevitable counter-measure to the activities of the most aggressive forces of imperialism' (Bulgarian Foreign Minister Petar Mladenov, *SWB* EE/7952/C/7–9) and especially to NATO and the remilitarisation of West Germany (Czechoslovak commentator Jirina Dupalova, ibid., C/10). The Polish commentator Hofman (1985, p. 8) argued that 'we have to conclude that relations in Europe are not better now than they were thirty years ago. Different, yes, but not better'.

The GDR Foreign Minister said that the WTO was a defensive alliance, defending peace and consolidating socialist co-operation and friendship, reliably protecting socialist construction (*SWB* EE/7952/C/11–12). 'The GDR's membership of this alliance stressed the force of the commitment to do everything so that war never again emanates from German soil' (ibid.).

The Central European reporting does not seem to have covered the structure of the WTO to the same extent as the Soviet articles and speeches (but see *SWB*, ibid., C/13, where it was covered in an interview with Hungarian Deputy Foreign Minister István Roska). However, the WTO's contribution to peace was covered in great detail. Hungarian Deputy Premier Lajos Czinege, speaking to the meeting of WTO Parliamentarians, told his audience that in fulfilling its aims the WTO had been maintaining peace 'not only in the military but in the political sense too' through its peace initiatives (MTI *Daily Bulletin*, vol. 20/134, 14 May 1985). The Bulgarian Foreign Minister Petar Mladenov, addressing a meeting in Sofia, said that the WTO 'became a generator of proposals and initiatives to the benefit of détente and for the promotion of all-European co-operation and at the same time a dynamic factor for their realisation' (*SWB* EE/7952/C/7–9). GDR Foreign Minister Oskar Fischer stated that the WTO had made 'more than 100 proposals to reduce step by step the danger of war by effective measures of arms limitation and disarmament' (ibid., C/11). Reports in the Polish party daily *Trybuna Ludu* claimed that 'The consistent activities of the socialist camp . . . ' had led to the 1963 Partial Test Ban Treaty, the 1968 Non-Proliferation Treaty, the SALT agreements, and the CSCE Final Act (ibid., C/16–17). (As discussed above, these were also successes claimed by Soviet articles, but in most cases the WTO played little or no visible part.)

Surprisingly, the non-Soviet coverage of the Anniversary does not seem to have made any particular mention of the rôle of the parties or overtly ideological matters. This is unlike the treatment in the Soviet media as outlined above.

As with the Soviet articles and speeches, the West was criticized for being aggressive, militaristic, and revanchist. Unlike the Soviet treatment the Central Europeans do not seem to have been quite so strident in their criticism as the Soviets. The West was criticized for the breakdown of the wartime alliance and the division of Europe (Bulgarian Foreign Minister Mladenov, ibid., C/7–9), and US President Reagan was seen to follow Truman, Churchill, Adenauer, and Dulles, for wanting 'to halt the progressive development in the world in order to advance imperialism' (Czechoslovak commentator Dupalova, ibid., C/10). Mention was even made of the USSR not having been allowed to accede to NATO (Hofman, 1985, p. 6). Hofman also saw a rise in jingoism in the USA, and a new militarism and revanchism in West Germany, which he depicted as a US bastion in Europe (p. 8). Nonetheless, no attempt was made to paint a picture of an inherently aggressive enemy, which some of the Soviet coverage seemed to do. While this may be seen as an example of each of the Soviet Union's allies acting as a bridge to the West at a time of renewed superpower confrontation it seems more likely to be evidence of a general difference in national foreign policy positions for each of the WTO member states.

Where the Soviet allies definitely concurred with the Soviet Union was in their assessment of the efficacy of the first thirty years of the WTO. The Czechoslovak Defence Minister Vaclavik's Order of the Day saw the history of the WTO as 'The decisive factor in preventing the aggressive forces of imperialism from unleashing a world war and in ensuring peace in Europe; it permanently ensures the collective security of its members and the inviolability of their frontiers' (*SWB* EE/7952/C/18). The Bulgarian Defence Minister Dzhurov saw the Treaty as having 'inaugurated a qualitatively different, higher stage in the relations among the socialist states . . . ' – it had become a reliable guardian, 'a powerful bulwark of all revolutionary forces and of the national liberation movements' (ibid., C/17–18). The GDR Foreign Minister Fischer saw the WTO as 'the main source of the positive changes which have been accomplished since the end of the Second World War in Europe. The decisive initiatives for a durable peace have emanated from it . . . ' (ibid., C/11–12 – this echoes the assessment by WTO C-in-C Kulikov, *Pravda*, 14 May 1985). The Hungarian Deputy Premier Czinege, in his address to the Parliamentarians' meeting, saw the WTO as having fulfilled its aims of guaranteeing socialist construction and maintaining peace, and that there had been thirty years of a 'decisive contribution to the development of the international situations' (MTI *Daily Bulletin*, vol. 20/134, 14 May 1985).

Overall it can be seen that the Soviet Union and the Central Europeans treated the 30th Anniversary of the signing of the Warsaw Treaty in general unison, but giving allowance for national requirements in their presentations.

CONCLUSIONS

Anniversaries are not just a time for reflexion, which the articles and speeches carried out admirably, but also a time to look to the future and consider what may happen next. This is an opportunity that all the presentations singularly missed. Having explained its history and justified its prolongation, they seemed to assume that stating what a good job the WTO was doing was a sufficient mark of the occasion. The only reference to the future was in calling for greater unity and cohesion, and greater co-ordination of affairs, which are standard calls in all intra-socialist bilateral and multilateral communiques. There was no attempt to hint at further structural developments (though Polish press comment reiterated almost verbatim Gorbachev's remark at the signing of the Protocol [*Pravda*, 27 April 1985] that the WTO states 'are forced to think how to further strengthen their defensive structures' – *SWB* EE/7952/C/16–17). Nor was there any attempt to signal concessions for the East-West negotiating fora, or to offer grounds for a relaxation of tensions. The articles merely restated existing positions, peace initiatives, and the anti-Western diatribe of the moment.

The 30th Anniversary of the signing of the Warsaw Treaty for Friendship, Co-operation, and Mutual Aid, appears to have been a chore, an event that had to take place, rather than a glorious time for celebration. With the exception of the Parliamentarians, who are not an official part of the structure, and ignoring the military historians, none of the participants at the meetings even had to travel from their normal place of residence. With the exclusion of any summit-level or ministerial meeting from the festivities, the Anniversary seems to have been organized to cause the minimum of fuss and disruption. Perhaps they would rather not have celebrated the occasion at all.

ANNIVERSARY BIBLIOGRAPHY

Address by Commander-in-Chief Kulikov to anniversary meeting: *Krasnaya Zvezda*, 14 May 1985, pp. 1, 3.

General of the Army A. Gribkov, 'Na strazhe mira i sotsializma', *Izvestiya*, 14 May 1985, p. 3.

'Gribkov addresses "Scientific Conference", May 14 1985', *SWB* SU/7952/c1/4, 16 May 1985.

Address of Secretary of the CPSU Central Committee K. V. Rusakov 'Alliance for Peace and Socialism', *Izvestiya*, 15 May 1985, p. 4.

Communique on the meeting of representatives of the Parliaments of the state-participants of the Warsaw Treaty, *Izvestiya*, 15 May 1985, p. 5.

SWB SU/7951/C – coverage of events in the USSR.

SWB EE/7952/C – coverage of events in Central Europe

Speech by deputy premier Lajos Czinege to Budapest meeting, MTI *Daily Bulletin* vol. 20, no. 134, 14 May 1985.

Article 'The shield of our peace' by Hungarian State Secretary for Defence Lt. Gen. Morocz Lajos (in *Népszabadság*) MTI *Daily Bulletin* vol. 20/135, 15 May 1985.

Gribkov, A., 'Brat'ya po klassu, Brat'ya po oruzhiyu' *Voennyi vestnik* 1985/5a

Gribkov, A., '30-let na strazhe mira i sotsializma', *Voenno-istoricheskii zhurnal* 1985/5b.

Hofman, Michal 'Firm Foundations' *Polish Perspectives* (Warsaw) vol. XXVIII/3, Summer 1985.

Katrich, A., 'Nadezhnyi shchit sotsialisticheskogo sodruzhestva', *Kommunist vooruzhennykhsyl* 1985/10.

Kulikov, V., 'Nadezhnyi shchit mira', *Kommunist* 1985/8.

Nezhinsky, L., 'An alliance for world peace and security', *International Affairs* (Moscow) 1985/6.

Shkarovskii, Viktor Stepanovich, *Na Strazhe Mira i Sotsializma* (Moskva: Izdatel'stvo *Planeta*, 1985).

Skorodenko, P. P., *Vo glave boyevogo soyuza: Kommunisticheskiye partii – sozdateli i rukovoditeli Organizatsiya Varshavskogo Dogovora* (Moskva: Voenizdat, 1985a).

Skorodenko, P. P., 'Nadezhnyi shchit mirnogo truda' *Kommunist Ukrainy* 1985/5-b.

Smorigo, N., 'Varshavskii Dogovor – nadezhnyi instrument ukrepleniya mezhdunarodnoi bezopasnosti' *Partiinaya zhizn'* 1985/10.

Svetlov, A., 'Varshavskii Dogovor na sluzhbe mira i bezopasnosti', *MEMO* 1985/5.

Yakovlev, A., 'Mezhdunarodnoe znacheniye Varshavskogo Dogovora', *MEMO* 1985/7.

6 Conclusions

SUMMARY OF CHAPTERS

This book has focused on Soviet and Central European writings on the WTO. I have attempted to show what the original documents and writings have said about the WTO, from its origins, through its structure and development, to an analysis of its documentary history and the WTO's rôle in the joint foreign policy of the socialist states. The question of the military rôle of the WTO, while featuring prominently in the original sources, has been shown, through the analysis of the structure and documents, not to amount to more than a loose assembly of intent to be an alliance.

Chapters 1 and 2, in detailing the historical roots and specific origins of the WTO, showed that while a form of military alliance already existed, the post-Stalin Soviet leadership took the opportunity of the West's London and Paris Agreements that incorporated the Federal Republic of Germany into the West's political and military alliance. A formal socialist alliance was created – and then nothing happened. As the preceding chapters showed, in its infancy the WTO was not only an extremely unsophisticated Organization, but in both political and military terms was largely ignored by the Soviet Union and its allies. The Organization as originally created in 1955 cannot have been designed as a significant body within the socialist community.

Chapter 3 discussed in depth the structural development of the WTO. This showed that while the original sources themselves are often scanty and at times contradictory, a fairly complete picture can be created of just how the structure of the WTO operates. Or, as is concluded, is designed not to operate. While quite a sophisticated system of political and military bodies has developed, the WTO is still not intended to be a full-time organization within the socialist community. In its early years the structure amounted to little more than a mechanism for issuing bland statements of propaganda to the Soviet cause. A military structure began to emerge, but this still did not amount to a useful multilateral alliance. It seemed to concentrate more on co-ordinating existing interrelationships and still seemed to operate mainly on a national or bilateral basis.

In foreign policy terms, the main overt reason for the WTO, no formal structure existed until late in 1976. This does not mean that foreign policy was not co-ordinated or carried out. Just that it was done inefficiently on an ad hoc basis, underlining the minimal scope of the WTO. The Organization, in both political and military terms, seems to have developed unevenly, almost unplanned, as if the formal structure was forced to adapt to the de facto unofficial mechanisms that emerged as the need arose. This is underlined by the fact that up to the early Gorbachev years there was still an extensive extra-structural series of bodies tied in formal documentary terms to the main structure. Foremost within this were the regular meetings of the deputy foreign ministers. While the newspaper reports from these meetings were very brief and generally uninformative, unofficial sources[N] cited these meetings as the primary forum for genuine debate and negotiation between the alliance members.

This must however be seen as being within the inter-state structure of the socialist community. Quite separate from the formal structure of the WTO remain the extensive and mainly bilateral inter-party ties. Official accounts of the WTO regularly contain remarks giving the parties a leading rôle in the delineation of foreign policy and military affairs. In its earliest meetings the WTO attendees were identified only by their state rôles; the second session of the PCC (1958) had first secretaries of the parties attending, but not generally as heads of delegations; it was only from the third session of the PCC (1960) that the WTO became formally dominated by party delegates. Yet to this day there is still a façade of placing the decisions and policies of the WTO in an inter-state context.

Official analyses do not restrict treatment of foreign or military policies to a discussion of the WTO. Even books and articles specifically on the WTO will refer to extra-structural meetings, policies shaped outwith the WTO (principally in party documents and decisions of party congresses), and issues outwith the immediate scope of the WTO (generally Soviet–US nuclear relations and other out-of-area topics). Chapter 4 showed that even within the formal documents of the WTO the issues covered are not dealt with exclusively by the WTO. Furthermore they are dealt with by the WTO only in the broadest terms. Even when it is acknowledged that the PCC policy is carried out by the foreign ministers (only formally convened within the structure in 1976) the ministers themselves do not seem to take the policy much further. Policies such as proposals to hold East–West conferences seem to be dealt with through formal bilateral diplomatic channels. There is as yet no evidence that a full-time WTO office exists to carry out policy on behalf of the combined members.[1] Chapter 4 also showed that the members themselves do not seem to see the concept of joint foreign policy in restrictive terms, arguing that national foreign policies are only co-ordinated by the WTO along the broadest lines and in broad ideological terms. The chapter concluded that the main significance was to see the WTO in these ideological terms. Where there were influences on national policies they occurred fully outwith the scope of the WTO.

Chapter 5 showed how the 30th Anniversary of the signing of the Warsaw Treaty was celebrated, and how the speeches and articles subtly rewrote the origins and development of the WTO. All in all, the occasion was shown to be something of a non-event – not even the Commander-in-Chief of the Joint Armed Forces of the WTO was acknowledged as such in the Soviet coverage of the keynote speech and meeting of the whole Anniversary.

PLACING THE WTO IN CONTEXT

The conclusion that would seem to be drawn from this analysis is that, in itself, the Warsaw Treaty and all that follows from it does not amount to very much, either in political or military terms. The best way to understand the WTO would be to place it in the context of the all-round relations of the Soviet Union with Central Europe. Indeed, this is where many official Soviet and Central European writers themselves place the Organization.

Menzhinskii *et al.*, 1980, p. 27), whose description of the WTO structure featured in Chapter 3, prefaced his discussion of that multilateral structure by writing that:

> Within the framework of the socialist community comprehensive (political, economic, cultural, scientific, etc.) and intensive co-operation between the fraternal states is realized . . . the leaders of the fraternal parties have regular meetings, as on the multilateral, so on the bilateral level: exchange visits, the Crimea meetings, conducting sessions of the Political Consultative Committee of the Warsaw Treaty Organization.

Menzhinskii was emphasizing that everything he was about to say about the WTO would have to be seen as lying within the wider context of the inter-party and inter-state relations of the socialist countries. The members of the WTO must be seen to interrelate outwith the context of the WTO. As Alexandrov (1980, p. 16) put it, 'The Warsaw Treaty Organization plays an important rôle in the life of world socialism, where co-operation is developing rapidly along all directions'.

In such an analysis, even a multilateral political-military alliance only has an important, not an overwhelming or even paramount rôle. In the life of world socialism, joint military or foreign policy is not seen as a particularly important means to strengthen the unity and cohesion of the alliance. It becomes just another means to that ideological end. Alexandrov stressed that 'All political aspects of the life and development of socialist society' were discussed through the bilateral and multilateral party links, and that 'no additional mechanism for such international activities is necessary' (p. 17). Such links were especially at the level of Central Committee Secretaries (ibid., p. 16). He went on to imply that the rôle of inter-state ties (and thus the WTO) was being minimized or circumvented (ibid., p. 17).

Even in military terms, the rôle of the WTO was minimized by its one-time Commander-in-Chief: Grechko (1977, p. 319) wrote that 'The [military] alliance of the socialist armies constitutes a part of the general economic, political, military and cultural co-operation between the fraternal states'. Similarly Tyranowski (1973, p. 118) stressed that through its rôle as a forum for 'adopting a joint political line, a common attitude' the WTO was more than just a framework to prepare for joint defence. He merely referred to the WTO as being 'one of the organizational forms of the community of socialist states' (ibid.).

Such an overall assessment of the rôle of the WTO was not even omitted from the 30th Anniversary analysis:

> Together with the fraternal socialist countries' [bilateral] treaties of friendship and mutual interest and their association within the framework of the Council for Mutual Economic Assistance, the Warsaw Treaty was a powerful international legal factor, cementing all the fraternal ties among European socialist countries. (Nezhinsky, 1985, p. 62)

In other words, when the WTO was being praised for its usefulness and efficacy, it was being placed within the overall socialist community as just another factor in the wider ideological rôle of cementing all the fraternal ties.[2]

Writing in 1980, Savinov, in a major analysis of the structure of the WTO, also placed the Organization within this wider context. After stressing the rôle of both bilateral and multilateral inter-party meetings to discuss policies in every field, he only then added that 'important problems are examined in the meetings of the Political Consultative Committee . . . ' (1980, p. 22). But even this minimization was extended, since he went directly on to add 'and in the sessions of the Council for Mutual Economic Assistance' (ibid.). More than this, he stated that the Crimea meetings between Brezhnev and the leaders of the fraternal parties and states 'have great significance' (ibid.), an assessment he later changed to 'One of the most important forms of co-operation . . . ' (ibid., p. 24).[3] Article 8 of the Warsaw Treaty was also interpreted as signifying that the states had agreed a

> readiness also further to develop bilateral and multilateral co-operation in all spheres of the economy, in the utilization of the attainments of scientific-technological progress for the further growth of the material and spiritual prosperity of the people of the socialist countries, to act together with the other country-members of the CMEA all the more to complete the Complex Programme . . . (ibid., pp. 22–3, p. 23)

Therefore not only was the WTO to be seen as just another facet of the overall ties, but that its multilateral significance and its military rôle were not to be seen as particularly important.

Savinov went on to discuss the particular issue of joint foreign policy, but stated that 'An integral element' of this was 'the mutual visits of the Ministers of Foreign Affairs of the fraternal countries, during which go on an exchange of views on questions of the co-ordination of practical activities, concrete actions on the international arena' (ibid., p. 26). These were issues also covered in the sessions of the WTO's Committee of Ministers of Foreign Affairs , but he saw as 'integral' non-WTO meetings – in fact bilateral meetings – for the formation of the practical activities of foreign policy (ibid.). In his assessment, the WTO's rôle was once again being limited and minimized, restricted to a general policy guidance rather than to prescribe national foreign policies. In this field, Savinov also mentioned periodic meetings of the deputy foreign ministers, both bilateral and multilateral, and he stated that:

> Close connexions exist between the corresponding executive departments of the Ministries of Foreign Affairs, between the Embassies of the fraternal countries. Traditional co-operation of the socialist countries [takes place] in the [UN] and in other international organizations. (Ibid.)

In this official assessment, the sessions of the Foreign Ministers within the formal structure of the WTO are just one small part of the overall foreign-policy relationships of the wider socialist community.

As this book has argued, the conclusion must be that the WTO is not as important as the prevailing image of it either as presented by the East or considered by the West. If the functions it carries out are carried out on a wider level outwith the Organization then, as Chapter 4 above concluded, the real purpose of the WTO must be seen in ideological terms. It is a symbol of the socialist community as an international-legal body; or, as one Central European specialist[N] put it, the formal relationships of both the WTO and the CMEA have become the symbolic framework of the interdependence and joint historical development of the bloc. While another specialist[N] claimed that since 1968 the USSR had not had a common policy towards its allies, merely a string of separate policies on defence, economics, or whatever, the former specialist pointed out that the WTO's symbolism has become that of being a body working against disintegration: the presence of a formal structure has required attention from the members, and thus a visible show of participation.

At the ultimate level, the ideological significance of the WTO has become one of bloc identity, which itself has become a realpolitik justification for the WTO. A Central European expert[N] argued that the West, in dealing with the leaders of the ruling parties, has accepted by default the post-war realities of Europe in which the leading parties are the de facto authorities.

One view quite prevalent in Central Europe[N] is that, in binding the states together within the socialist community, the USSR has been acting as the region's *gendarme*. By forcing the members themselves to accept the symbol of unity, it has contained the bickering and animosity over, for example, what remain the unresolved issues of borders and ethnic minorities in the region.[4] While the formation of a military alliance and the WTO might be seen as one source of the peace that has existed in the region since the Second World War, it has also been pointed out[N] that this has only stopped Central Europe itself from sorting out the roots of the prevailing problems and issues. It has stopped the states reaching a level of political development and geopolitical stability more conducive to a working and effective alliance.[5]

THE WTO IN THE GORBACHEV PERIOD

The Warsaw Treaty party and state leaders met Mikhail Gorbachev for the first time in his new leading rôle (he had never been listed as attending a WTO meeting – see Chapter 3, footnote 6) on 13 March 1985, at a 'friendly meeting' in Moscow. They were gathered 'in connexion with the death of K. U. Chernenko'. Despite its ad hoc nature, the meeting was specifically described as a WTO meeting (*Izvestiya*, 15 March 1985). In carrying out their exchange of views all the standard topics of past WTO meetings were covered, and in particular questions of détente and disarmament (ibid.).

Twice, however, the report referred to the wider ideological question of unity:

> Common resolve was expressed also in the future to improve all-round political interaction, economic, ideological, and other co-operation . . .
>
> It was stressed, that in conditions of a complicated international situation the consolidation of the unity and cohesion of the fraternal countries, the greater co-ordination of their activities on the international arena acquire special significance. (Ibid.)

The issue of unity and cohesion is not new to the WTO. Arguably the whole concept of establishing the Organization was to further this aim, and in some form or another the issue has appeared in all the main Warsaw Treaty documents from the very beginning. Behind this, however, the issue has a greater meaning, though one of ideology rather than the practicalities of organizing a political-military alliance.

But, as the first meeting with Gorbachev showed he, like his predecessors, saw the need for the WTO to express an interest in the closer co-operation of its members, and in all fields. Unlike his predecessors Gorbachev made this interest public within official Warsaw Treaty documentation. Brezhnev raised the issue in a report to the CPSU Central Committee in 1965; Gorbachev mentioned it just over a month after becoming General Secretary of the CPSU.

In his speech to the reception following the signing of the Protocol extending the Treaty, Gorbachev referred once again to the WTO's willingness to dissolve itself in conjunction with the dissolution of NATO. Noting that NATO 'does not have such an intention' and was in fact acting aggressively and building up its conventional and nuclear arms, he concluded: 'And this makes us think now of further enhancing the Warsaw Treaty Organization' (*Pravda*, 27 April 1985). The rest of the speech again covered general WTO issues. In conclusion, and presumably by way of a toast, he said:

> To the further co-operation of our parties and states, their stronger unity and cohesion on the principles of Marxism–Leninism and socialist internationalism!
>
> Let the fraternal alliance of socialist countries – the Warsaw Treaty – grow stronger! (Ibid.)

Once more, Gorbachev was pointing out the rôle of the WTO in advancing the ideological issue of unity.

The question of further enhancing the WTO did not go away, but the issue took several years to resolve itself. Six months after Gorbachev's remarks, the PCC met in Sofia (22–23 October 1985). The opening paragraph of the Statement issued explained that there had been 'a fruitful discussion of topical problems of further developing the co-operation of the state-participants of the Warsaw Treaty' (*Pravda*, 24 October 1985).

A month later, when Gorbachev was returning from his Geneva summit (21 November 1985) with US President Reagan, an extraordinary meeting was held in Prague of the WTO's 'highest leaders' (party and state leaders plus foreign ministers). Tagged on to the terse resumé of the limited international issues arising from Gorbachev's report, the article stated that the parties and states were unanimous in seeing that their unity and cohesion in every field was of paramount importance (*Pravda*, 22 November 1985). This mild wording was similar to that emanating from the meeting at Chernenko's funeral rather than Gorbachev's speech after the Protocol extending the Treaty.

Meeting four months later, the foreign ministers also discussed the question of unity, cohesion, and the structure to effect it. Towards the end of their Communique, it was stated that:

> The states represented at the meeting reaffirm the importance of their defence alliance for ensuring their security and peaceful development, for strengthening European and universal peace. They will further closely co-operate in international affairs, in outlining and implementing an agreed policy of peace, security, and international co-operation. (*Pravda*, 21 March 1986)

This statement seemed strongly to be saying that, a year after Gorbachev's accession in the USSR and his consequent leading rôle in the WTO, the purpose of that Organization would remain one of delineating the general aims and principles. The WTO's activities in this wider field would not be augmented. The Communique went on to place the rôle of the WTO in its wider context, by referring to the significance of the CMEA framework and the even wider constructive co-operation of the WTO's governments, parties, public organizations, and movements 'concerned with the destinies of peace on Earth' (ibid.).

For over a year this status quo remained. The formal and informal structures of the Organization carried on much as before. Compared to the published sources of the first thirty years, in the Gorbachev period there was slightly more openness in these documents. For example the report of a meeting of the deputy foreign ministers for the first time listed who had attended (*Pravda*, 3 September 1986). The scope of meetings in the military structure was also enhanced.

The Military Council session of 12–14 November 1986 discussed the results of the Reagan–Gorbachev summit at Reykjavik (*Pravda*, 15 November 1986), a political subject not previously held to be within the purview of the Military Council. The report of the meeting continued with a statement stressing the rôle of the Central European countries in ensuring peace, and made particular reference to the reduction of conventional arms and the preservation of bloc parity with NATO (ibid.). Previously the Military Council had limited itself to the discussion of issues connected with joint training.

In December 1986 the Committee of Ministers of Defence met, and for the first time issued a Communique (*Pravda*, 4 December 1986) rather than a general report on the results of the meeting. Once again the attendees were listed for the first time for such a meeting, including reference to leading staff from the national Ministries of Defence and from the Joint Command. This meeting was also unusual since it too discussed political matters – the Reykjavik summit, and the initiatives of the Budapest PCC session of the previous June.[6]

The Gorbachev period of the WTO continues to lay great emphasis on the rôle of the Political Consultative Committee as the general co-ordinating mechanism of the WTO. Under the new Soviet leadership the PCC has met annually. While this is a doubling of the frequency of meetings to that of the Brezhnev era, it still does not fulfil the promise of the first PCC Communique to meet 'as necessity arises, but not less than twice a year' (*Pravda*, 29 January 1956). These PCC sessions have continued to publish joint documents on single issues. One in particular 'On the Military Doctrine of the state-participants of the Warsaw Treaty' issued by the Berlin session (28–29 May 1987) has become the focus of a series of articles and publications.[7] Unlike any of the other single-issue documents the PCC has ever issued, the question of military doctrine (as evaluated by the WTO) of the alliance has become a campaign in itself.

The Communique that accompanied the 1987 PCC session (*Izvestiya*, 30 May 1987) also signalled the first apparent changes to the formal structure of the WTO since the Bucharest Reforms of 1976. After more than a year's documentary silence on the question of 'enhancing the Warsaw Treaty Organization', two new bodies were added, once again to the political structure. Furthermore, for the first time these two bodies make non-Soviet participation in policy formation a structural reality. The eleventh and final section of the Communique stated that

When questions of interaction in the framework of the Warsaw Treaty were discussed, the participants in the meeting declared for imparting greater dynamism to co-operation in the foreign policy sphere, for upgrading its mechanism and for the steady observance of the principles of equality and mutual responsibility in the system of political relations among the allied states. They attach importance to enhancing the activity and initiative of every allied state in international affairs in the interests of conducting a concerted foreign policy course.

In this context it was decided to set up a multilateral current mutual information group consisting of representatives of the state-participants of the Warsaw Treaty.

It has been decided to create a special commission of the state-participants of the Warsaw Treaty on questions of disarmament, consisting of representatives of the ministries of foreign affairs and ministries of defence, to exchange views and information on questions of arms limitation and disarmament, especially nuclear disarmament, including the discussion of initiatives of allied states and the working out of joint proposals in this field. The creation of the commission is called on to facilitate the still more active participation of all the state-participants of the Warsaw Treaty in joint efforts in the field of arms limitation and disarmament. (*Izvestiya*, 30 May 1987)

As with the history of the structural development of the WTO, the formal changes seem to be codifying and endorsing what was already happening informally. Prior to this PCC session, information was already being exchanged, for example at the meeting in Warsaw of 'editors of the central bodies of the presses of the country-participants of the Warsaw Treaty' discussing the presentation of peace policy (*Pravda*, 22 March 1986). Discussion of arms limitation was taking place, such as at the 'regular meeting of working groups of experts [of WTO states] on reducing armed forces and conventional arms in Europe' held in Sofia (*Pravda*, 14 March 1987).[8]

Where the proposals for structural changes suggested by Gorbachev and the Soviet Union were apparently blocked by the Central Europeans in 1986, this time they must have been satisfied with the situation. Certainly the wording of the Communique does seem to stress both the rôle which each state will be playing and also the advisory, rather than prescriptive, status of the bodies formed.

Since the Berlin PCC, *Pravda* has reported regular meetings of the two bodies. The 'working group of experts' that first met before the Berlin PCC has continued to meet, in Budapest (December 1987), Sofia twice more

(February 1988, June 1988), and Bucharest (December 1988). It would seem important that while this body has not met on a strictly rotational basis, Bucharest has proved to be one of the venues. Romania, it seems, continues to play its part in the evolving structure, and in fact views this new body worthy of attention and within the limits of its national foreign policy.

A second body began regular meetings after the Berlin PCC. This is described as a 'multilateral group of current mutual information'. Unusually it has almost exclusively met in Warsaw. Its first meeting (12 September 1987) was headlined is *Pravda* as 'meeting of a group', briefly stating that it was a regular session consisting of representatives of the Warsaw Treaty state-participants, and that it 'carried out an exchange of information and views on some current international questions' (*Pravda*, 13 September 1987). The third meeting, given a verbatim report in *Pravda*, added that it was attended by deputy minister of foreign affairs of Poland Jaroszek in his capacity as PCC General Secretary[9] (*Pravda*, 13 November 1987). When this group met again in January 1988 it was attended by another Polish deputy foreign minister, who was not there in an official Warsaw Treaty capacity (*Pravda*, 21 January 1988). The sixth session of this group stated that 'in particular' it discussed security and co-operation in Europe (*Pravda*, 14 April 1988).

After meeting exclusively in Warsaw, a seventh regular session of the multilateral group of current mutual information (referred to for the first time by its initials) met in Bucharest. Even more detail was given about the matters under discussion. As at the sixth session European peace and security was mentioned. In addition to this the settlement of conflicts in other regions of the world was discussed, and an exchange of information took place on the members' foreign policy activities (*Pravda*, 24 November 1988). As with the meetings of the 'working group of experts', the participation of Romania is informative, showing its active rôle in the WTO in the Gorbachev period.

While the multilateral group of current mutual information is direct evidence of the Berlin PCC statement, the press reports of the working group of experts would only indicate that a second new PCC body has come into operation. The detailed description of its composition and activities in the Communique has never been repeated in the truncated press information. On balance, however, it would appear that the formal structure of the WTO is alive and thriving.

On the other hand, the informal activities of the WTO are also thriving. *Pravda* published what was described as a WTO 'Proposal' to NATO for a moratorium on military spending (11 April 1987), though this did not coincide with any meeting. (Two such free-standing documents had been issued in 1984 – see Appendix 2.) The Presidents of the Parliaments of the member states met in Warsaw (*Pravda*, 4 July 1987) and issued a message to the CSCE states.

To deal with issues of the moment the Gorbachev period has continued to call ad hoc meetings outwith the formal structure, rather than call a full PCC session as was envisaged when the Organization was established. For example, to inform his allies of the outcome of the Washington summit with US President Reagan and the signing of the INF Treaty, Gorbachev held a meeting in Berlin of 'leading statesmen' of the the Warsaw Treaty states (*Pravda*, 12 December 1987). Likewise when Soviet Foreign Minister Shevardnadze sought to inform the Warsaw Treaty foreign ministers of the results of his meeting in Moscow with the then US Secretary of State Shultz, there was a meeting in Prague, but it was not a proper session of the Committee of Ministers of Foreign Affairs (*Pravda*, 27 February 1988). The foreign ministers also held a separate meeting, again not a session of the CFM, in Warsaw during the full PCC convocation (*Pravda*, 17 July 1988). This was the first time that such a division of work within a PCC session had been stated.

One innovation to the informal WTO structure was that in June 1988 delegates of the Warsaw Treaty states met during the UN Special Session on Disarmament in New York. What is more, a formal Memorandum was issued titled 'Security through disarmament' (*Pravda*, 5 June 1988). Prior to this meeting *Pravda* had noted get-togethers of deputy foreign ministers at the United Nations, but these had been of the wider socialist world community.

GORBACHEV'S 'NEW SECURITY CONCEPT'

That under Gorbachev there has been a move by the Soviet leadership to develop a new security policy was greeted with marked enthusiasm in at least some official Central European quarters.[N] According to one specialist[N] speaking in the spring of 1986 'the perception of military security has changed completely'. This expert dated evidence of such a change in thinking back to Gorbachev's official visit to France in October 1985. In a speech to the French parliamentarians, he had signalled a move in the Soviet arms-negotiating position. Gorbachev, talking of medium-range nuclear weapons in Europe, claimed that 'we consider it possible to conclude a corresponding agreement separately, outside direct connexion with the problem of space and strategic arms' (*Vizit* . . . , p. 49).

This offer was repeated in part 2 of the Sofia PCC Communique (*Pravda*, 24 October 1985).

By the time of the 27th Congress of the CPSU, this apparent shift in basic negotiating positions had become a full security policy. In part 4 of his keynote Political Report, Gorbachev discussed the 'fundamental principles' of 'an all-embracing system of international security'. Such a system would embrace not just military and political aspects, but would also be intimately tied to economic and humanitarian concerns. The military 'fundamental principles' were standard concerns of WTO documents, such as the arms race and the disbanding of military alliances; the political sphere again included concerns seen in WTO references to principles of international relations. Even the economic sphere of the new security concept contained issues covered in the sections on wider international affairs in some WTO documents, such as ending economic discrimination (sanctions, blockades) and a new world economic order covering such things as Third World debt and shifting military investment to civil development and the peaceful use of outer space. Gorbachev's concept of humanitarian aspects to security began with 'co-operation in the dissemination of the ideas of peace, disarmament, and international security', as part of moves for greater mutual understanding and concord; then went on through genocide apartheid, and other forms of discrimination; 'international co-operation in the implementation of the political, social, and personal rights of people'; questions of divided families, marriage, and contacts between people and organizations; and finally co-operation in culture, art, science, education and medicine (*Materialy* . . . , pp. 74–6).

The aim of such principles (which Gorbachev saw as stemming logically from the CPSU Programme, and in keeping with 'our concrete foreign policy initiatives' – ibid., p. 76) was 'to make peaceful coexistence the highest principle of state-to-state relations' (ibid.). (Such a paramount importance for peaceful coexistence should surely have already been explicit, including from the history of WTO documents and materials.) The importance of this analysis, however, was later explained[N] as being that such new thinking strived to maintain 'an optimal level of security which is just enough' within a military balance, a move from conceiving equality of numbers to that of equality of capabilities. The level of security would also be conceived in terms where relaxation in political, economic or humanitarian spheres of security would be seen to contribute to the military balance, and so become a factor in Soviet considerations of balances or imbalances at all levels of the military sphere, a redifinition of Soviet numbers and expenditures(ibid.).

Whether or not this did indicate a genuine shift in Soviet security thinking, or was just one side of the continuing internal Soviet debate or factional dispute, is of course unclear. Gorbachev did, however, in his address to the 11th Congress of the SED (18 April 1986) go on to offer what was seen in the West as an indication of a further shift. Towards the end of his speech he stated that the USSR suggested 'substantial reductions in all components of the land forces and tactical air forces of the European states and the relevant forces of the USA and Canada deployed in Europe . . . [covering] the territory of all of Europe – from the Atlantic to the Urals' (*Pravda*, 19 April 1986). He also tied this in to simultaneous reductions in 'operational-tactical nuclear weapons'.[10] As another apparent shift in Soviet policy, Gorbachev went on to state that 'The question of dependable verification at every stage of this process offers itself. Both national technical means and international forms of verification are possible including, if need be, inspection on site' (ibid.). Such positions went on to be included in the bilateral Soviet–US INF Treaty and in the CSCE follow-up agreements.

It must be stressed that the speech in France, the Political Report to the CPSU Congress, and Gorbachev's address to the SED Congress, were all unilateral Soviet moves, with no obvious official WTO involvement. The WTO did eventually participate in this process, in the PCC Communique from Budapest (11 June 1986).

Opening part 2 of the Communique, and referring back to the goals and tasks set by the previous PCC session (Sofia, 23 October 1985) it was stated that 'The allied socialist states strive to create an all-embracing international security system covering both the military and political, and economic and humanitarian fields' (*Pravda*, 12 June 1986). This was using, unattributed, the Gorbachev/CPSU wording, rather than the original Warsaw Treaty call for an all-European system of collective security. The Communique went on directly to specify that the fraternal countries' foreign-policy line was 'expressed in the decisions of the Congresses of their leading parties . . . ' The PCC covered the familiar WTO issues and proposals but included the offer on verification 'up to and including on-site inspection. The states represented at the meeting are prepared to reach agreement also on any additional verification measures.' (ibid.) This took, unattributed, Gorbachev's proposal from the SED Congress, but also extended it slightly.

It must also be stressed that, in the same period since Gorbachev's accession, Soviet security interests have still largely focused on the super-power relationship and nuclear weapons, neither of which is directly covered by the WTO. While the Central European countries have an interest in these matters they do not directly participate in the questions of a Soviet–US summit, a nuclear test moratorium, or Star Wars; nor indeed are these matters associated with their national foreign or security policies.

The PCC continued to pay attention to the Euromissile question, by supporting the USSR in its campaign on the issue leading up to the INF Treaty, for example in part 3 of the PCC Communique (*Pravda*, 12 June 1986).

'UNITY AND COHESION' WITH GORBACHEV

The Central European states were still being asked to pledge an interest in strengthening their unity and cohesion, and in developing co-operation in all fields. In the Communique of the Budapest PCC (ibid.), part 4 opened by stating that the meeting devoted special attention to these matters, and particularly noted that the states wanted to 'increase active co-operation in international affairs, in the elaboration and transition into life of a co-ordinated foreign policy . . . ' (ibid.)

While calls for unity and cohesion have always been a factor in the states' multilateral and bilateral relations, it seems strange that this PCC session should have seen the need to give a separate mention to co-ordinating their foreign policies. Was that not what the WTO and PCC were there for anyway? This would seem to confirm the conclusions of Chapter 4 , that the WTO has not until now done more than co-ordinate the basic directions of the foreign policies to be carried out nationally. Asked about the striving for unity and cohesion, Central European specialists[N] are quite blasé about the matter. They see it as just another piece of lip-service to the USSR. This too would seem to confirm that the WTO does no more than issue generalized statements that do little to affect national policies.

The Budapest PCC Communique followed the reference to unity and cohesion by repeating the willingness for mutual dissolution with NATO and then immediately referred to exchanging experience in such matters as social construction, exchanges in economics, science, technology, and culture, 'and widening contacts between work collectives, the public, local and tourist contacts, and of deepening co-operation in other spheres . . . (ibid.) At this extent, unity and cohesion seems to become a catch-all for what is in fact an ideological commitment to bind the socialist states together into a wider community. While this would explain the need for a rider for the WTO to have to mention foreign policy co-operation separately, it raises the question of what was happening in this field during the first 30 years of co-operation.

One military expert[N] could not explain this, and could only repeat that under Gorbachev's new security concept, there was for the first time a genuine multilateral consultation in defining joint security, a genuine bringing-together of all the Warsaw Treaty states. This expert argued that, for the first time, the Central European countries were given the opportunity to voice their concerns and opinions directly, and before a Soviet–US summit (for example the Sofia session of the PCC in 1985, prior to the Reagan–Gorbachev meeting in Geneva in November 1985), and they were also given an immediate report by Gorbachev afterwards (the Prague 'highest leaders' meeting, 21 November 1985). 'This would never have happened under Brezhnev', said the expert, who described it as an example of 'a more mutual and democratic concept' of Soviet relations with Central Europe. Gorbachev, he said, was also self-critical, not just accusing his partners of a lack of understanding but pointing to his and the USSR's own faults and weaknesses.

Officially, even in the Gorbachev period, the WTO has given only 'a historical contribution' to the work of integration:

> The fraternal states supremely execute the decisions and further improve the mechanism of their political co-operation, *including by means of the regular and efficient carrying out of collective and bilateral meetings at the highest level.* (Savinov, 1986, pp. 244–5, emphasis added)

This underlines the fact that even in a period of enhanced intra-bloc co-operation, the WTO has not been seen as the sole, or even the most important, means of working for the unity and cohesion of the socialist countries.

CENTRAL EUROPE AND THE WTO

Speaking in 1986, more than one Central European specialist[N] was adamant that the non-Soviet WTO states were not interested in broadening the WTO's official co-ordinating rôle. While at that time they welcomed the greater opportunity for discussion between members of the alliance afforded by Gorbachev's new-style leadership, Central Europe wanted this co-operation to take place on an extra-structural level. The structural changes revealed at the Berlin PCC (*Pravda*, 23 June 1987) can be seen as evidence that the WTO is indeed developing not as a supranational prescriptive organization, but as a forum for the co-ordination of mutually-agreed general policy. One specialist[N] argued that the offical meetings such as the Committee of Ministers of Foreign Affairs would be delayed if it was known in advance that there would not be agreement that could be expressed in an official report. This need not happen to unofficial meetings occuring on an ad hoc basis.

Secondly, any extension to the formal co-ordination of foreign policy would, it seems,[N] involve the onus for individual countries to open up their national policies to the perusal of, and therefore to official objections from, the allies. This was not just on the level of the Soviet Union relating to Central Europe, but also to relations within Central Europe. It would mean that if one country wished to visit or be visited by leaders from another country outwith the alliance (for example British Prime Minitser Thatcher visiting Hungary or Poland's Jaruzelski visiting China) then it would have to ask its allies for their views on this, raising tensions and objections to an official, structural level, of what are at present national foreign policies. Such moves are currently considered to be part of the national foreign policy prerogative of each state.[N]

The deputy foreign ministers met regularly within the scope of the WTO, but outwith the formal structure, from 1968 onwards. Several sources[N] stated that it was in these meetings that real negotiation of policy and disagreement between the member states took place. The deputy foreign ministers met three times in 1986 but have not been reported in *Pravda* as having met since then on behalf of the WTO. It would seem unlikely that the Gorbachev period would remove such a useful tool of Warsaw Treaty co-ordination without good reason. It would appear that the increased co-operation and discussion within the formal structure has obviated the need for the meetings of deputy foreign ministers. In particular the two bodies established by the PCC in 1987, including national representatives from the ministries of defence and foreign affairs (*Izvestiya*, 30 May 1987) would seem to satisfy for the moment the Central European demands for more attention to be paid to their own, Central European, security needs, as opposed to the USSR's super-power policies.

SOVIET RELATIONS WITH CENTRAL EUROPE

Warsaw Treaty bloc relations do not take place in a vacuum, and the rôle of the WTO is itself to be seen within the overall context of Soviet relations with its Central European allies. What, then, can be said about *perestroika* and *glasnost'*, to the USSR's political and economic restructuring in a spirit of political openness? Certainly it has had a marked efect on bloc relations, but once again it must be pointed out that Soviet political changes are internally-generated, and are the result of a new leadership emerging within the USSR. Any discussion of the WTO, and of consequent changes in the East–West political-military balance, must be placed firmly in this context. In an era of rapidly-moving events, all that can be done is to draw tentative conclusions.

The signing of the Protocol extending the Warsaw Treaty to the year 2015 binds together the current state-participants within the limits of international law. How those states carry out their Treaty obligations is debatable, but as discussed above even before Gorbachev there was quite some leeway. The one point that could not be questioned was the one of ideological unity. The members had to be seen to cohere as an alliance of socialist states. What is now open to question is how the socio-political changes currently taking place in most of the allied states will affect the wider rôle of the alliance as an element of East–West confrontation.

Significantly, the Organization is still functioning at an official level. Each state, including Romania, is hosting meetings within that structure. Each state is able to put its signature to joint documents, including the Communique (*Pravda*, 18 December 1988) and Statement (*Pravda*, 30 January 1989) issued by the Committee of Ministers of Defence. This Statement is evidence that the Alliance is able to engage in a carefully-orchestrated peace offensive against NATO. In this way the various proposals to NATO covered by the CFM (*Pravda*, 31 March 1988) shows bloc support for Bulgarian co-operation with Romania for a Balkan nuclear-free zone, and Czechoslovak co-operation with the GDR on a Central European zone, and the ability of Czechoslovakia to make an independent proposal to NATO (*Pravda*, 9 March 1988) for a 'zone of trust, co-operation, and good-neighbourliness' along the NATO–WTO line of contact.

Gorbachev's various unilateral arms-reduction moves, beginning with his speech to the United Nations on 8 December 1988[11] must be seen as a move independent of the Soviet allies, since there was no offical WTO prior approval for such an initiative. It was, however, followed by various 'unilateral' moves by other Warsaw Treaty states – for example Hungary (*The Independent*, 21 December 1988), Poland (*The Guaradian*, 4 January 1989, and *The Daily Telegraph*, 27 February 1989), and the GDR (*The Guardian*, 24 January 1989). This implies some level of unofficial co-operation and agreement. But once again these moves took place independent of a declared multilateral initiative from the WTO.

At the same time, other relations within the bloc would seem to belie the apparent unity. The Central European response to the internal reforms in the Soviet Union have been varied. At one extreme, Ceauşescu in Romania has continued his extreme form of central command. This has not stopped the normal flow of bilateral ties with the USSR. At the other extreme, Hungary has legalized the formation and activity of political parties other than the ruling Hungarian Socialist Workers' Party (*The Guardian*, 12 January 1989, 13 February 1989), is rewriting its constitution, and is even removing the red star from the state emblem (*The Guardian*, 25 January 1989). The Hungarian press is openly discussing the possibility of rewriting Hungary's commitments to if not membership of the Warsaw Treaty Organization (*The Independent*, 10 March 1989, 17 April 1989). Officially, Hungary is seeking closer ties and perhaps even associate membership of the European Communities (*The Daily Telegraph*, 18 February 1989).[12] Relations between these two putative allies have at the same time deteriorated to the extent that Hungary appealed directly to the United Nations for it to intervene against Romania's continuing policy of rural systemization (*The Guardian*, 15 March 1989).

What is perhaps most interesting is that despite this more open display of variety in the internal policies of the allies, the Organization has apparently managed to remain coherent and develop to the satisfaction of the Central European allies. Behind or above it all, the USSR has by its own internal actions been a driving-force for change within the alliance.

The changes in Soviet foreign policy are integral to the Soviet internal reforms. Speaking in Kiev, CPSU General Secretary Gorbachev stated that:

> Our foreign policy serves the cause of perestroika also in the sense that it clears the way to more extensive economic co-operation with the outside world, to the country's joining in the world economic processes . . .
>
> Such are the major components of a deep change for the better in the Soviet Union's status in the world. All of them are working for socialism's renewal. (*Pravda*, 24 February 1989)

But Gorbachev did not see this as a purely Soviet matter, nor that a change in Soviet relations with the West could be made in isolation. The USSR was also altering its attitude to its socialist allies, and redefining the basis of the socialist alliance. His speech continued:

> Many socialist countries are now seeking ways and forms of going over to a new quality of life, to society's consolidation on the basis of revealing its potential in a socialist democracy. Every country resolves its problems in a sovereign way, seeks its own answers to questions of the life of its own people. The multiformity of movement towards

> the essentially common goal is a source of the vitality and strength of socialism.
>
> In keeping with these conditions of the new thinking, we are not only in theory but also in practice restructuring our relations with the socialist countries. (Ibid.)

If this statement is true, then the Warsaw Treaty Organization, as a function of the Stalinist heritage, and an excuse for the Brezhnev doctrine of political uniformity, could indeed be under practical revision. It could in fact begin to operate within the ideological principles stated in the Preamble to the treaty and reiterated throughout the documents of the WTO. In theory, the WTO could support a variety of national policies. Given the limited scope of operation permitted by its formal documentation, it could even be argued that the WTO may be beginning to operate in the manner which a superficial reading of the Treaty might suggest was intended.[13]

NATO AND THE WTO

The WTO does not operate in isolation. As a formal political-military alliance it is in confrontation with the West's political-military alliances. Despite the documentary rhetoric on the part of the WTO, the confrontation continues. In 1988, at a time when the casual observer might have thought that the Cold War was well into a thaw, the then Commander-in-Chief of the WTO Kulikov[14] wrote that 'in ensuring the reliable security of their nations [the Warsaw Treaty states] cannot ignore the fact that certain forces in the West are carrying out preparations for another world war' (Kulikov, 1988, p. 78). Such statements, so reminiscent of the earliest years of the WTO, sit strangely with the new political thinking of the means to a lasting peace (ibid., p. 32), of the defence policy of reasonable sufficiency (ibid., pp. 80–1). Kulikov repeated the interpretation that imperialism was inherently aggressive and was therefore the source of the threat to world peace (ibid., p. 28) but at the same time repeated the WTO policy of calling for talks between the General Secretary of the WTO[15] and the Secretary-General of NATO (ibid., p. 49).[16]

So what is NATO to make of this, and the various proposals on the conventional balance for example the Statement from the WTO Committee of Ministers of Defence (*Pravda*, 30 January 1989)? How is NATO to respond to a re-invigorated political-military alliance of the socialist states? It would not be too circumspect to point out that the new public face of socialism, both through Gorbachev's direct diplomacy with western leaders and the internal changes in many of the allied states, is presenting a need for a fundamental rethink of the political and military threat that is perceived by the West.

In some ways, NATO itself has not changed its position from that of the pre-Gorbachev era. In March 1988 the Heads of State and Government met in Brussels and issued a Statement 'Conventional Arms Control: the Way Ahead'.[17] Paragraph A.1 stated that in the view of the Heads of State and Government, 'The Soviet Union's military presence in Europe, at a level far in excess of its needs for self-defence, directly challenges our security as well as our hopes for change in the political situation in Europe'. In other words, NATO felt cowed under an aggressive Soviet military machine while still hoping to roll back the Iron Curtain and liberate politically and economically the states of Central Europe. Paragraph A.2 went on to describe the Soviet military presence on its allies' soil as 'a shadow over the whole of Europe'.

Other parts of the Statement, as with most documents issued by NATO, continued to present the image of an open NATO countering a WTO closed to public scrutiny, a defensive NATO with no military ambitions, not seeking surprise attack or superiority in any military means and above all not presenting any nuclear threat. Paragraph B.8 of the statement, in words similar to those used by Gorbachev and the WTO, stated that 'Security in Europe involves not just military, but also political, economic and, above all, humanitarian factors'. To NATO, these factors were western democratic values being upheld by a free Alliance which looked forward 'to a Europe undivided' (ibid.).

This is not to argue for or against either of the political-military alliances in Europe. It is more to compare and contrast their ideological basis and aims. In many ways the overt statements and positions sound the same, but are fronting for quite different political visions. Peace, freedom, and democracy, can mean different things to different people. As the introduction to the NATO Statement quoted above pointed out, 'The military confrontation in Europe is the result, not the cause, of the painful division which burdens this continent.'

Internally to NATO there are many issues which remain the same whichever Soviet leadership sits in the Kremlin. The conclusions of the Harmel Report of 1967 on the basis for relations with the Warsaw Treaty states were reaffirmed in a Statement on the Ministerial Meeting of the North Atlantic Council held in Reykjavic in June 1987.[18] At the same time as calling for co-operation with the WTO states while being ready to defend the West, it is still the opinion that 'It is the consistent and primary aim of Soviet policy to undermine the cohesion of the Alliance and, in particular, to separate Europe from the United States' (Beugal, 1986, p. 14). After 40 years of NATO and over 30 years of the WTO, the aims and principles stated in the Preamble to the North Atlantic Treaty are not being called into question. What is under discussion is how a cohesive western alliance can maintain its position in the face of a rapidly-evolving 'enemy'. It is accepted that the Soviet bloc is a complex entity (for example Pick, 1988) and that the Gorbachev position on democratization excludes any change in the leading rôle of socialism and the Party (for example Feldbrugge, 1988, p. 16). Against this, NATO also is discussing the fine-tuning of its own internal basis, for example the size and contribution of the European element, the best means to show commitment to the defence of Europe and the Alliance, the European needs to be taken into account in the bilateral Soviet–US talks. (See, for example, the report *NATO in the 1990s* by Parliamentarians of the North Atlantic Committee – *The Guardian*, 18 May 1988.) Ultimately, how much trust and good faith should be placed on Gorbachev's new-look USSR? If the aim of *perestroika* is to make socialism more efficient and more resilient in its political confrontation with the West, then how best can Western political-military security be maintained?

FINAL CONCLUSIONS

The WTO exists because of the existing political-economic-social-military division of Europe. Given that the socialist community has had the resilience to exist throughout the entire post-war period, the WTO must be accepted as a logical possibility. That it has not been shown to operate as the West would expect is due to an insufficient understanding of what the socialist community entails. It is to be hoped that this book has gone some way to providing the basis for an informed reapraisal of the political and military ties of the socialist bloc.

It is accepted that this book has been unable to be comprehensive. The statutes of the various WTO bodies, both as they first existed and as some were revised in 1969, still remain 'perfectly secret'.[N] There is still the question of the 'other documents' agreed in 1969 and those referred to in the preamble to the Legal Convention. Finally, despite continued evolution, there is the problem of the mix between the offical structure and the extra-structural bodies, and also the balance between the state and party inputs to the alliance. The machinery seems to exist, even if not in the form of a full-time office of civil servants, for multilateral co-operation somewhat closer to that envisioned in the founding documents and in the

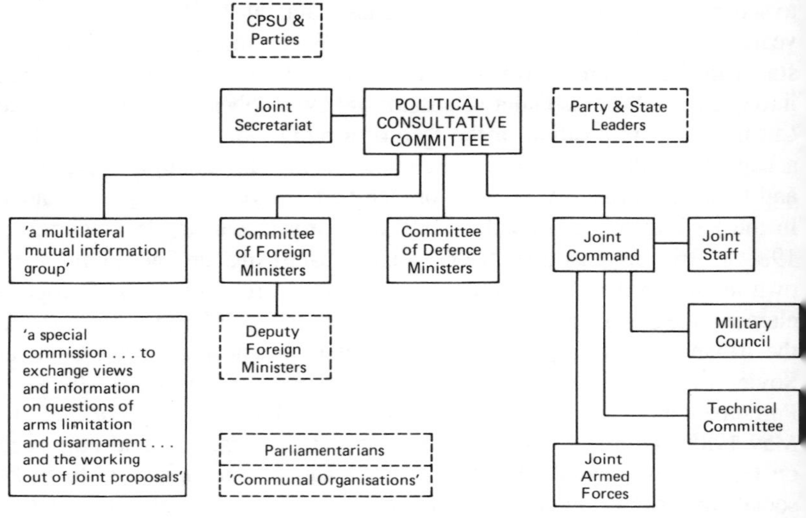

SOURCES As in Figure 4; PCC Communique 1987

—— denotes bodies within the formal structure

– – – denotes bodies within the informal structure

FIGURE 5 *WTO formal and informal structure, 1987*

communique of the first session of the Political Consultative Committee. But even under Gorbachev the USSR is still going it alone on various issues of international policy, including military policy that directly affects and involves its WTO allies.

This is not to conclude that the WTO is entirely unimportant. If only because it is still the sole multilateral political alliance of the socialist states and that it includes a military element, it is arguably more significant than the CMEA. It must therefore be studied more deeply. However, Western interest in the WTO as the West's nemesis perhaps obscures the real issues of the national and bilateral activities of the individual states, activities such as arms-sales and the supply of military advisers abroad that are carried out beyond the formal scope of the WTO.

There are the questions of the economic development of the individual states, the nature of their political and military activities and reliability, the qualified level of national Central European independence on certain matters, and the all-important interrelationships of the member-states, at both party and state levels, not just between the Soviet Union and the individual Central European states but also amongst the non-Soviet countries themselves. Once these and other issues and relationships can be properly undrestood, the *military* significance, potentials, and activities of the WTO's members, both nationally and multilaterally, can be analysed properly, and placed correctly within the scope of the socialist community. Then the workings of these relationships, either through the WTO or elsewhere, can be correctly analysed and responded to by the West.

The simple number-crunching of tanks and other military hardware is not enough. Even the definition and analysis of doctrines and strategies can never replace the understanding of the political and ideological basis of the states which operate those tanks.

Appendix 1: Selected Documents

THE WARSAW TREATY (1955)

Treaty of Friendship, Co-operation and Mutual Assistance

between the People's Republic of Albania, the People's Republic of Bulgaria, the Hungarian People's Republic, the German Democratic Republic, the Polish People's Republic, the Rumanian People's Republic, the Union of Soviet Socialist Republics, and the Czechoslovak Republic

The contracting parties,

Reaffirming their desire for the organization of a system of collective security in Europe, with the participation of all the European states, irrespective of their social and state systems, which would make it possible to combine their efforts in the interests of securing peace in Europe,

Taking into consideration at the same time the situation obtaining in Europe as the result of the Paris Agreements, which provide for the formation of a new military grouping in the shape of the 'Western European Union' together with a remilitarized West Germany in the North Atlantic alliance, which increases the threat of another war and creates a menace to the national security of the peaceloving states,

Convinced that, under these circumstances, the peaceloving states of Europe should take the necessary measures for safeguarding their security, and in the interests of maintaining peace in Europe,

Guided by the purposes and principles of the United Nations Charter,

In the interests of further strengthening and promoting friendship, co-operation, and mutual assistance, in accordance with the principles of respect for the independence and sovereignty of states, and also with the principle of non-interference in their internal affairs,

Have resolved to conclude this Treaty of Friendship, Co-operation, and Mutual Assistance, and have appointed as their authorized representatives:

The Presidium of the People's Assembly of the People's Republic of Albania – Mehmet Shehu, Chairman of the Council of Ministers of the People's Republic of Albania,

The Presidium of the People's Assembly of the People's Republic of Bulgaria – Vylko Chervenkov, Chairman of the Council of Ministers of the People's Republic of Bulgaria,

The Presidium of the Hungarian People's Republic – András Hegedüs, Chairman of the Council of Ministers of the Hungarian People's Republic,

The President of the German Democratic Republic – Otto Grotewohl, Prime

Minister of the German Democratic Republic,

The State Council of the Polish People's Republic – Józef Cyrankiewicz, Chairman of the Council of Ministers of the Polish People's Republic,

The Presidium of the Grand National Assembly of the Rumanian People's Republic – Gheorghe Gheorghiu-Dej, Chairman of the Council of Ministers of the Rumanian People's Republic,

The Presidium of the Supreme Soviet of the Union of Soviet Socialist Republics – Nikolai Aleksandrovich Bulganin, Chairman of the Council of Ministers of the USSR,

The President of the Czechoslovak Republic – Viliam Siroký, Prime Minister of the Czechoslovak Republic,

Who, having presented their credentials, found to be executed in due form and in complete order, have agreed on the following:

Article 1

The contracting parties undertake, in accordance with the Charter of the United Nations Organization, to refrain in their international relations from the threat or use of force, and to settle their international disputes by peaceful means so as not to endanger international peace and security.

Article 2

The contracting parties declare their readiness to take part, in the spirit of sincere co-operation, in all international undertakings intended to safeguard international peace and security and they shall use all their energies for the realization of these aims.

Moreover, the contracting parties shall work for the adoption, in agreement with other states desiring to co-operate in this matter, of effective measures towards a general reduction of armaments and prohibition of atomic, hydrogen, and other weapons of mass destruction.

Article 3

The contracting parties shall take council among themselves on all important international questions relating to their common interests, guided by the interests of strengthening international peace and security.

They shall take council among themselves immediately, whenever, in the opinion of any one of them, there has arisen the threat of an armed attack on one or several state-participants of the treaty, in the interests of organizing their joint defence and of upholding peace and security.

Article 4

In the event of an armed attack in Europe on one or several state-participants of the treaty by any state or group of states, each state that is a party to this treaty shall, in the exercise of the right to individual or collective self-defence in accordance with Article 51 of the Charter of the United Nations Organization, render the state or states so attacked immediate assistance, individually and in agreement with other state-participants to this treaty, by all the means it may consider necessary, including the use of armed force. The state-participants to this treaty shall immediately take council among themselves concerning the necessary joint measures to be adopted for the purpose of restoring and upholding inter-national peace and security.

In accordance with the principles of the Charter of the United Nations Organization, the Security Council shall be advised of the measures taken on the basis of the present article. These measures shall be stopped as soon as the Security Council has taken the necessary measures for restoring and upholding inter-national peace and security.

Article 5

The contracting parties have agreed on the establishment of a joint command for their armed forces, which shall be placed, by agreement among these parties, under this command, which shall function on the basis of jointly defined principles. They shall also take other concerted measures necessary for strengthening their defence capacity, in order to safeguard the peaceful labour of their peoples, to guarantee the inviolability of their frontiers and territories and to provide safeguards against possible aggression.

Article 6

For the purpose of holding the consultations provided for in the present treaty among the parties to the treaty, and for the purpose of considering problems arising in connection with the implementation of this treaty, a political consultative committee shall be formed in which each state-party to this treaty shall be represented by a member of the government, or any other specially appointed representative.

The committee may form auxiliary bodies for which the need may arise.

Article 7

The contracting parties undertake not to participate in any coalitions and alliances, and not to conclude any agreements the purposes of which would be at variance with those of the present treaty.

The contracting parties declare that their obligations under existing treaties are not at variance with the provisions of this treaty.

Article 8

The contracting parties declare that they will act in the spirit of friendship and co-operation with the object of furthering the development of, and strengthening the economic and cultural relations between them, adhering to the principles of mutual respect for their independence and sovereignty, and of non-interference in their internal affairs.

Article 9

The present treaty is open to be acceded to by other states – irrespective of their social and state systems – which may express their readiness to assist, through participation in the present treaty, in combining the efforts of the peaceloving states for the purpose of safeguarding the peace and security of nations. This act of acceding to the treaty shall become effective, with the consent of the state-participants to this treaty, after the instrument of accession has been deposited with the government of the Polish People's Republic.

Article 10

The present treaty is subject to ratification, and the instruments of ratification shall be deposited with the government of the Polish People's Republic.

The Treaty shall take effect on the date on which the last ratification instrument is deposited. The government of the Polish People's Republic shall advise the other state-participants to the treaty of each ratification instrument deposited with it.

Article 11

The present treaty shall remain in force for 20 years. For the contracting parties which will not have submitted to the govern-ment of the Polish People's Republic a statement denouncing the treaty a year before the expiration of its term, it shall remain in force throughout the following ten years.

In the event of the organization of a system of collective security in Europe and the conclusion of a general European treaty of collective security to that end, which the contracting parties shall unceasingly seek to bring about, the present treaty shall cease to be effective on the date the general European treaty comes into force.

Done in Warsaw, on May 14, 1955, in one copy each in Russian, Polish, Czech, and German languages, all the texts being equally authentic. Certified copies of the present treaty shall be transmitted by the government of the Polish People's Republic to all the parties to this treaty.

In witness whereof the authorized representatives have signed the present treaty and have fixed thereto their seals

By authorization of the Presidium of the People's Assembly of the People's Republic of Albania – *Mehmet Shehu*,

By authorization of the Presidium of the People's Assembly of the People's Republic of Bulgaria – *Vylko Chervenkov*,

By authorization of the Presidium of the Hungarian People's Republic – *András Hegedüs*,

By authorization of the President of the German Democratic Republic – *Otto Grotewohl*,

By authorization of the State Council of the Polish People's Republic – *Józef Cyrankiewicz*,

By authorization of the Presidium of the Grand National Assembly of the Rumanian People's Republic – *Gheorghe Gheorghiu-Dej*,

By authorization of the Presidium of the Supreme Soviet of the Union of Soviet Socialist Republics – *Nikolai Aleksandrovich Bulganin*,

By authorization of the President of the Czechoslovak Republic – *Viliam Siroký.*

Note: Rodionov, and Malt'sev (1980), both give on their page ten the following list of dates for the ratification of the Warsaw Treaty. The dates in brackets are explained as the date of the handing over of the documents of ratification to the government of the Polish People's Republic.

19 May	the Sejm of the Polish People's Republic.
21 May	the President of the German Democratic Republic (24 May)
25 May	the President of the Supreme Soviet of the USSR (1 June)
25 May	an extraordinary session of the State Assembly of the Hungarian People's Republic (2 June)
26 May	the President of the Czechoslovak Republic (27 May)
28 May	the third extraordinary session of the People's Assembly of the People's Republic of Bulgaria (31 May)
28 May	an extraordinary session of the People's Assembly of the People's Republic of Albania (4 June)
30 May	a session of the Great National Assembly of the Rumanian People's Republic (3 June).

Article 10 of the Treaty states that 'The Treaty shall take effect on the date on which the last ratification instrument is deposited.' Thus the Treaty came into effect on 4 June 1955, the date of Albania's deposition of ratification, but, unlike the treatment of the Legal Convention in the same official volumes, no date is given by Rodionov or Mal'tsev for the coming into effect of the Treaty. The official table of ratification footnotes that 'since 1962 the representative of Albania has not taken part in the work of the Warsaw Treaty Organization'. Presumably this is why most Warsaw Treaty historians do not wish the 4th June date to be registered. Strangely, Yakubovskii *did* specify June 4 as the date of the Treaty coming into force (1971, p. 22) and Savinov did the same (1980, p. 11).

FORMATION OF JOINT COMMAND (1955)

Formation of Joint Command of the Armed Forces of the State-Participants to the Treaty of Friendship, Co-Operation and Mutual Assistance

Under the Treaty of Friendship, Co-operation and Mutual Assistance between the People's Republic of Albania, the People's Republic of Bulgaria, the Hungarian People's Republic, the German Democratic Republic, the Polish People's Republic, the Rumanian People's Republic, the Union of Soviet Socialist Republics, and the Czechoslovak Republic, the state-participants to the treaty have taken the decision to form a joint command of their armed forces.

This decision envisages that general questions pertaining to the strengthening of the defence capacity and to the organization of the joint armed forces of the state-participants to the treaty will be examined by the Political Consultative Committee, which will take appropriate decisions.

In the capacity of Commander-in-Chief of the Joint Armed Forces, assigned by the states, signatories of the treaty, has been appointed Marshal of the Soviet Union *I. C. Konev.*

The deputy commanders-in-chief of the Joint Armed Forces are appoined the ministers of defence and other military leaders of the state-participants to the treaty, who are vested with the command of the armed forces of each state-participant of the treaty, allotted to the Joint Armed Forces.

The question of participation of the German Democratic Republic in measures pertaining to the armed forces of the joint command will be examined later.

Under the Commander-in-Chief of the Joint Armed Forces is created a staff of the Joint Armed Forces of the state-participants of the treaty, in the composition of which will include permanent representatives of the general staffs of the state-participants of the treaty.

The location of the staff is *the city of Moscow.*

Distribution of the joint armed forces on the territories of state-participants of the treaty will be carried out in accordance with the requirements of mutual defence in agreement among these states.

LEGAL CONVENTION (1973)

Convention concerning the legal status, privileges and immunities of the Staff and other administrative bodies of the Joint Armed Forces of the state-participants of the Warsaw Treaty

The governments of the People's Republic of Bulgaria, the Hungarian People's Republic, the German Democratic Republic, the Polish People's Republic, the Socialist Republic of Romania, the Union of Soviet Socialist Republics, and the Czechoslovak Socialist Republic,

guided by the principles of the Treaty on friendship, co-operation, and mutual assistance, signed in Warsaw on 14 May 1955,

taking into account the Decision of the state-participants of the Warsaw Treaty, taken at the session of the Political Consultative Committee on 17 March 1969 in the city of Budapest,

noting that the general tasks and appointment of the Staff and other bodies of administration of the Joint Armed Forces are defined by documents, accepted by the state-participants of the Warsaw Treaty,

bearing in mind the Statute of the Joint Armed Forces and Joint Command of the state-participants of the Warsaw Treaty,

being conscious, that for the fulfilment of the tasks, laid on the staff and

other bodies of administration of the Joint Armed Forces, they should [be granted] legal capacity, privileges and immunities,
have come to agreement on the following:

Article 1

1. The Staff of the Joint Armed Forces consists of generals, admirals, and officers of the state-participants of the Warsaw Treaty, which under the fulfilment of official duties are granted privileges and immunities in connexion with the present Convention.

   In the Staff of the Joint Armed Forces work also employees, apportioned by the state [where the staff is located], part of whom enjoy the privileges and immunities in the conditions provided for in the present Convention. Categories and numbers of employees, enjoying the privileges and immunities, are co-ordinated by the Staff of the Joint Armed Forces with the General (Main) staffs of the armies of the state-participants of the Convention. A nominal roll of these employees annually is communicated by the Staff of the Joint Armed Forces to the General (Main) staffs of the armies of the state-participants of the Convention.
2. For the purposes of the present Convention the term Staff of the Joint Armed Forces stands also for the other bodies of administration of the Joint Armed Forces of the state-participants of the Warsaw Treaty.
3. The place of residence of the Staff of the Joint Armed Forces is the city of Moscow.

Article 2

The Staff of the Joint Armed Forces of the state-participants of the Warsaw Treaty is a legal entity and in aim of the carrying out of problems, for which it was created, it is capable:

(a) to conclude agreements;
(b) to acquire, lease, and [dispose of] equipment;
(c) to appear in court.

Article 3

1. The Staff of the Joint Armed Forces enjoys on the territory of each state-participant of the present Convention the legal status, privileges and immunities to be provided for in the present Convention.
2. Premises of the Staff of the Joint Armed Forces, its property, assets, and documents, irrespective of the place of their situation, enjoy immunities from any form of administrative and legal interference with the exception, that the Staff itself is denied immunities in some individual instances.
3. The Staff of the Joint Armed Forces is free from basic taxes and dues on the territories of each of the state-participants of the present Convention. This condition does not apply to payment for the actual condition of maintenance and the communal public services.

4. The Staff of the Joint Armed Forces is free from customs charges and of the restrictions on the [import] and export of goods, intended for the officials' use.
5. The Staff of the Joint Armed Forces enjoys on the territory of each of the state-participants of the present Convention no less favourable conditions on relation first and foremost, and tariffs and to rates of mail, telegraph and telephone connexions, than that, which in this country is utilized by the national military command or diplomatic representatives.

Article 4

1. The officials of the Staff of the Joint Armed Forces on the territory of each state-participant of the present Convention for the fulfilment of their official duties are granted the following privileges and immunities:

   (a) inviolability of all papers and documents;
   (b) the same customary privileges and terms of their personal baggage, which are granted to officials of diplomatic representations in the present country;
   (c) freedom from personal duties and from [basic] taxes and dues in relation to salary allowance (wages), of payments to individuals of the personnel of the Staff of the Joint Armed Forces posted to their countries;
   (d) immunity from personal arrest or detention, and also from the jurisdiction of legal and administrative institutions in relation of all activities, which must be accomplished by them in the capacity of officials.

The status of points «b» and «c» apply to members' families, living together with officials of the Staff of the Joint Armed Forces.

2. The Chief of Staff of the Joint Armed Forces and his deputies, in addition to the privileges and immunities, stated in point 1 of the present article, enjoy on the territories of all the state-parties of the present Convention privileges and immunities, given in this country to diplomatic representatives. Appointed persons receive diplomatic cards.
3. The privileges and immunities, provided by the present article, are being granted to be mentioned in their persons exclusively in the interests of the carrying-out of their official [duties].
   The Commander-in-Chief of the Joint Armed Forces by agreement with the Minister of Defence of the corresponding state has the right and duty to retract the immunity of officials of the Staff in every event, when immunity impedes the implementation of justice and the denial of immunity does not prejudice the aims, in connexion with which it was granted.
4. Officials of the Staff of the Joint Armed Forces and members of their

families are presented by the Staff special identity cards, confirming the right in privilege and immunity.

Officials of the Staff of the Joint Armed Forces and members of their families are free from compulsory residence permits and registration. They are registered by the Staff of the Joint Armed Forces.

5. The status of points 1, 2, 3, and 4 of the present article do not apply to the mutual relations of the officials of the Staff of the Joint Armed Forces and the members of their families with the bodies of the country, the citizens with which they are, or the country, on the territory of which they always live.
6. Persons, who enjoy the privileges and immunities, envisaged in the present Convention, are obliged to respect the laws of the state, on the territory of which they are situated, and not to interfere in the internal affairs of the given state.

Article 5

In the event of the denial by the Commander-in-Chief of the Joint Armed Forces of the immunity of an official of the Staff, provided for by Article 4 of the present Convention, in relation of this person, who committed a criminal or administrative offence, conforms the legislation of the country, on the territory of which the offence [was committed], and affects the bodies of military justice, competent for the question of the pursuit of the punishable deed.

Bodies of military justice of the state-participants of the present Convention are able mutually to address amongst themselves with the petition to deny legal aid in relation to separate matters. Such denial will be examined [sympathetically].

Article 6

1. The present Convention will be subject to ratification of the signing by its states in conformity with their constitutional procedures.
2. Ratification papers will be placed in the keeping of the Government of the Union of Soviet Socialist Republics, which is nominated depository of the present Convention.
3. The Convention will enter into force on the day of the handing over to the custody of the deposition of the ratification documents by any three of the states. In relation to other states, signing the Convention, it comes into force on the day of the handing over to custody of their ratificatiorn documents.
4. Possibly vexed questions, arising from the interpretation and application of the present Convention, will be resolved by the state-participants of the given Convention through discussions between the national commands or through diplomatic channels, or found by other measures according to agreement.
5. The present Convention is composed in one specimen in the Russian language. The Convention will be handed over to the custody of the Government of the Union of Soviet Socialist Republics, which will

distribute certified copies of it to the governments of all the other signatories of it of the states, and also to notifiy these governments and the Staff of the Joint Armed Forces on the handing over to custody of each document.

To the certification of which the undersigned, of due form on such authorized agents, signed the present Convention.

Concluded in the city of Moscow 24 April 1973.

Mal'tsev (1980) mentions in a footnote on p. 160 that the Convention came into force on 21 November 1973. This does not seem to have been recorded in the Soviet press at the time.

PROTOCOL OF EXTENSION (1985)

Protocol

On prolonging the period of validity of the Treaty of Friendship, Co-operation, and Mutual Assistance, signed in Warsaw on May 14, 1955.

The member states of the Treaty of Friendship, Co-operation, and Mutual Assistance – the People's Republic of Bulgaria, the Hungarian People's Republic, the German Democratic Republic, the Polish People's Republic, the Socialist Republic of Romania, the Union of Soviet Socialist Republics, and the Czechoslovak Socialist Republic – have decided to sign the present protocol and agreed to the following:

Article 1
The Treaty of Friendship, Co-operation and Mutual Assistance, signed in Warsaw on May 14, 1955, shall remain in force for the next twenty years. For the contracting parties, which a year before the expiry of this period of time shall not present to the Government of the Polish People's Republic statements of denunciation of the treaty, it shall remain in force for another ten years.

Article 2
The present protocol is subject to ratification. The instruments of ratification shall be presented for deposition to the Government of the Polish People's Republic.

The protocol shall enter into force on the day of the presentation for deposition of the last instrument of ratification. The Government of the Polish People's Republic shall inform the other member states of the treaty of the presentation for deposition of each instrument of ratification.

Done in Warsaw on April 26, 1985, one copy in the Bulgarian, Hungarian, German, Polish, Romanian, Russian, and Czech languages, all texts being of equal value. Certified copies of the present protocol shall be sent by the Polish People's Republic to all the other parties to the protocol.

For the People's Republic of Bulgaria:
Todor Zhivkov, General Secretary of the Central Committee of the Bulgarian Communist Party and President of the State Council of the People's Republic of Bulgaria.

For the Hungarian People's Republic:
János Kádár, General Secretary of the Hungarian Socialist Workers' Party.

For the German Democratic Republic:
Erich Honecker, General Secretary of the Central Committee of the Socialist Unity Party of Germany and President of the State Council of the German Democratic Republic.

For the Polish People's Republic:
Wojciech Jaruzelski, First Secretary of the Central Committee of the Polish United Workers' Party and Chairman of the Council of Ministers of the Polish People's Republic.

For the Socialist Republic of Romania:
Nicolae Ceauşescu, General Secretary of the Romanian Communist Party and President of the Socialist Republic of Romania.

For the Union of Soviet Socialist Republics:
Mikhail Gorbachev, General Secretary of the Central Committee of the Communist Party of the Soviet Union.

For the Czechoslovak Socialist Republic:
Gustáv Husák, General Secretary of the Central Committee of the Communist Party of Czechoslovakia and President of the Czechoslovak Socialist Republic.

Appendix 2: Chronology of Meetings

This Appendix lists all the known meetings of bodies, both formal and extra-structural, of the WTO. It covers the period from the formation to the end of 1988.

In the 'Body Meeting' column, names placed within quotation marks are the description used in the documentary source. (Appendix 3 contains a Documentary History listing these sources.)

Date	*Place*	*Body Meeting*
1954		
Nov. 29–Dec. 2	Moscow	CECSPSE
1955		
May 11–May 14	Warsaw	CECSPSE
1956		
Jan. 27–28	Prague	PCC
1958		
May 24	Moscow	PCC
1959		
Apr. 27–28	Warsaw	Foreign Ministers
1960		
Feb. 4	Moscow	PCC
Mar. 28–29	Moscow	PCC
Aug. 3–5	Moscow	First Secretaries
Aug. 12[1]		[governments' Statement]
Sept. 8–9	Warsaw	Defence Ministers
1962		
Jan. 30–Feb. 1	Prague	Defence Ministers
June 7	Moscow	PCC
1963		
Feb. 28	Warsaw	Defence Ministers
Jul. 25	Moscow	First Secretaries and Government Heads
Jul. 26	Moscow	PCC

1964[2]

1965

Jan. 19	Warsaw	Defence Ministers
Jan. 19–20	Warsaw	PCC
May 10–18	sub-Carpathian military district	Ministers of Defence, Chiefs of Staff, heads of MPAs, and others
May 14	Moscow	military representatives and diplomats
Nov. 24–25	Warsaw	Commander-in-Chief, deputy Defence Ministers

1966

May 27–28[3]	Moscow	Defence Ministers
June 17[4]	Moscow	Foreign Ministers
Jul. 4–6	Bucharest	PCC
Nov. 14–17	Budapest	«miltary leaders»

1967

Feb. 8–10	Warsaw	Foreign Ministers
Nov. 13–17	Dresden	«leaders of army cadres»

1968

Feb. 26–27	Berlin	deputy foreign ministers
Mar. 6–7	Sofia	PCC
Oct. 29–30	Moscow	Defence Ministers
Nov. 26–29	Bucharest	«military leaders»

1969

Feb. 12–13	GDR	«military representatives»
Mar. 17	Budapest	PCC
May 12–16	Warsaw	«Chiefs of the General Staffs»
May 20–21	Berlin	deputy foreign ministers
Oct. 30–31	Prague	Foreign Ministers
Oct. 30–Nov. 3	Prague	«military leaders»
Dec. 3–4[5]	Moscow	Party and State leaders
Dec. 9–10	Moscow	MC
Dec. 22–23	Moscow	CDM

1970

Jan. 26–27	Sofia	deputy foreign ministers
Apr. 27–28	Budapest	MC
May 21–22	Sofia	CDM
June 21–22	Budapest	Foreign Ministers
Aug. 20	Moscow	PCC
Aug. 31–Sept. 2[6]	Dresden	«generals and officers of the MPAs»

Oct. 27–30	Varna, Bulgaria	MC + «chief army officers»
Nov. 17–20[7]	Prague	
Dec. 2	Berlin	PCC
1971		
Feb. 18–19	Bucharest	Foreign Ministers
Mar. 2–3[8]	Budapest	CDM
Mar. 15–19	Budapest	«Chiefs of the General Staffs»
May 12–15	Berlin	MC + «delegations»
Aug. 2[9]		
Oct. 26–29	Warsaw	MC + «army leaders»
Nov. 30–Dec. 1	Warsaw	Foreign Ministers + «groups of advisers and experts»
1972		
Jan. 25–26	Prague	PCC
Feb. 9–10	Berlin	CDM
Apr. 11–12	Bucharest	MC
Jul. 31[10]		
Oct. 17–20	Minsk, USSR	MC + «military leaders»
1973		
Jan. 15–16	Moscow	Foreign Ministers
Feb. 6–8	Warsaw	CDM
Apr. 24	Moscow	deputy foreign ministers[11]
May 16–17	Sofia	MC
Jul. 30–31[12]		
Oct. 18–19[13]	Dresden	«leaders of army political bodies»
Oct. 30–Nov. 1	Prague	MC + «military leaders»
1974		
Feb. 6–7	Bucharest	CDM
Mar. 26–27	Budapest	MC
Apr. 17–18	Warsaw	PCC
Nov. 19–21	Berlin	MC + «delegations»
1975		
Jan. 7–8	Moscow	CDM
Jan. 29–30	Moscow	deputy foreign ministers
Mar. 19–20	Warsaw	deputy foreign ministers
Apr. 22–24[14]	Moscow	
May 14	Budapest	Central Committee of the Hungarian Socialist Workers' Party, Council of Ministers of the Hungarian People's Republic 'commemorative conference'
May 14–15[15]	Warsaw	Parliamentarians
May 19–21	Warsaw	MC + «delegations»

June 3–4	Prague	«delegates of communal organizations»
Jul. 31–Aug. 1[16]	Helsinki	
Aug. 5–6[17]	Moscow	
Oct. 27–30	Bucharest	MC + «military leaders»
Nov. 18–19	Prague	CDM
Dec. 15–16	Moscow	Foreign Ministers
1976		
May 25–27	Kiev	MC
June 22–23[18]	Varne	
–[19]		
Nov. 25–26	Bucharest	PCC
Dec. 10–11	Sofia	CDM
1977		
Feb. ?21–23[20]	Berlin	deputy foreign ministers
May 16–20	Prague	MC
May 25–26	Moscow	CFM
Jul. 5–8[21]	Leningrad	Parliamentarians
–[22]		
Sept. 5	Moscow	
Oct. 17–20[23]	Sofia	Mc + «military representatives»
Oct. 26[24]	«Staff of the JAFs»	
Nov. 29–Dec. 2	Budapest	CDM
1978		
Feb. 16[25]	«Staff of the JAFs»	
Apr. 24–25	Sofia	CFM
May 16–19	Budapest	MC + «delegations»
–[26]		
Oct. 16–19	Berlin	MC + «delegations»
Nov. 22–23	Moscow	PCC
Dec. 4–7	Berlin	CDM
1979		
Apr. 23–26	Warsaw	MC + «delegations»
May 14–15	Budapest	CFM
–[27]		
Sept. 3–6[28]	Minsk	«ideological workers»
Oct. 6[29]		
Oct. 16–17	Prague	Parliamentarians
Oct. 29–31	Bucharest	MC + «delegations»
Nov. 22[30]	«Staff of the JAFs»	
Dec. 4–6	Warsaw	CDM
Dec. 5–6	Berlin	CFM

1980		
May 14–15	Warsaw	PCC
May 15	Budapest	«gala evening . . . a cultural programme was presented by the art ensembles of the Soviet Southern Army Group stationed in Hungary, the Silesia military zone of the Polish People's Army, and the Hungarian People's Army.»
May 20–23	Moscow	MC + «delegations»
June 16–18	Minsk	Parliamentarians
June ?20–?22[31]	Warsaw	«MPA workers»
Jul. 8–9	Prague	deputy foreign ministers
Oct. 15–17	Prague	MC + «delegations»
Oct. 19–20	Warsaw	CFM
Dec. 1–3	Bucharest	CDM
Dec. 5	Moscow	Party and State leaders
1981		
Jan. 19–20	Berlin	deputy foreign ministers
Apr. 21–23	Sofia	MC + «delegations»
Oct. 27–30	Budapest	MC + «delegations»
Dec. 1–2	Bucharest	CFM
Dec. 1–4	Moscow	CDM
1982		
Apr. 26–29	Berlin	MC + «delegations»
Oct. 20–22	Warsaw	MC + «delegations»
Oct. 21–22	Moscow	CFM
1983		
Jan. 4–5	Prague	PCC
Jan. 11–13	Prague	CDM
Jan. 27–28	Bucharest	deputy foreign ministers
Apr. 6–7	Prague	CFM
Apr. 26–28	Bucharest	MC + «delegations»
June 28	Moscow	Party and State leaders
Oct. 13–14	Sofia	CFM
Oct. 20	Berlin	extraordinary CDM
Oct. 26–29	Lvov	MC + «delegations»
Nov. 9–10	Sofia	Parliamentarians
Dec. 5–7	Sofia	CDM
Dec. 20–21	Warsaw	deputy foreign ministers
1984		
Jan. 11[32]		Proposal issued
Feb. 14[33]	Moscow	Party and State leaders

Mar. 5[34]		Proposal delivered
Apr. 19–20	Budapest	CFM
Apr. 24–26	Prague	MC + «delegations»
May 3–4	Warsaw	deputy foreign ministers
May 7[35]		Appeal delivered
Oct. 17–19	Sofia	MC + «delegations»
Dec. 3–4	Berlin	CFM
Dec. 3–5	Budapest	CDM
1985		
Mar. 1	Moscow	deputy foreign ministers
Mar. 13[36]	Moscow	Party and State leaders
–[37]		
Apr. 26	Warsaw	Party and State leaders

* * *

May 13	Central House of the Soviet Army, Moscow	«Soviet military figures, JAF representatives» (Kulikov report)
May 13	Prague, Ministry of Defence	«JAF representatives», meeting with Czechoslovak Minister of Defence
May 13	Warsaw	«military historians»
May 13	Poland	«chairmen of military youth bodies»
May 13–15	Budapest	Parliamentarians
May 14	Bol'shoi Theatre	«solemn gathering of represent–atives of Moscow working people and the USSR Armed Forces»
May 14	Sofia	«official meeting»
May 14	GDR	«WTO defence attachés in GDR», meeting with GDR Defence Minister
May 14	Székesfehérvár, Hungary	«WTO defence attachés in Hungary», meeting with Hungarian Defence Minister
May 14–15	Academy of the Social Sciences, Moscow	«scientists, diplomats, Warsaw Treaty national military leaders, guests from Asian socialist countries and Cuba»

End of the first 30 years

May 20–23	Budapest	MC + «delegations»
–[38]		

Oct. 22–23[39]	Sofia	PCC
Nov. 12–14	Berlin	MC
Nov. 21[40]	Prague	«highest leaders»
Dec. 2–5	Berlin	CDM
1986		
Mar. 8	Budapest	deputy foreign ministers
Mar. 19–20	Budapest	CFM
Mar. 21	Warsaw	«editors of the central bodies of the presses of the country-participants of the Warsaw Treaty» participated in a «round table» session of representatives of party newspapers etc. on how to propagandize peace policies
Apr. 9[41]		Appeal delivered
–[42]		
Apr. 16	GDR Party Congress	joint statement on US bombing of Libya
Apr. 23–25	Warsaw	MC
June 10–11	Budapest	PCC
June 27[43]	Berlin	deputy foreign ministers
Sept. 2	Warsaw	deputy foreign ministers
Oct. 14–15[44]	Bucharest	CFM
Nov. 12–14	Bucharest	MC + «senior executives of the defence ministries and the command agencies of the Joint Armed Forces»
Dec. 1–3	Warsaw	CDM + «leading staff of the Ministries of Defence . . . and the Joint Command»
1987		
Jan. 22	Warsaw	deputy foreign ministers
Mar. 13	Sofia	«regular meeting of working groups of experts [of WTO states] on questions of reducing armed forces and conventional arms in Europe»
Mar. 13	Moscow	ambassadors of Warsaw Treaty states with USSR chief delegate to the Vienna nuclear and space weapons talks
Mar. 24–5	Moscow	CFM
Apr. 10[45]	Proposal	
Apr. 16–8	Minsk	MC

May 28–9	Berlin	PCC
Jul. 1–3	Warsaw	Presidents of Parliaments of Warsaw Treaty states
Sept. 11	Warsaw	«multilateral group of current mutual information»
Sept. 24–6	Prague	MC
Oct. 13	Warsaw	multilateral group . . .
Oct. 28–9	Prague	CFM
Nov. 11–2	Warsaw	multilateral group . . .
Nov. 24–5	Bucharest	CDM
Dec. 11	Berlin	«leading statesmen»
Dec. 15–6	Warsaw	multilateral group . . .
Dec. 17–8	Budapest	working group of experts . . .
1988		
Jan. 19–20	Warsaw	multilateral group . . .
Feb. 2–3	Sofia	working group of experts . . .
Feb. 23	Prague	Foreign Ministers
Mar. 29–30	Sofia	CFM
Apr. 12–3	Warsaw	multilateral group . . .
May 11–3	Sofia	MC
June 4	New York	delegates to UN Special Session on Disarmament
June 7	Warsaw	Defence Ministers[46]
June 16–7	Sofia	working group of experts . . .
Jul. 5–8	Moscow	CDM
Jul. 15–6	Warsaw	PCC
Jul. 16	Warsaw	Foreign Ministers[47]
Oct. 3–5	Budapest	MC
Oct. 17–8	Prague	CDM
Oct. 28–9	Budapest	CFM
Nov. 17–8	Moscow	Foreign Ministry experts
Nov. 23	Bucharest	multilateral group . . .
Dec. 7	Bucharest	working group of experts
Dec. 8–9	Moscow	Defence Ministry experts
Dec. 17	Sofia	CDM
1989		
Jan. 30[48]		CDM Statement

Appendix 3: Documentary History

Appendix 3 details the official source of all the relevant documents issued by the meetings listed in Appendix 2 (Chronology).

* denotes documents listed in the official 'Documents and Materials' volumes (Rodionov, 1975; Mal'tsev, 1980; Mal'tsev, 1986).

† denotes those listed in the earlier volumes, but not in Mal'tsev (1986).

‡ denotes documents listed in the earlier volumes, not listed in Mal'tsev (1986), but which were included in the Hungarian-language edition of 1985.

Date	*Body*	*Document/source*
1954		
Dec. 2	Moscow Conference	Declaration of the Governments
1955		
May 14	Warsaw Conference	*Treaty, *Pravda*, May 15 *Joint Command, *Pravda*, May 15 *communique, *Pravda*, May 15
1956		
Jan. 28	PCC	*communique, *Pravda*, Jan. 29 *Declaration, *Pravda*, Jan. 29
1958		
May 24	PCC	*communique, *Pravda*, May 27 *Declaration, *Pravda*, May 27 *draft non-aggression treaty, *Pravda*, May 27
1959		
Apr. 28	Foreign Ministers	*Communique, *Pravda*, Apr. 29
1960		
Feb. 4	PCC	Communique, *Pravda*, Feb. 5 *Declaration, *Pravda*, Feb. 5
1961		
Mar. 29	PCC	*Communique, *Pravda*, Mar. 31
Aug. 5	First Secretaries	Report, *Pravda*, Aug. 6
Aug. 12/13	'governments'	*Statement [on West Berlin], *Pravda*, Aug. 14

Sept. 9	Defence Ministers	*Report, *Pravda*, Sept. 10
1962		
Feb. 1	Defence Ministers	*Report, *Pravda*, Feb. 2
June 7	PCC	*Declaration, *Pravda*, June 10
1963		
Feb. 20	[Geneva Disarmament Committee]	*draft non-aggression treaty, *Pravda*, Feb. 21
Feb. 28	Defence Ministers	report, *Kr. Zv.*, Mar. 1
Jul. 25	First Secretaries and Government Heads	*Resolution, *Pravda*, Jul. 27
Jul. 26	PCC	*Communique, *Pravda*, Jul. 28
1965		
Jan. 19	Defence Ministers	report, *Pravda*, Jan. 20
Jan. 20	PCC	*Communique, *Pravda*, Jan. 22
May 14	10th Anniversary	report, *Pravda*, May 15
May 18	military leaders	report, *Pravda*, May 19
Nov. 25	C-in-C, deputy defence ministers	report, *Pravda*, Nov. 26 + *Kr. Zv.*, Nov. 27
1966		
June 17	Foreign Ministers	*Report, *Pravda*, June 18
Jul. 6	PCC	Communique, *Pravda*, Jul. 7 *Statement on US Aggression in Vietnam, *Pravda*, Jul. 8 *Declaration on Strengthening Peace and Security in Europe, *Pravda*, Jul. 9
Nov. 17	military leaders	report, *Pravda*, Nov. 19
1967		
Feb. 10	Foreign Ministers	*report: In the interests of European Security, *Pravda*, Feb. 11
Nov. 18	leaders of army cadres	report, *Pravda*, Nov. 19
1968		
Feb. 27	deputy foreign ministers	report, *Pravda*, Feb. 28
Mar. 8	PCC	*Communique, *Pravda*, Mar. 9 *Declaration on the Threat to Peace Created by the Expansion of US Aggression in Vietnam, *Pravda*, Mar. 9

		*Statement on nuclear non-proliferation [excluding Romania], *Pravda*, Mar. 9
Oct. 30	Defence Ministers	report, *Pravda*, Oct. 31
Nov. 29	military leaders	report, *Pravda*, Nov. 30
1969		
Feb. 13	military representatives	report, *Kr. Zv.*, Feb. 14
Mar. 17	PCC	*Communique, *Pravda*, Mar. 18
		*Address to the European Countries, *Pravda*, Mar. 18
May 16	Chiefs of the General Staffs	report, *Pravda*, May 17
May 21	deputy foreign ministers	*Report, *Pravda*, May 22
Oct. 31	Foreign Ministers	*Statement [concerning all-European conference], *Pravda*, Nov. 1
Nov. 3	military leaders	report, *Izvestiya*, Nov. 5
Dec. 4	Party & State leaders	*Communique, *Pravda*, Dec. 5
		*Statement: Put an end to aggression in Vietnam, *Pravda*, Dec. 5
Dec. 10	MC	report, *Pravda*, Dec. 11
Dec. 23	CDM	*Report, *Pravda*, Dec. 24
1970		
Jan. 27	deputy foreign ministers	*Report, *Pravda*, Jan. 28
Apr. 28	MC	report, *Pravda*, Apr. 29
May 22	CDM	*Report, *Pravda*, May 23
June 22	Foreign Ministers	*Communique, *Pravda*, June 24
		*Memorandum [on questions concerning the holding of an all-European conference], *Pravda*, June 27
Aug. 20	PCC	*Communique, *Pravda*, Aug. 21
Oct. 30	MC, chief army officers	report, *Pravda*, Oct. 31
Dec. 2	PCC	Communique, *Pravda*, Dec. 2
		*Statement: Strengthening Security and Developing Peaceful Co-operation in Europe, *Pravda*, Dec. 4
		*Statement: Aggravation of

		Situation in the Region of Indochina, *Pravda*, Dec. 4 *Statement: For the Restoration of a Lasting Peace in the Middle East, *Pravda*, Dec. 4 *Statement: End Imperialist Provocations Against the Independent States of Africa, *Pravda*, Dec. 4
1971		
Feb. 19	Foreign Ministers	*Communique, *Pravda*, Feb. 20
Mar. 3	CDM	*Report, *Pravda*, Mar. 4
Mar. 19	Chiefs of the General Staffs	report, *Pravda*, Mar. 20
May 15	MC	report, *Pravda*, May 16
Aug. 2	Crimea	†report
Oct. 29	MC, army leaders	report, *Pravda*, Nov. 2
Dec. 1	Foreign Ministers	*Communique, *Pravda*, Dec. 3
1972		
Jan. 26	PCC	Communique, *Pravda*, Jan. 27 *Declaration on Peace, Security and Co-operation in Europe, *Pravda*, Jan. 27 *Statement on the Continuation of US Aggression in Indochina, *Pravda*, Jan. 27
Feb. 10	CDM	*Report, *Pravda*, Feb. 11
Apr. 12	MC	report, *Pravda*, Apr. 13
Jul. 31	Crimea	†report
Oct. 20	MC, military leaders	report, *Pravda*, Oct. 21
1973		
Jan. 16	Foriegn Ministers	*Report, *Pravda*, Jan. 17
Feb. 8	CDM	*Report, *Pravda*, Feb. 9
Apr. 24		*Legal Convention *Kr. Zv.*, Apr. 27
May 17	MC	report, *Pravda*, May 18
Jul. 31	Crimea	†report
Nov. 1	MC, military leaders	report, *Pravda*, Nov. 2
1974		
Feb. 7	CDM	*Report, *Pravda*, Feb. 8
Mar. 28	MC	report, *Pravda*, Mar. 29
Apr. 18	PCC	Communique, *Pravda*, Apr. 19

		*Statement 'For a lasting and just peace in the Middle East', *Pravda*, Apr. 20 *Statement 'For a lasting peace in Vietnam and for ensuring the just national interests of the Vietnamese people', *Pravda*, Apr. 20 *Statement 'Stop the Outrages and Persecution of Democrats in Chile', *Pravda*, Apr. 20
Nov. 21	MC	report, *Pravda*, Nov. 22
1975		
Jan. 8	CDM	*Report, *Pravda*, Jan. 9
Jan. 30	deputy foreign ministers	*Report, *Pravda*, Feb. 1
Mar. 20	deputy foreign ministers	report, *Pravda*, Mar. 22
May 15	Parliamentarians	*Document 'For peace, security, co-operation, and rapprochement between the people of Europe', *Pravda*, May 17
May 21	MC	report, *Pravda*, May 22
June 4	representatives of communal organizations	*Report, *Pravda*, June 7
Oct. 30	MC, military leaders	report, *Pravda*, Oct. 31
Nov. 19	CDM	*Report, *Pravda*, Nov. 20
Dec. 16	Foreign Ministers	*Communique, *Pravda*, Dec. 17
1976		
May 27	MC	report, *Pravda*, May 28
Nov. 26	PCC	*Communique, *Pravda*, Nov. 27 *Declaration 'For fresh advances in international relaxation, the strengthening of security, and the development of co-operation', *Pravda*, Nov. 27 *Proposal [to CSCE states, on nuclear no-first-use], *Pravda*, Nov. 28 *Draft Treaty [on nuclear no-first-use], *Pravda*, Nov. 28
Dec. 11	CDM	*Report, *Pravda*, Dec. 12

1977		
Feb. 23	deputy foreign ministers	report, *Kr. Zv.*, Feb. 24
May 20	MC	report, *Pravda*, May 21
May 26	CFM	*Communique, *Pravda*, May 27
Jul. 8	Parliamentarians	*Appeal [to CSCE Parliaments and Parliamentarians, *Pravda*, Jul. 7
Oct. 20	MC, military reps	report, *Pravda*, Oct. 21
Dec. 2	CDM	*Report, *Pravda*, Dec. 3
1978		
Apr. 25	CFM	*Communique, *Pravda*, Apr. 27
May 19	MC	report, *Pravda*, May 20
Oct. 19	MC	report, *Pravda*, Oct. 20
Nov. 23	PCC	*Communique, *Pravda*, Nov. 24 *Declaration, *Pravda*, Nov. 24 ‡Statement on the Middle East situation [excl. Romania], *Pravda*, Nov. 25
Dec. 7	CDM	*Report, *Pravda*, Dec. 8
1979		
Apr. 26	MC	report, *Pravda*, Apr. 27
May 15	CFM	*Communique, *Pravda*, May 16
Oct. 17	Parliamentarians	*'Appeal of the representatives of the parliaments of the states-participants of the Warsaw Treaty to the parliaments of the country participants of the North Atlantic Alliance' *Izvestiya*, Oct. 18
Oct. 31	MC	report, *Pravda*, Nov. 1
Dec. 6	CDM	*Report, *Pravda*, Dec. 7
Dec. 6	CFM	*Communique, *Pravda*, Dec. 6
1980		
May 15	PCC	*Communique, *Pravda*, May 16 *Declaration, *Pravda*, May 16 *Statement [calling for a world summit], *Pravda*, May 16
May 23	MC	report, *Pravda*, May 24
June 18	Parliamentarians	*Communique, *Pravda*, June 17 *Appeal to the parliaments and parliamentarians of the states of Europe and the world, *Pravda*, June 19

June 22?	MPA workers	report, *Kr. Zv.*, June 25
Jul. 9	deputy foreign ministers	report, *Pravda*, Jul. 10
Oct. 17	MC	report, *Pravda*, Oct. 18
Oct. 20	CFM	*Communique, *Pravda*, Oct. 21
Dec. 3	CDM	*Report, *Pravda*, Dec. 4
Dec. 5	Party and State leaders	*Report, *Pravda*, Dec. 6
1981		
Jan. 20	deputy foreign ministers	report, *Pravda*, Jan. 21
Apr. 23	MC	report, *Pravda*, Apr. 24
Oct. 30	MC	report, *Pravda*, Oct. 31
Dec. 2	CFM	*Communique, *Pravda*, Dec. 3
Dec. 4	CDM	*Report, *Pravda*, Dec. 5
1982		
Apr. 29	MC	report, *Pravda*, Apr. 30
Oct. 22	MC	report, *Pravda*, Oct. 23
Oct. 22	CFM	*Communique, *Pravda*, Oct. 23
1983		
Jan. 5	PCC	*Communique, *Pravda*, Jan. 6 *Political Declaration, *Pravda*, Jan. 7
Jan. 13	CDM	*Report, *Pravda*, Jan. 14
Jan. 28	deputy foreign ministers	report, *Pravda*, Jan. 29
Apr. 7	CFM	*Report, *Pravda*, Apr. 8
Apr. 28	MC	report, *Pravda*, Apr. 29
June 28	Party and State leaders	*Report, *Pravda*, June 29
Oct. 14	CFM	*Communique, *Pravda*, Oct. 15
Oct. 20	extraordinary CDM	*Communique, *Pravda*, Oct. 22
Oct. 29	MC	report, *Pravda*, Oct. 30
Nov. 10	Parliamentarians	*Communique, *Pravda*, Nov. 13 *Appeal to the Parliaments of states-participants of the Conference on Security and Co-operation in Europe, *Pravda*, Nov. 13
Dec. 7	CDM	*Report, *Pravda*, Dec. 8
Dec. 21	deputy foreign ministers	report, *Pravda*, Dec. 22
1984		
Jan. 11[1]		*'On the question of the

		liberation of Europe from chemical weapons', *Pravda*, Jan. 11
Feb. 14	Party and State leaders	report, *Pravda*, Feb. 15
Mar. 5		*Proposal of the state-participants of the Warsaw Treaty to the state-members of NATO regarding talks on the question of the non-increase and reduction of military spending, *Pravda*, Mar. 6
Apr. 20	CFM	*Communique, *Pravda*, Apr. 21
Apr. 26	MC	report, *Pravda*, Apr. 27
May 4	deputy foreign ministers	report, *Pravda*, May 5
May 7		*Appeal on the mutual non-use of military force and the maintenance of relations of peace between the states-participants of the Warsaw Treaty and the states-members of NATO, *Pravda*, May 8
Oct. 19	MC	report, *Pravda*, Oct. 20
Dec. 4	CFM	*Communique, *Izvestiya*, Dec. 6
Dec. 5	CDM	*Report, *Pravda*, Dec. 6
1985		
Mar. 1	deputy foreign ministers	‡Report, *Pravda*, Mar. 2
Mar. 13	Party and State leaders	report, *Izvestiya*, Mar. 15
Apr. 26	Party and State leaders	*Communique, *Pravda*, Apr. 27 *Protocol, *Pravda*, Apr. 27
May 14		speech by K. V. Rusakov [on the 30th Anniversary] *Izvestiya*, May 15
May 14	Parliamentarians	*Communique, *Izvestiya*, May 15

* * *

May 23	MC	report, *Kr. Zv.*, May 25
Oct. 23	PCC	*Communique, *Pravda*, Oct. 24 *Statement 'For the elimination of the nuclear threat and a turn

		for the better in European and world affairs', *Pravda*, Oct. 24
Nov. 14	MC	report, *Pravda*, Nov. 15
Nov. 21	'highest leaders'	*Report, *Pravda*, Nov. 22
Dec. 5	CDM	report, *Izvestiya*, Dec. 6
1986		
Mar. 8	deputy foreign ministers	report, *Pravda*, Mar. 9
Mar. 20	CFM	*Communique, *Pravda*, Mar. 21
Apr. 8		Address [on European nuclear free zones], *Pravda*, Apr. 9
Apr. ?16		Statement [on the US bombing of Libya], *Pravda*, Apr. 17
Apr. 25	MC	report, *Izvestiya*, Apr. 26
June 11	PCC	Communique, *Pravda*, June 12 Address of the states-participants of the Warsaw Treaty to the country-participants of NATO, and to all European countries, with a programme of reducing armed forces and conventional arms in Europe, *Pravda*, June 12
June 27	deputy foreign ministers	report, *Népszabadság*, June 28
Sept. 2	deputy foreign ministers	report, *Pravda*, Sept. 3
Oct. 15	CFM	Communique, *Pravda*, Oct. 17
Nov. 14	MC	report, *Pravda*, Nov. 15
Dec. 3	CDM	Communique, *Pravda*, Dec. 4
1987		
Jan. 22	deputy foreign ministers	report, *Pravda*, Jan. 23
Mar. 13	group of experts	report, *Pravda*, Mar. 14
Mar. 13	ambassadors	report, *Pravda*, Mar. 14
Mar. 25	CFM	Communique, *Pravda*, Mar. 26 Statement 'Towards the development of the all-European process and the intensification of the conclusions of the Vienna meeting', *Pravda*, Mar. 26 'Statement of the state-participants of the Warsaw Treaty on the question of the prohibition

		of chemical weapons', *Pravda*, Mar. 27
Apr. 10		'Proposal by the Warsaw Treaty Organization to NATO' on moratorium on increasing military spending, *Pravda*, Apr. 11
Apr. 18	MC	report, *Pravda*, Apr. 19
May 29	PCC	Communique, *Izvestiya*, May 30 Statement 'On the Military Doctrine of the state-participants of the Warsaw Treaty', *Izvestiya*, May 30 Statement 'On overcoming under-development and establishing a New International Economic Order', *Izvestiya*, May 30
Jul. 3	Parliamentarians	Communique, *Pravda*, Jul. 4 'Message to the Parliaments and Parliamentarians of the countries participating in the Conference on European Security and Co-operation', *Soviet News*, Jul. 15
Sept. 11	multilateral group	report, *Pravda*, Sept. 13
Sept. 26	MC	report, *Pravda*, Sept. 27
Oct. 13	multilateral group	report, *Pravda*, Oct. 14
Oct. 29	CFM	Communique, *Pravda*, Oct. 30 Statement 'On the increase of the effectiveness of the Conference on Disarmament in Geneva', *Pravda*, Oct. 31
Nov. 12	multilateral group	report, *Pravda*, Nov. 13
Nov. 25	CDM	Communique, *Pravda*, Nov. 27
Dec. 11	leading statesmen	report, *Pravda*, Dec. 12
Dec. 16	multilateral group	report, *Pravda*, Dec. 17
Dec. 18	group of experts	report, *Pravda*, Dec. 19
1988		
Jan. 20	multilateral group	report, *Pravda*, Jan. 21
Feb. 3	group of experts	report, *Pravda*, Feb. 4
Feb. 23	Foreign Ministers	report, *Pravda*, Feb. 24
Mar. 30	CFM	Communique, *Pravda*, Mar. 31 Address, *Pravda*, Mar. 31
Apr. 13	multilateral group	report, *Pravda*, Apr. 14
May 13	MC	report, *Pravda*, May 14
June 4	UN delegates	Memorandum 'Security through

		disarmament', *Pravda*, June 5
June 7	Defence Ministers	report, *Pravda*, June 8
June 17	group of experts	report, *Pravda*, June 18
Jul. 8	CDM	Communique, *Pravda*, Jul. 9
Jul. 16	PCC	Communique, *Pravda*, Jul. 17 Statement 'On the negotiations for a reduction in armed forces and military arms in Europe', *Pravda*, Jul. 17
Jul. 16	Foreign Ministers	report, *Pravda*, Jul. 17
Oct. 5	MC	report, *Pravda*, Oct. 6
Oct. 18	CDM	report, *Pravda*, Oct. 19
Oct. 28	CFM	Declaration 'On measures for strengthening confidence and disarmament in Europe', *Pravda*, Oct. 29
Oct. 29		Communique, *Pravda*, Oct. 30
Nov. 18	Foreign Ministry experts	report, *Pravda*, Nov. 19
Nov. 23	multilateral group	report, *Pravda*, Nov. 24
Dec. 7	group of experts	report, *Pravda*, Dec. 8
Dec. 9	Defence Ministry experts	report, *Pravda*, Dec. 11
Dec. 17	CDM	Communique, *Pravda*, Dec. 18
1989		
Jan. 30		CDM Statement, *Pravda*, Jan. 30

Appendix 4: The Bilateral Treaties

Table 1 indicates the bilateral treaties of friendship, co-operation, and mutual assistance that have been signed between the member-states of the Warsaw Treaty.[1] These treaties, originating in the post-war period before the signing of the Warsaw Treaty are considered to be part of the 'first stage' of military co-operation between the allies (Grechko, 1977, p. 330; Alexandrov, p. 17; Yakubovskii, 1976; Lototskii, p. 347). The most fundamental difference between these and the Warsaw Treaty is that the latter makes a point of not referring to socialist internationalism in any shape or form (Tyranowski, p. 105; see also Meissner, 1966, p. 249). In addition it is explained that:

> All the treaties contain resolutions on the development of economic and cultural associations and relations of friendship and co-operation between the people of the contracting countries, and the obligation to co-operate with all states in the cause of securing universal peace and security in accordance with the Charter of the [United Nations]. (Bakhov, p. 5)

So they seem to go further in these fields, too, than does the Warsaw Treaty.

Many of the arguments supporting the bilateral treaties are similar to those used to defend the Warsaw Treaty – for example that they were a response to imperialist aggression (Grechko, 1977, p. 331; Kozlov, p. 211), and that they are defending the revolutionary gains of the signatories (Kozlov, p. 211; Alexandrov, p. 17). Once again, the military construction of the signatories is seen to be under the dominant support of the USSR and the Soviet army's experience (Yakubovskii, 1976). Alexandrov likewise places the bilateral treaties alongside 'corresponding firm ties' in the spheres of politics, economics and culture, that are assisting in leading to 'an awareness of the emergence of a new international community' (p. 17). As with the Warsaw Treaty in its practice, the bilateral treaties are seen as having the fundamental principles of Marxism-Leninism, common political aims and tasks, and 'the principles of organizing political education and training in the armed forces' (Grechko, 1977, p. 330).

The Soviet Union and the WTO regularly offer the dismantling of the WTO in return for the dismantling of NATO, usually suggesting that the military structures should go first as part of an interim deal. This would make little difference to the Soviet bloc, since the basis of its military relations are not dependent on multilateral co-ordination under the Warsaw Treaty,[2] rather under the bilateral treaties or just individual arrangements as the stationing of the Soviet forces and TNFs in Central Europe. It is arguable that even the

TABLE 1 *The bilateral treaties*

	USSR	*GDR*	*CzSR*	*PPR*	*SRR*	*PRB*	*HPR*	*PRA*
USSR	–	–	12Dec43	21Apr48	4Feb48	18Mar48	18Feb48	9Jul46
	–	12Jun64	27Nov63	8Apr65	7Jul70	14May67	7Sep67	
	–	7Oct75	6May70	–	–	–	–	
GDR	–	–	6Jun50	–	–	–		
	12Jun64	–	17Mar67	15Mar67	1Oct70	7Sep67	18May67	–
	7Oct75	–	3Oct77	28May77	10Jun77	14Sep77	24Mar77	–
CzSR	12Dec43	–	–	10Mar47	21Jul48	23Apr48	16Apr49	–
	27Nov63	17Mar67	–	1Mar67	16Aug70	26Apr68	14Jun68	–
	6May70	3Oct77	–	–	–	–	–	–
PPR	21Apr48	6Jun50	10Mar47	–	26Jan49	29May48	18Jun48	–
	8Apr65	15Mar67	1Mar67	–	12Nov70	6Apr67	16May68	–
	–	28May77	–	–	–	–	–	–
SRR	4Feb48	–	21Jul48	26Jan49	–	16Jan48	24Jan48	–
	7Jul70	1Oct70	16Aug70	12Nov70	–	19Nov70	24Feb71	–
	–	10Jun77	–	–	–	–	–	–
PRB	18Mar48	–	23Apr48	29May48	16Jan48	–	16Jul48*	16Dec47
	14May67	7Sep67	26Apr67	6Apr67	19Nov70	–	10Jul69	–
	–	14Sep77	–	–	–	–	–	–
HPR	18Feb48	–	16Apr49	18Jun48	24Jan48	16Jul48*	–	–
	7Sep67	18May67	14Jun68	16May68	24Feb71	10Jul69	–	–
	–	24Mar77	–	–	–	–	–	–
PRA	9Jul46	–	–	–	–	16Dec47		

* Meissner (1966, p. 240) says it was in June. This must be a typographical error, since he later (1967, p. 581) says it was in July.

SOURCES Meissner (1966); Mackintosh (1969); Staar (1982).

bilateral treaties are not entirely necessary, since, even though an argument for the Warsaw Treaty was to allow more effective co-operation than that afforded under the bilateral arrangements they are also inter-state agreements which would be subject to party guidance in the same way that the WTO is controlled. Party guidance of state affairs has never been on offer for dismantling. The one principle which has been rigorously defended above all else is the continuation of the leading role of the parties.

Officially the Warsaw Treaty was never intended to supersede the arrangements of the bilateral treaties. In his opening Statement to the Warsaw Conference in 1955, Bulganin reminded the delegates that:

> Nearly all our countries are bound with one another by bilateral treaties of friendship and mutual assistance, which have played *and continue to play* an important part in safe-guarding European peace and security. (*Pravda*, 12 May 1955; my italics)

Virtually the same wording was used by Menzhinskii, when he argued that the events of the 1950s additionally required the Warsaw Treaty:

> The bilateral treaties of the fraternal socialist countries played and continue to play a prominent role as an effective and efficient instrument in securing the mutual security against imperialist aggression, strengthening international peace, and developing between them comprehensive co-operation. (p. 28)

Menzhinskii had, in fact, stated (p. 27) that the importance of the bilateral treaties was *supplemented* by the Warsaw Treaty.

The most forthright presentation of how the bilateral treaties and the Warsaw Treaty must be seen as complementary aspects of the states' inter-relations was made by Savinov in 1980. In an extended passage on the matter, he wrote that:

> The agreed basis of the co-ordination of foreign policy in the framework of the Warsaw Treaty strengthens itself by the presence of the enduring bilateral treaties of relations, which cement all the state-members of the Warsaw Treaty. (p. 20)
>
> The bilateral treaties between the state-participants of the [WTO] are strengthened in the bilateral obligations resulting from membership of the Organization of the Warsaw Treaty, the strivings of the contracting countries actively to participate in the improvement of all forms of co-operation in the fields of politics, economics, and defence, are borne out. These treaties incorporate a provision that the sides, taking part in the decision-making structure, observe their obligations resulting from the Warsaw Treaty. (ibid.)
>
> The inseparable connexion and [complementary] relationship of the Warsaw Treaty and the bilateral treaties . . . were repeatedly noted by the leaderships of the fraternal parties of the socialist countries. (p. 21)

Even in relation to the WTO's 30th Anniversary it was asserted that:

> Together with the fraternal socialist countries' [bilateral] treaties of friendship and mutual interest and their association within the framework of the Council for Mutual Economic Assistance, the Warsaw Treaty was a powerful international legal factor, cementing all the fraternal ties among European socialist countries. (Nezhinsky, p. 62)

In other words, all these various ties, both bilateral and multilateral, are to be seen as complementary factors, not just to the defence of socialism or the commitment to joint political action, but to the paramount ideological interest of the overall membership of the European socialist community. Since, as this book concludes, the WTO was just one element in the context of international socialism, then it does not matter how many other ties, either bilateral or multilateral, also exist – they all work together to the common aim. One more treaty merely reinforces the rest; one fewer, for example the dissolution of the Warsaw Treaty, again would not matter, since the overall context of mutual socialist activity is not diminished.

Appendix 5: Notes on Albania and Romania

NOTE ON ALBANIA

In the early post-war years, Albania was not incorporated fully into the bilateral treaty system. Its inclusion in the Warsaw Treaty was its first formal participation in the collective defence community. According to Kobal (1974, p. 242), however, from 1955 to the 1960s, Albania was objecting to being forced to maintain large military forces.[1]

The PCC met on 28–29 March 1961 (see Appendix 2) but Albania did not send party representatives, and its chief delegate was only the 'First Vice-Chairman of the Council of Ministers, Minister of Defence' rather than the First Secretary of the ruling party as with the other states. On 3–5 August 1961, the First Secretaries of the Warsaw Treaty states met in Moscow and issued a Communique on the German question, but on August 8 Albania issued its own proposals for a German settlement. On 12 December 1961 the Albanian Embassy in Moscow was closed, the Soviet staff was withdrawn from Tirana, and the other non-Soviet Warsaw Treaty states reduced their diplomatic representation to the level of Chargé d'Affairs. Finally, on 7 June 1962, a PCC session was held in Moscow at which Albania was not represented.

According to the remaining members, it was Albania's decision not to participate, though there is confusion over when this began. Menzhinskii states that Albania was not an active member from 1961 (footnote, p. 30), while Tyranowski (1973, p. 106) writes that 'Beginning with 1962, Albania did not take any part in the conferences of the [PCC]', though he only refers to Albania as non-participatory rather than actually 'withdrawn'.[2] Kozlov is more outspoken and says that Albania 'by virtue of the position taken by its leaders' hadn't been active 'since 1963' (p. 212). A Polish source even writes that Albania 'functioned within its [WTO's] structure only until 1964' (Czyzewski, p. 7). Technically it was not until 13 September 1968 that Albania fully distanced itself from the WTO, passing a law to that effect (Meissner, 1983, p. 360a), in response to the events in Czechoslovakia.

Writing for the 10th anniversary,[3] WTO Chief of Staff Batov (p. 112) listed the states which founded the Warsaw Treaty, but did not give any footnote or rider to the listing of Albania, implying that the Soviet Union at that time did not consider Albanian non-participation as final. However, the 1966 PCC Statement on US aggression in Vietnam (*Pravda*, 8 July 1966) spoke of the Statement expressing the policy of 'the parties to the Warsaw Treaty', which could be interpreted to imply that at that time Albania, not a participant to the Statement, was not considered to be a party to the Warsaw Treaty.

During the 30th Anniversary, Gribkov, in a footnote (1985b, p. 83) shirked the question of the founding membership of the WTO, by writing of the Treaty's 'participants at the present time', and so did not have to mention Albania. This was also the method used by Smorigo (p. 27).

Albania did not participate in the first WTO multilateral exercises of October 1961 (Yakubovskii, 1975b, p. 282) and so was only fully a member of the WTO during the virtually-moribund stage of the Organization. It would seem that the question of Albania's rôle and political-military policy need be of little concern to a study of the WTO.

NOTE ON ROMANIA

Since 1964, Romania has had an openly maverick and recusant rôle within the WTO, distancing itself from military and party-political activities, but participating in the WTO structure, including putting its signature to virtually every PCC document. Romania's claim is that the country is rigorously following the parts of the Treaty (and the later official interpretations) claiming that the WTO is founded on 'the principles of respect for the independence and sovereignty of states, and also with the principle of non-interference in their internal affairs'.

This attitude came into the open in 1964, when, under the guise of its attempts at mediating in the Sino-Soviet dispute, the Rumanian Workers' Party[4] issued a *Statement on the Stand of the Rumanian Workers' Party Concerning the Problems of the International Communist and Working Class Movement* which was 'Adopted by the Enlarged Plenum of the Central Committee of the RWP Held in April 1964'[5] (April 15–22). Section 4 (of seven sections), on 'The World Socialist System', includes the following passages:

> By promoting in the international arena a qualitatively new system of relations, unprecedented in history, the Communist and workers' parties in the socialist countries have placed at the foundation of these relations the *principles of* national independence and sovereignty, equal rights, mutual advantage, comradely assistance, non-interference in internal affairs, observance of territorial integrity, the principles of socialist internationalism.
>
> *As . . . fully confirmed by historical experience, these principles form the immutable law and guarantee of the development of the entire* world socialist system. They have imposed themselves as an objective necessity for the development of relations of co-operation, for securing the unity of action and cohesion of a community of independent states, with equal rights. Any curtailment or violation of these principles can be only a source of misunderstanding and discord.
>
> . . . the socialist countries achieve their unity of action in all domains, economic as well as political, by reciprocal consultations, the joint elaboration of certain common stands as regards the major problems of principle,

> and not by establishing unique solutions by some super-state authority. This is the only correct and possible way of developing co-operation among sovereign and equal states; it guarantees the adoption of realistic and efficient solutions and secures a lasting basis for the common efforts aiming at the implementation of the decisions or general line line that have been adopted.
>
> . . . specific and individual interests cannot be presented as general interests, as objective requirements of the development of the socialist system.
>
> [*The text then included a call for notice to be taken of national-historical conditions.*]
>
> *The strict observance of the basic principles of the new-type relations among the socialist countries is the primary prerequisite of the unity and cohesion of these countries and of the world socialist system performing its decisive role in the development of mankind.* (Rumanian Workers' Party; italics in original)

In his discussion of the *Statement*, Floyd mainly concentrates on the application of the references elsewhere in the text to economic relations and the CMEA, but his general conclusions are that the *Statement* clearly signalled Romanian defiance of the Soviet Union and Khrushchev – 'by 1965, Rumania was no less free of Russian control than was Yugoslavia . . . ' (footnote 39, p. xii). But, unlike Yugoslavia, or Hungary's line in 1956, the Romanians have never completely cut their ties with the bloc; and in other ways, particularly over the leading rôle of the party, Romania has been decidedly hardline. Since 1964, Romania has walked a narrow line between national lattitude and bloc unity or solidarity. In military terms, this has been manifested in Romania refusing to take a full part in multilateral field exercises (but sends observers, and has taken part in staff exercises – see the chronology in Kulikov, 1980b), on the grounds that military forces must not be placed on another's territory (arguing the national sovereignty and non-interference principles).

Romania has guest status in the non-aligned movement, and according to Ceauşescu, it is up to non-aligned countries to unite in order to challenge super-power domination and so offer solutions to international problems (Tismaneanu, 1985).

It was no doubt Romania that was behind opposition to Brezhnev's calls in 1965 for greater political control within the WTO (see Chapter 3), though whether this could have been achieved without support from the other members, and whether it would have made the Organization more efficient (by whatever criterion) or even more significant in the face of overall party influence, is open to debate. By 1976, at the time of the Bucharest Reforms to the political mechanisms, Romania was apparently strongly in favour of strengthening the political aspects of the Treaty, and was calling for the introduction of 'the principle of consensus in the adoption of all decisions in this military-political alliance' (Tanjug in English, November 26, discussing a book on the Warsaw Treaty published in Romania, *SWB* EE/5376/C/14, 29 November 1976). The Romanians were pushing for greater priority to be given to the political aspects of the Treaty, and 'improving the system of providing information on all the problems which relate to peace and security in Europe' (ibid.). In view of the extent of the Bucharest political reforms, it is debatable just how much Romania actually agreed with the final reorganization, or just what more change Romania was demanding and did not get (despite hosting the PCC session) let alone how it has acted within the WTO since 1976. Certainly as it stands, national views and the needs of the non-Soviet members are not yet perfectly catered for.

In military terms, the question of Romania's role in the WTO is a moot point. Just how distant is Romania from WTO practice, and does this matter in terms of bloc security?

Despite the work of Jones (for example, 1981) detailing Romania's 'people's defence' policy, it must be remembered that this is based largely outwith the regular army. The 1972 Law on the 'Organization of the National Defence' created a policy of 'Emphasizing resistance via lightly armed units of "Patriotic Guards" . . . the Romanian law diluted the role of the professional army' (Nelson, 1986a). In formal military terms, therefore, 'the RPA itself still resembles its allies, with a fairly standard WTO organization, large number of officer schools and emphasis on close political control' (Rakowska-Harmstone *et al.* 1981, p. 216) though it has been removed 'structurally . . . from WTO integration' (ibid., p. 221).

While Romania has broken away from general reliance on bloc military equipment (ibid., p. 218; Erickson, 1981, p. 162) this has resulted more recently in the realization of the need for access to (mainly Soviet) more-modern weapons (Nelson, 1986a). Overall, however, in bloc terms, this need not be seen as unusual, since bloc equipment is *not* standard (see Erickson, 1981, p. 163).

But, even in military terms, is Romania's position significant? Geostrategically, Bulgaria (and even Hungary) are more important. In an alliance that claims to be purely defensive, Romania if attacked by, say, NATO, would presumably defend itself, which would hold up an attack on the USSR from that direction. In the final analysis, even if Romanian doctrine differs, Romania has not apparently distanced itself completely from the WTO military structure. Several Central European sources[N] denied that the Romanian position caused problems; a familiar response was to point out that no alliance, not even NATO, had uniform participation. (While this might be because, even in otherwise off-the-record talks, admission of Romanian dissidence was still beyond the pale, it could also be suggested that unconcern over Romania was further evidence of the lack of impact of the WTO on both military and political national policies.)

In political terms, too, the limited nature of Romania's autonomy has also been confirmed. In 1985, the US Ambassador to Romania resigned, claiming that Ceauşescu 'had "outfoxed" the US by exaggerating his independence from Moscow . . . ' (David Buchan in *The Financial Times*, 17 May 1985).

> Mr Funderbuck also complained that Washington had ignored evidence, collected by his embassy, that Romanian independence of Moscow was a sham. He cited growing economic links between Bucharest and Moscow, large numbers of Soviet civilians in the country, and the Romanian transfer of Western technology and exports of arms to the Soviet Union. (Ibid.)

Various Central European specialists,[N] when questioned about this, confirmed this assessment. One such expert went on to argue that Romania 'couldn't afford' to leave the WTO, and wished to influence it from within. To influence the WTO internally, Romania would of course have to have a measure of active participation. As noted in Chapter 4, Romanian participation in the political processes of the WTO is virtually perfect. Romania's national foreign policy,[6] while perhaps expressing its goals more stridently, does not conflict with overall WTO joint foreign policy.

A further example of Romanian conformity was to be expressed by Ceauşescu in a speech on 20 December 1985, where he was 'calling on the Soviet bloc to take a more offensive propaganda line against the West' and included 'a pledge to co-operate more closely with the Warsaw Pact members in the future' (Robin Gedye in *The Daily Telegraph*, 21 December 1985). While this could be just another example of a Romanian ability to keep in with all sides, it could also serve to confirm that Romanian independence from all aspects of the WTO is perhaps generally overrated.

Appendix 6: Note on the Leading Military Staff

This appendix discusses the WTO Commanders-in-Chief (C-in-C) and Chiefs of Staff (C-of-S). For a discussion of the positions of C-in-C, C-of-S, and General Secretary, see Chapter 3. Both Yakubovskii (1975b) and Kulikov (1980b) have chronologies which include the dates of appointment of the C-in-C and C-of-S:

The Commanders-in-Chief

Name	*Date of Appointment*
Konev	14 May 1955
Grechko	25 July 1960
Yakubovskii	8 July 1967
Kulikov	5 January 1977

The Chiefs of Staff

Name	*Date of Appointment*
Antonov	14 May 1955
Batov	30 October 1962
Kazakov	24 November 1965
Shtemenko	5 August 1968
Gribkov	12 October 1976

In Yakubovskii, the date is given, then a description of the post – for example 'Commander-in-Chief of the Joint Armed Forces' – and then the name of the new occupant. The description and name are interspersed with the word *naznachen*: '[he was] appointed.' Kulikov repeats this format, until the appointments of Gribkov (Chief of Staff, 1976) and Kulikov (Commander-in-Chief, 1977); in both these cases the format becomes the date followed by 'The Governments of the state-participants of the Warsaw Treaty appointed . . . ' and the name.

This subtlety implies either that the earlier appointments emerged, or that it was only with the later appointments that a consensus of the governments occurred, or that the authors wished to *imply* that there had been a consensus. With both formats, and all interpretations, it underlines that however the appointments were arrived at, they are not formulated within the official structure of the WTO, and are not to be seen as appointments from the PCC, the WTO's top body. It has been suggested[N] that in 1968 Czechoslovakia and

Romania called for the C-in-C not to be a Soviet, but that the USSR described such an idea as 'the voice of the enemy'. Whether by the appointment of Gribkov and Kulikov such objections to the perpetual Soviet holding of the posts had been shelved is of course still unknown.

Both Kulikov and Yakubovskii footnote each appointment with the rider that the dates given are for the date of publication of the appointment in the Soviet press, with the exception of Konev and Antonov. Kulikov (1980b) dates their appointment from May 14, in the context of describing the extablishment of the Joint Command as part of the proceedings of the Warsaw Meeting, with no footnote about the press. Yakubovskii (1975b) describes the decision to create the Joint Command, and the appointment of Konev and Antonov, as part of a separate entry from the signing of the Treaty, with a footnote that it was the date of publication in the Soviet press. The *Bol'shaya Sovetskaya Entsiklopediya* entry for the Warsaw Treaty states that Grechko took over the the C-in-C post from Konev in June 1960, a month before the press announcement, and that Grechko continued in this capacity until July 1967, three months after his appointment as Soviet Minister of Defence. This reinforces the conclusions in Chapter 3 that these leading posts are not full-time appointments.

On 3 February 1989, *Pravda* published an article on page 7 titled 'Naznachen glavnokomanduiushchim' (A commander-in-chief was appointed). In it it was stated that 'The governments of the state-participants of the Warsaw Treaty were satisfied with the request of Marshall of the Soviet Union V. G. Kulikov for his release from the appointment as Commander-in-Chief of the Joint Armed Forces of the state-participants of the Warsaw Treaty in connection with the appointment as the general inspector of the group of general inspectors of the Ministry of Defence of the USSR . . . ' He was replaced by first deputy minister of defence of the USSR general of the army P. G. Lushev. The post of Chief of Staff of the Joint Armed Forces was also changed at about the same time.

Notes

1 The Early Post-war Period

1. The 'second stage' beginning with the formation of the WTO.
2. See, for example, Timothy Dunmore's *The Stalinist Command Economy: The Soviet State Apparatus and Economic Policy, 1945–1953* (London: Macmillan, 1980)
3. Such developments could also, perhaps, be seen in the progress of the Council For Mutual Economic Assistance.

2 The Specific Origins of the Warsaw Treaty

1. At the Berlin Conference, Molotov had in fact proposed that a collective European security treaty replace both the EDC *and* NATO.
2. Britain, France, the FRG, Italy, Belgium, the Netherlands, Luxembourg, the United States, and Canada. In the commentaries immediately following the Paris Conference, the USSR objected to the 'London and Paris' agreements, but, as with Western sources, later omitted the reference to London.
3. France, Britain, Holland, Italy, Belgium, Luxembourg, West Germany.
4. In 1986, a Central European military expert[N] was adamant that, owing to the nature of modern war, the speed of events, and the problem of communication during war, the non-Soviet armies in the WTO would 'of course' have access to and control over theatre nuclear warheads.
5. This note was sent to: France, Great Britain, Austria, Albania, Belgium, Bulgaria, Hungary, the GDR, the Netherlands, Greece, Denmark, Iceland, Italy, Luxembourg, Norway, Poland, Rumania, Turkey, Finland, Czechoslovakia, Switzerland, Sweden, Yugoslavia, and the USA. The People's Republic of China was offered observer status to the meeting (*Pravda*, 14 November 1954). The list was explained as being states with diplomatic relations with the USSR.
6. The *Soviet News* coverage of the note referred, mistakenly, to the 'West European Alliance'.
7. This was the only such text supplied to the National Library of Scotland, and was in the form of a supplement to *New Hungary* 22 (January 1955).
8. Unofficially, however, and behind the scenes, on returning from his attendance at the Moscow celebrations of the anniversary of the October Revolution in 1954, Hungarian party leader Rákosi had leaked that a Warsaw Treaty was going to be signed. He did this for his own internal factionalism against Nagy, who did not support the idea of the alliance.[N]

The treatment of the foreign policy issues behind such a decision were not so openly forthright at the time – see Saburov's speech above. It is also useful to note that it was a party figure, Rákosi, who did not attend the Moscow Conference (which was an inter-state meeting), who brought such a decision to Hungary. In its early years, the WTO tried hard to present itself as an inter-state body with no party input.

9. The CMEA Treaty can be discounted since it has a worldwide membership, and its activities – trade and economic development – are also carried out by its members outwith the CMEA. The Warsaw Treaty limits the members' foreign policy activities and is the only multilateral tie of an ideological nature that formally defines a Soviet bloc.
10. Molotov was busy in Vienna, concerned with the Austrian State Treaty.
11. Khrushchev did, however, make an appearance to observe the signing of the Moscow Declaration, but he was not accorded specific treatment, being placed half-way down the list of persons at the ceremony (*Pravda*, 3 December 1954).
12. This was similar to the use made of the CMEA. That the CMEA was moribund in its early years, see George Schöpflin *The Soviet Union and Eastern Europe: A Handbook* (London: Anthony Blond, 1970) pp. 151, 237.

3 The Structural Development of the WTO

1. Tismaneanu reports that 'in 1958, Khrushchev made the unexpected decision to withdraw the Soviet troops that were stationed in Romania' (p. 59a–b).
2. A similar treaty was signed with Czechoslovakia in 1968. For an analysis of its provisions and how they compare with the earlier treaties, see R. Waring Herrick, 'The Soviet Military Intervention: terms of the Soviet troop-stationing treaty imposed on Prague' in Radio Liberty *Research Bulletin* (CRD 379/68) 23 October 1968, no. 24 (2469).
3. From the original Moscow Conference of 1954 and the Warsaw Conference of 1955, through all the PCC meetings until 1961 inclusive, there was an official observer from the People's Republic of China; North Korea and Mongolia also sent observers to the PCC meetings of 1960 and 1961 (see fn. 6 below). Since 1962 there have been no observers at PCC meetings, 'although Mongolian, North Korean, and Cuban observers attend the joint manoeuvres' (Walker, p. 563).
4. John Erickson writes that 'the whole apparatus of the pact, ponderous as it is, is largely irrelevant to Soviet *operational* purposes; it appears to be a high price to pay for a few hand-picked non-Soviet formations to fight in the first attack echelon' (1982c, pp. 165/8, my italics). Rakowska-Harmstone et al argue that 'The Soviet Union has attempted to solve the problem of East European reliability by fragmenting national military forces along service lines, detaching elite and specialized

units from national control and incorporating these units into a "Greater Sociailst Army" built around the [Soviet Armed Forces] and under the operational control of the Soviet General Staff' (1981, pp. v–vi; see also fn. 20 below).

5. In *military* terms, Article 4 of the Treaty limits mutual assistance to being 'in case of an attack in Europe. This means that it does not cover armed attacks launched outside Europe' (Tyranowski, p. 112). *Strategic Survey* 1970 states (p. 28) that this was only made explicit in May 1970, by an official Polish handbook on the WTO. Tyranowski argues that documents from the PCC, or other WTO bodies, that express views on what amount to out-of-area issues 'express their interest taken in problems of world importance, according to the principle that peace is indivisible' (p. 116).
6. Unpublished research by myself on the compleat lists of those stated as attending all WTO meetings.
7. Tyranowski, writing in 1971, explains that consultations due to military threat or attack have not arisen (p. 107). This indicates that the military interventions in Hungary and Czechoslovakia were not carried out under the auspices of the WTO, but at most in its name.
8. For an in-depth discussion of PCC documents, see Menzhinskii (pp. 35–6) who divides them, in ascending order, into 'communique', 'declaration', 'appeal', 'resolution', 'statement', and 'draft international treaty'.
9. Malcolm Mackintosh says that the Defence Ministers themselves merely rubber-stamp decisions taken by the Military Council (1974, p. 123a). But see the specific discussion on the Committee of Ministers of Defence.
10. The question of consensus is also affected by bilateral bargaining (both during PCC meetings and during exchange bilateral visits of the leaders)[N]. Romania, for example, is said[N] of late to have increased the frequency of offering support (or non-objection) in the WTO, in exchange for Soviet economic aid under non-WTO auspices.
11. Under the Budapest Reforms, the ministers of defence were formed into a separate Committee, and their deputies became the Deputy Commanders of the Joint Armed Forces.
12. The original document in *Pravda* is just headed 'Formation of Joint Command . . . ', but in Mal'tsev (1980) it is described as 'Resolution for the creation of a Joint Command . . . '
13. This is also how Shtemenko describes it (p. 189a).
14. Alexandrov describes the Joint Command as being 'the Committee of Defence Ministers, the Military Council, and the Staff of the Joint Armed Forces' (p. 24) though this seems too broad. The Commander-in-Chief with his Soviet and non-Soviet deputies comprise the *military* leadership of the Joint Armed Forces, though they obviously need the administrative services of the Staff and the Military Council. The defence ministers need not be military men, so theirs must be more

of a policy-advice, or political, function. Meissner states that the active military leadership rests with the Joint Command and not the Committee of Ministers of Defence (1983, p. 361b).

15. Romania was excluded from the planning and execution of the intervention. See also fn. 7 above.
16. Shtemenko does, however, say that 'collective measures are taken for the suppression of counter-revolutionary and aggressive acts against socialist countries' (p. 168a), but this seems to be the only time such a function has been described. But see also fn. 7 above.
17. The forces of the GDR were only incorporated into the Joint Command after the PCC resolution of 28 January 1956. The Communique states that 'its armed contingents be incorporated into the Joint Armed Forces' (*Pravda* 29 January 1956). Meissner confirms that it is the whole of the GDR's National People's Army that is allotted to the JAFs (1983, p. 361b). See also Erickson (1981, p. 152).
18. In practice, however, as with the Commander-in-Chief, the Chief of Staff has always been 'chosen' as a Russian.
19. Mackintosh was writing in 1974. In July 1978, a WTO Deputy Commander-in-Chief, Marshal of Aviation A. I. Koldunov, designated as 'Commander of the Air Defence Forces', was identified.[N] Erickson (1981, p. 157) reports that an 'Assistant to the C-in-C for Rear Services/Logistics' had been identified in May 1980, but he had earlier remarked (ibid., pp. 154–5) that the WTO lacked 'any specific mobilization mechanism and logistical support'.

    I would argue that until any of these functions can be seen in practice, their Staff designations must be regarded as merely putative part-time posts (see also fn. 4 above).
20. In discussing 'Political activities in WTO military exercises', Jones details that during pauses in the action, political discussions, speeches, and film and stage performances, take place (1984, p. 71). This seems to me to be a strange way to simulate offensive, or even defensive, operations.
21. Mackintosh suggests that the Military Council 'probably includes the "Inspector General"' [a post he does not explain or define], and states that it does include a senior Soviet political officer and 'a military representative of Lieutenant-General or Vice-Admiral rank from each of the East European armed forces' (1974, p. 123b), but he does not give a source for this.
22. Mackintosh, for example, argues that the 'Soviet leaders got down to the task of reorganizing the Pact' *after* the Czechoslovak crisis, though he does acknowledge that pre-crisis there had been some criticism of the WTO in Central European journals.
23. Kobal does not quote a source for this information, which was not covered by the session's communique.
24. Further evidence of the scope of what would be in the reforms, and suggesting that Johnson's claims of 'detailed planning' for them (1978,

p. 254) might be a bit exaggerated is that, between 19–28 September 1968, the Commander-in-Chief visited all the members' countries to discuss reorganization.

25. Albania had formally withdrawn from the Treaty the previous September.
26. Kobal (p. 207) claims without quoting a source that the session was preceded by *three* days of bilateral negotiations.

    In view of the Soviet penchant for bilateral relations seen both in the retention of the bilateral treaties and in, for example, Brezhnev's speech (*Pravda*, 30 September 1965) it was presumably the Soviet delegation that held up the session.
27. For an extensive analysis of the Legal Convention, see Jones (1986).
28. It must be remembered that the CMEA comprises the Warsaw Treaty member states, plus Mongolia, Vietnam, and also Cuba which is a member of the non-aligned movement.
29. 'Romania, which refuses to participate in the joint political activities of the WTO political administrations, has a system of party committees in the military very similar to the system of party committees in the Yugoslav armed forces. The Romanians established this system in 1964' (Jones, 1984, p. 68).

4 Analysis of the Documents and Materials, 1955–85

1. A booklet published by Novosti in 1984, *The Warsaw Treaty Organization: Alliance for Peace*, comments that 'The states-parties to the Warsaw Treaty have long been proposing to the Western powers that a peace treaty be concluded with the two German states . . . ' and refers to 'a special statement on the matter' by the governments and dates it as being issued on August 12. The booklet thus seems to be referring to the second extra-structural meeting.
2. *SWB* explains that 'The Albanian radio and agency transmitted the text of a long statement, said to have been circulated by "the leader of the Albanian Workers' Party delegation" to the other delegation heads on 3rd August, the opening day of the conference.' While the document expressed support for the Soviet line on Germany, it also proposed that, should the Western states refuse to attend a peace conference, the socialist states should meet and conclude a separate peace treaty with the GDR. They should also 'envisage taking measures to raise [their] defence potential and combat readiness. The document concluded with a call to rally round the USSR' (EE/711, 9 August 1961). This was in fact the start of Albania's open rift with the WTO.
3. *Soviet News* 4897 (29 July 1963) issued a composite report on these three summit-level meetings, but quoted part of the Party and State leaders' Resolution, attributing it to the PCC.
4. See in particular A. Ross Johnson, *The Warsaw Pact's Campaign for 'European Security'* Rand Project R-505-PR, November 1970.

5. Quite another matter would be actions by individual Central European states, either in arms-trade to the Third World or through the sending of technical advisers. Once again these must be seen as national *bilateral* agreements, and are not covered either by the formal or informal *multilateral* WTO. (See M. Radu [ed.] *Eastern Europe and the Third World* New York: Praeger, 1981.) A Polish pamphlet spoke of Polish soldiers spending 'months and years of their life and work on peace mission . . . They have performed these missions for over thirty years in various regions of the world: Korea, Vietnam, Laos, Cambodia, Nigeria, the Middle East' (Czyzewski, p. 27). This was describing activities outwith the WTO. See also Gasparini, 1985.
6. The differentiation between political and military détente had already been created, in the Communique of the 1974 PCC, but these expressions were only linked by implication to the CSCE process in what might have been a reference to the Mutual and Balanced Force Reduction talks of Vienna.
7. Such a proposal had in fact first been mentioned by the WTO in the 1956 PCC Declaration.
8. Another regional issue that the WTO does *not* cover is the war in Afghanistan. Up to the 30th Anniversary, this matter was only mentioned once, by the PCC 1983 Political Declaration, where paragraph 79 calls for a settlement through the Afghan-Pakistan talks under the auspices of the United Nations.

   However, in an article in *Népszabadság* (14 May 1980 – MTI *Daily Bulletin* vol. 15/136) WTO C-in-C Marshal Kulikov argued that 'The leading circles of the United States are now making desperate efforts to falsify the meaning of the friendly assistance provided for the Afghan people.' It was not made clear if this was actually aid from the Warsaw Treaty Organization, from its individual states, or just from the Soviet Union.
9. Note that in 1971 the foreign ministers were meeting outwith the formal structure of the WTO.
10. This is the gist of section 1, 'The Contemporary World: its main tendencies and contradictions'. Aspects of section 4 'Basic Aims and Directions of the Party's Foreign Policy Strategy' somewhat qualify such an assertion, and argue more that co-operation is still possible and desirable.
11. See, for example, Elizabeth Teague, '*Pravda* raises specter of revisionism' Radio Liberty *Research* RL206/85, no. 26 (3335), 26 June 1985.
12. The WTO does not seem to talk in terms of a Soviet nuclear umbrella. In fact, I know of only one such comment: 'The defence of the socialist countries is guaranteed by the joint defensive might above all by those of the Soviet Union. The nuclear missile shield of the world's first socialist country is a reliable barrier in the way of the warmongering plans of the imperialist aggressors' (Nezhinsky, p. 63).
13. It was argued[N] that this could have been a reason why Gierek was

unable to 'grasp his chance' for internal and foreign policy changes. In the mid-1980s there was a joke in Hungary that 'The economists were Polish but the economic success was Hungarian.' It would, however, be unwise to be too simplistic in analysing Poland's politics.

5 The Thirtieth Anniversary

1. For a complete list of the known anniversary meetings, see Appendix 2.
2. For a list of the known anniversary articles, see the specific bibliography for the Anniversary at the end of this chapter.
3. There was no corresponding article in *Pravda* in 1985, but page 4 of the May 14 issue did have a small article covering the May 13 'solemn gathering' and another announcing the publication of the Skorodenko book (for which see fn. 2 above).
4. Article 9 of the Warsaw Treaty.
5. Svetlov refers to 'military' and 'international-legal' measures. For the former he lists: no new theatre or intermediate nuclear weapons in Europe; nuclear free zones; a ban on chemical weapons; the non-increase and then reduction in military budgets; and the mutual reduction of forces. For the latter he lists: a treaty on the no-first-use of nuclear weapons; a non-aggression treaty; and confidence-building measures in conjunction with the Stockholm Conference (pp. 32–3). The 1984 session of the Committee of Foreign Ministers called for a ban on nuclear weapons, a ban on chemical weapons, a nuclear test ban, confidence-building measures, the non-militarization of space, European nuclear-free zones, a general nuclear freeze, the non-first use of nuclear weapons, and action on military budgets.
6. Canada, France, the Federal Republic of Germany, Italy, Japan, the UK, and the USA, met in Bonn for their 11th regular economic summit, on 2–4 May, 1985 (*Keesings* XXXI 33635). Being only ten days before Rusakov gave his address, this would indicate that in this instance, at least part of the speech was prepared close to the time of its delivery, This shows both an attempt at topicality (the meeting was reported in *Pravda* on May 3rd and 5th, 1985, p. 5), but also a limited time for multilateral consultation on the keynote address of the 30th Anniversary.
7. As I argue in Chapter 4, the internal-security rôle is a question of ideological, not military, security.

6 Conclusions

1. *The Daily Express* (21 November 1986) reported a 'direct approach' from the WTO for talks on conventional arms, but explained it as from 'the Soviet Union, which sent the message through Italy'. NATO

insisted on East-West talks on a bilateral basis, since NATO was not a supranational body.

2. Equally, the CMEA can be seen as just another aspect in the ties of the socialist community. Its significance could be assessed in these political rather than practical terms given that, like the WTO, it could be seen as generally unimortant as regards its overtly-perceived functions. For a recent analysis of the CMEA see Arie Bloed *The External Relations of the Council for Mutual Economic Assistance* (Dordrecht: Martinus Nijhoff Publishers, 1988).
3. Savinov was referring to the multilateral sessions outwith the WTO (1970–73 inclusive) and the series of bilateral meetings from 1976 onwards. The post-Brezhnev leaderships discontinued these meetings. See Appendix 2.
4. It has even been suggested[N] that the Romanian leadership has told the USSR that Romania considers that the USSR only holds Bessarabia 'on lease'.
5. In general, the USSR's possible rôle as *gendarme* and arbiter does not seem to be discussed in Western literature.
6. For example Kulikov (1988), and Alexei Arbatov 'Military Doctrines' in *Disarmament and Security 1987 Yearbook* (Moscow: Novosti, 1988).
7. The bodies of the military structure have continued to play an enhanced rôle.
8. Despite being described as a regular meeting this appears to have been the first such meeting reported in *Pravda*.
9. His WTO rôle was only until the PCC met in Warsaw in July 1988. See the discussion of the post of PCC General Secretary in Chapter 3.
10. This is the Soviet description of such weapons as the shorter-range rockets deployed in the GDR and Czechoslovakia as a response to the USA's cruise and Pershing-II weapons. See the report of the extraordinary Committee of Ministers of Defence, *Pravda*, 22 October 1983.
11. 'As recently as two weeks ago, Mr Miklos Nemeth, Hungary's Prime Minister, told Western journalists that there was "no question" of any Soviet withdrawal without concessions from NATO. In Prague, sources suggessted that the Czechoslovak leadership was also taken aback and would be reluctant to see many Soviet troops leave.' Richard Bassett 'Offer by Kremlin surprises East' in *The Times*, 9 December 1988.
12. In view of the increasing use of the European Community as a political alliance, for example towards Libya (a putatively socialist country), or Iran, it would be interesting to see how Hungary could square membership of the WTO with closer relations with the European Communities. Article 7 of the Warsaw Treaty expressly forbids participating states to enter into coalitions, alliances, and agreements 'the purposes of which would be at variance with those of the present treaty'.
13. However, as this book has argued, the way the Organization has

operated in practice is very different. The WTO is ultimately the vehicle of the hidden agenda of intra-bloc relations.

14. Kulikov was replaced as Commander-in-Chief by General of the Soviet Army Petr Georgievich Lushev (*Pravda*, 16 February 1989).
15. The most recent sessions of the PCC have reiterated that the WTO General Secretary, as described in chapter 3 above, is a part-time post held by a deputy foreign minister of the member state hosting the next session of the PCC. It is a post incomparable with the full-time post of NATO Secretary-General – see fn. 9 above.
16. The two current Commanders-in-Chief did meet, informally, in London, during a conference organized by the Royal United Services Institute (*The Guardian, The Times*, 19 May 1989).
17. Originally published in *NATO Review* 36/2, April 1988, the Statement was reprinted as an Annex to the NATO brochure *Conventional Forces in Europe: The Facts*, also published in 1988.
18. The text was published in *NATO Review* 35/3, June 1987.

Appendix 2: Chronology of Meetings

1. Kulikov (1980b) dates this statement August 12; Yakubovskii (1975b) dates it as August 13. *Pravda* published it on August 14, dated August 13. There is no indication of how this statement was agreed between the various governments, or whether there was a formal meeting to agree on it.
2. Yakubovskii (1975b) and Kulikov (1980b) list only military manouevres as taking place in 1964.
3. A source[N] comments: 'Unpublicised meeting (following unpublicised meeting of deputy ministers in February) to consider proposed changes in the WP JAF structure in preparation for PCC meeting, Bucharest, 4–6 July' and cites *Borba* [the Jugoslav party newspaper] as its source.
4. Yakubovskii (1975b) and Kulikov (1980b) both give the sole date of this meeting as June 17. *Pravda* gives no starting date, but comments that it ended on June 17.
5. The original documents for this meeting list the attendee countries, which were the members of the WTO, without specifying it as a WTO meeting. Yakubovskii (1975b) does not list it, but Kulikov (1980b) does, and states that it was attended by the leaders of the 'country-participants of the Warsaw Treaty'.
6. This meeting is listed by both Yakubovskii (1975b) and Kulikov (1980b).
7. Yakubovskii (1975b) and Kulikov (1980b) list this as 'A military-science conference of leading workers of the rear of the allied armies . . . '
8. This was deferred from a meeting planned for December 21–23, 1970 – see *Izvestiya*, December 23.

9. The party leaders met in the Crimea. Although there was a wider attendance than the members of the WTO – it was in fact the membership of the CMEA – who discussed wider Party issues, this meeting was listed by Yakubovskii (1975b) and Kulikov (1980b), and its final document was included in Mal'tsev (1980). However, as Appendix 3 indicates, this document was excluded from Mal'tsev (1986).
10. As fn. 9 above.
11. The text of this treaty was published in *Krasnaya zvezda* on April 27, 1973, and listed its signatories without giving them any State or Party designation. Yakubovskii (1975b) and Kulikov (1980b) specify that the signatories were the deputy foreign ministers. Both these sources, plus Menzhinskii (1980, p. 39, footnote) say that it came into force on November 21, 1973, after full ratification.
12. See fn. 10 above.
13. This is listed by Yakubovskii (1975b) and Kulikov (1980b)
14. See fn. 6 above.
15. Yakubovskii (1975b) and Kulikov (1980b) describe this as 'a military-science conference of the Joint Armed Forces, dedicated to 20 years of the Warsaw Treaty Organization.' Cf. also fn. 7 above.
16. Kulikov (1980b) lists this as a meeting between Brezhnev and the Party leaders of the Warsaw Treaty countries at the CSCE, 'in the course of which took place an exchange of views on questions of the extending of fraternal relations between parties and countries, and also on some questions of an international character and questions, concerning the all-European meeting'. The role of detente was emphasized.
17. Kulikov (1980b) refers to this as 'a meeting of leading staff of military-scientific bodies of the general (Main) staffs, military publishers, and chief editors of the military-theoretical journals of the armies of the state-participants of the Warsaw Treaty'.
18. According to Kulikov (1980b), this was 'a meeting of leading staff of the political bodies of the armed forces of the state-participants of the Warsaw Treaty, dedicated to an exchange of experience in the fields of ideological activities.'
19. Kulikov (1980b) lists that in July–August, 1976, there were meetings in the Crimea. See also fn. 12 above.
20. The starting-date for this meeting is unclear.
21. Despite listing the Parliamentarians' meeting of 1975, Kulikov (1980b) omits mention of this one.
22. See fn. 19 above.
23. Kulikov (1980b) lists this as a meeting 'of chief editors of the central military newspapers of the countries of the Warsaw Treaty' covering ideological and military-educational problems, and 'the psychological training for war'.
24. Kulikov (1980b) includes reference to this 'theoretical conference' attended by representatives of 'all the fraternal armies of the state-participants of the Warsaw Treaty', in honour of the 60th anniversary

of the Great October socialist revolution.

25. Similar to note 24 above, this time a 'scientific conference' on the 60th anniversary of the Soviet Armed Forces
26. See fn. 22 above.
27. See fn. 22 above.
28. Kulikov (1980b) reports that, 'The participants of the meeting exchanged experiences of work concerning the training of the personnel of the fraternal armies in the spirit of socialist patriotism and internationalism, in the spirit of irreconcilability/intransigence to bourgeois and revisionist ideologies.'
29. Kulikov (1980b) lists that Brezhnev gave a speech in Berlin, where he 'announced the acceptance of the Soviet government, after consultation with the governments of the other state-participants of the Warsaw Treaty, the agreement to the unilateral reduction in the order of the number of Soviet forces in Central Europe, and also to reduce the quantity of nuclear [*sredstv* – means] of medium range, based in the western regions of the USSR, in the event if NATO fails in the plans of the supplementary allocation of nuclear weapons in West Europe.'

    This appears to be the only arms-proposal Kulikov refers to that is not otherwise part of a formal WTO meeting.
30. Kulikov (1980b) includes another 'theoretical conference' by representatives 'of all the fraternal armies of the state-participants of the Warsaw Treaty', and mentions its 'theme': 'the strengthening of the unity and co-operation of the countries of the socialist commmunity in the principle of Marxism-Leninism and socialist internationalism.' Compare this with fn. 25 above.
31. The actual dates are unclear, and were not included in the report in *Krasnaya Zvezda* (June 25).
32. There is no mention in the coverage in *Pravda* of a meeting having issued this document.
33. This was an ad hoc meeting during Andropov's funeral events. There was no corresponding meeting after Brezhnev's death.
34. The text in *Izvestiya* (March 6) indicates only that 'On agreement between the states-participants . . . ' the Proposal was delivered. There is no indication of a full meeting having taken place.
35. The text in *Pravda* (May 8) implies that the Appeal was delivered without a specific prior meeting, as a follow-on from the Prague PCC of January 1983. The covering text merely says that 'On agreement between them [the state-participants of the WTO] on May 7, 1984, a message . . . ' was sent.
36. This was an ad hoc meeting during Chernenko's funeral. See also fn. 32 above.
37. *SWB* SU/7951/C/1 (15 May 1985) refers to a Soviet TV broadcast including a recorded statement by Kulikov 'said to have been made at a March meeting of the Warsaw Treaty Military Council members and generals and officers of the staff of the Joint Armed Forces'. *Pravda*

in that month had no mention of such a meeting.

38. According to the end of the CFM meeting of 3–4 December 1984 (*Izvestiya*, December 6), a further regular session of the CFM was scheduled for Warsaw in June of 1985. This meeting never took place. The next recorded meeting of the CFM occurred in Budapest on 19–20 March 1986. I was told by a Central European specialist[N] that this delay was caused by the accession of Shevardnadze as Soviet Foreign Minister with no previous foreign policy experience, and by the major theoretical upheaval caused by Gorbachev's new security concepts (for which see Chapter 6).
39. This PCC session was scheduled for January 1985, but a 'Joint Announcement' (*Pravda*, 15 January 1985) reported that the session was 'postponed till a later date which is to be agreed'. This was presumably due to Chernenko's ill-health.
40. Gorbachev held this 'mutual discussion' during his return from his Geneva summit with US President Reagan.
41. *Pravda* (April 9) treated this as with fn. 35 above.
42. The BBC World Service news reported on April 15 that the Warsaw Treaty representatives at the Stockholm Conference had issued a joint statement on the US bombing of Libya. This was never reported in the Soviet press, but on April 16 the BBC news reported the statement issued from the GDR Party Congress which was published in *Pravda* on April 17.
43. This was reported in *Népszabadság* and *Neues Deutschland*, but not in the Soviet press, as a meeting to hear a report from the chief Soviet delegate at the Geneva nuclear and space weapons talks.
44. Although described[N] as a regular meeting, this would seem to have been timed to permit Soviet Foreign Minister Shevardnadze to report on the just-ended Reagan–Gorbachev mini-summit in Reykjavik.
45. No meeting corresponds to this Proposal.
46. This took place during the Shield-88 military exercise, the first time such a meeting was announced.
47. This is the first such meeting announced as held during a session of the PCC. The foreign ministers attend PCC sessions but this is an example of the ministerial elaboration discussed in Chapter 4 above.
48. This Statement was issued independently, but resulted from the CDM session of the previous December.

Appendix 3: Documentary History

1. This was not dated in *Pravda*, was dated January 10 in Mal'tsev (1986), but dated January 11 (the date of publication in *Pravda*) in the Hungarian edition of 1985.

Appendix 4: The Bilateral Treaties

1. These treaties are published in full under the UN Treaty Series. Meissner (1979) discusses and compares their content and development (see also Meissner 1966 and 1967).
2. Arguably, though, the West would be left with the Western European Union, which the WTO seems to have ignored since the Preamble to the Warsaw Treaty, since it has never mentioned it in relation to the dissolution of opposing blocs.

Appendix 5: Notes on Albania and Romania

1. Kobal also mentions Albanian objections to 'a large Soviet presence', but does not explain what arrangement this was, and whether it was advisers or troops.
2. Commenting on the mechanism for withdrawal from the Treaty, Tyranowski is adamant that Article 11 of the Treaty must be adhered to verbatim. But he adds that 'in the absence of conditions justifying such notice, a party may withdraw from the Warsaw Treaty only with the consent of the remaining parties' (p. 104).

   Article 1 of the Protocol extending the Treaty applies the same conditions for withdrawal as Article 11 of the Treaty (see Appendix 1).
3. *Voennyi vestnik* described the author as 'General of the Army P. Batov, twice Hero of the Soviet Union', and did not refer to his WTO post. (Six months later Batov was replaced by Kazakov). This concurs with the analysis of the post of C-in-C showing that position also not to appear to be full time.
4. Romania dropped the Slav spelling of its name in 1965, and in the same year also changed the name of its ruling party.
5. The text is in William E. Griffith (ed.) *Sino-Soviet Relations, 1964–1965* (Cambridge, MA/London: The MIT Press, 1967) pp. 269–96.
6. For a comprehensive summary of Romanian foreign policy, see Mututshika (1986).

Bibliography

Adam, Rachel (1984) 'Dialogue across the "Iron Curtain"', *The New Statesman*, 12 October.

Ágh, Atilla (1984) 'Rediscovery of Europe', paper presented to the European Association of Development Research and Training Institutes, Madrid Conference, September.

Ágh, Atilla (1985) 'The role of small countries and the perspectives of European co-operation', *Ulkopolitikka – Utrikespolitik*, 2/1985.

Akhtamzyan, Professor A. (1986) 'Leninist Principles of the International Policy of the CPSU and the Soviet State', *International Affairs* (Moscow) 3/1986.

Alexandrov, Valentin Alekseevich (1980) *The Warsaw Treaty and Peace in Europe* (Moscow: Novosti).

Andras, Charles (1978) 'A Summit with Consequences', Radio Free Europe *Research* RAD Background Report/271 (Eastern Europe) 14 December.

Arkin, William M. and Chappell, David (1983) 'The Impact of Soviet Theatre Nuclear Force Improvements', ADIU *Report* vol. 5/4, July–August.

Asmus, Ronald D. (1985) 'Chemical-Free-Weapons Zone in Central Europe?', Radio Free Europe *Research* RAD Background Report/74, 9 August.

Asmus, Ronald D. (1985) 'East Berlin Defends Foreign Policy Toward Western Europe' Radio Free Europe *Research* RAD Background Report/85, 30 August.

Bakhov, A. S. (1971) *Organizatsiya Varshavskogo Dogovora (pravovye aspekty)* (Moskva: Nauka).

Banks, Arthur S. *et al.* (eds) (1985) *Political Handbook of the World, 1984–1985* (Binghampton, NY: CSA Publications/State University of New York).

Batov, P. (1965) 'Boevoe sodruzhestvo', *Voennyi vestnik* 5/1965.

BBC Monitoring Service *Summary of World Broadcasts* [*SWB*], Section 1 (USSR), Section 2 (East Europe).

"B.D.B." (1985) 'Soviet Forces in the GDR: Changes at the Top, Problems Below the Surface', Radio Free Europe *Research* RAD Background Report/83, 30 August.

Bloed, Arie (1988) *The External Relations of the Council for Mutual Economic Assistance* (Dordrecht: Martinus Nijhoff Publishers).

Bloed, Arie (1980) 'The Warsaw Treaty Organization and Disarmament: the impact of individual member-states on the policy of the organization', *Coexistence* vol. 17/1, April.

Bloom, Bridget (1984) 'NATO Strategy: issues swept under the carpet', *Financial Times*, 30 May, p. 25.

Bol'shaya Sovetskaya Entsiklopediya, 3rd edn. (Moskva: *Sovetskaya*

Entsiklopediya) also its *Ezhegodniks*.

Booth, Ken (1975) 'Soviet Defence Strategy', in John Baylis *et al.*, *Contemporary Strategy: Theories and Policies* (London: Croom Helm).

Boyes, Roger (1985) 'First East bloc summit for Gorbachov: Warsaw Pact leaders to renew alliance', *The Times*, 16 April.

Boyes, Roger (1985) 'Warsaw Pact Summit: Wrinkles on the face behind the iron mask', *The Times*, 25 April.

Braun, Aurel (1981/82/83/84/85) 'Warsaw Treaty Organization', in Richard F. Starr (ed.), *Yearbook on International Communist Affairs* (Stanford, CA: Hoover Institute Press, Stanford University).

Broadhurst, Arlene Idol (ed.) (1982) *The Future of European Alliance Systems: NATO and the Warsaw Pact* (Boulder, Co.: Westview Press).

Brown, Archie; Fennell, John; Kaser, Michael; and Willetts, H. T. (eds) (1982) *The Cambridge Encyclopedia of Russia and the Soviet Union* (Cambridge: Cambridge University Press).

Buchan, David (1985) 'White House backs Romania on tariffs', *The Financial Times*, 17 May, p. 2.

[Buda Press] (1970) 'Organizational Progress within Warsaw Treaty', *Weekly Bulletin/English Bulletin*, vol. IX/138, 23 September.

Bulgarian Academy of Sciences (ed.) (1985) *Information Bulgaria* (Oxford: Pergamon Press).

Bykov, Oleg (1985) 'Different Approaches to the Key Problem of World Politics', in P. N. Fedoseyev, *et al.* (eds), *Peace and Disarmament, Academic Studies 1984* (Moscow: Progress).

Cahen, Alfred (1986) 'Relaunching the Western European Union: implications for the Atlantic Alliance', *NATO Review* 34/4 August.

Caldwell, Lawrence T. (1975) 'The Warsaw Pact: Directions of Change', *Problems of Communism*, vol. XXIV, September–October.

Carrington, Lord (1985) 'One year at NATO', *NATO Review* 33/4 August.

Cason, Thomas (1983) 'The Warsaw Pact', in Michael Sodaro and Sharon L. Wolchik (eds), *Foreign and Domestic Policy in Eastern Europe in the 1980s, trends and prospects* (London: Macmillan).

Clawson, Robert W. and Kaplan, Lawrence S. (eds) (1982) *The Warsaw Pact: Political Purpose and Military Means* (Wilmington, Delaware: Scholarly Resources Inc).

Colton, Timothy J. (1981) 'The Impact of the Military on Soviet Society', in Seweryn Bialer (ed.) *The Domestic Context of Soviet Foreign Policy* (Boulder, Co.: Westview Press/London: Croom Helm).

Cornwell, Rupert (1985) 'SPD, E. Berlin in N-free zone talks', *Financial Times*, 25 September, p. 2.

Crowley, Edward L. *et al.* (1968) *Prominent Personalities in the USSR* (Metuchen, NJ: The Scarecrow Press, Inc.).

Czyzewski, Ireneusz (1985) *The Peace Policy of Poland* (Warsaw: Interpress).

Dawisha, Karen (1988) *Eastern Europe, Gorbachev, and Reform: The Great Challenge* (Cambridge: Cambridge University Press).

Dawisha, Karen and Hanson, Philip (1981) *Soviet-East European Dilemmas Coercion, Competition, and Consent* (London: Heinemann/Royal Institut of International Affairs).

de Jager, General Cornelis (1986) 'NATO's strategy', *NATO Review* 34/. October.

Dibb, Paul (1988) *The Soviet Union: The incomplete superpower* (London Macmillan/International Institute for Strategic Studies).

Dibblin, Jane (1985) 'Across the Divide' *New Statesman,* 15 March.

'Disarmament: the main Soviet proposals' (1983) (Moscow: Novosti).

Dragnich, Alex N. (1980) 'Warsaw Treaty Organization', in *1980 Yearboo on International Communist Affairs* (Stanford, CA: Hoover Institute Press Stanford University).

Erickson, John (1982a) 'The Soviet View of Deterrence: A General Survey' *Survival,* vol. XXIV/6, November–December.

Erickson, John (1982b) 'Stability in the Warsaw Pact?', *Current History,* vol 81/478, November.

Erickson, John (1985) 'The Warsaw Pact: From Here to Eternity?', *Curren History*, vol. 84/505, November.

Erickson, John (1982c) 'The Warsaw Pact: Past, Present, and Future', in Milorad M. Drachkovitch (ed.) *East Central Europe: Yesterday, Today Tomorrow* (Stanford, CA: Hoover Institute Press).

Erickson, John (1981) 'The Warsaw Pact: the shape of things to come?', in Dawisha and Hanson (1981).

Fedoseyev, P. N. *et al.* (eds) (1985) *Peace and Disarmament, Academic Studies 1984* (Moscow: Progress).

Feldbrugge, Professor Ferdinand J. M. (1988) 'Gorbachev's reforms', *NATO Review* 36/6 December.

Fejtö, François (1974) *A History of the People's Democracies* (Harmonds worth: Penguin/Pelican).

Fesefeldt, Joachim (1984) *The Warsaw Pact at the Madrid CSCE Follow up Meeting and the CDE (except Rumania)* (Köln: Bundesinstitut fü ostwissenschaftliche und internationale Studien, 40).

Floyd, David (1965) *Rumania: Russia's Dissident Ally* (London: Pal Mall Press).

Fülöp Mihály (1985) 'The Council of Foreign Ministers and the Hungarian Peace Treaty of 1947', *Külpolitika* (Budapest) 4.

Gabanyi, Anneli Ute (1984) *Rumania's Individualist Positions at the Madrid CSCE Follow-up Conference and at the CDE* (Köln: Bundesinstitut fü ostwissenschaftliche und internationale Studien, 47).

Galvin, General John R. (1988) 'The INF Treaty – no relief from the burden of defence', *NATO Review* 36/1 February.

Gasparini, Emilio (1987) 'East-South economic relations: growing burden o communist client states', *NATO Review* 35/4 August.

Gasparini, Emilio (1985) 'East-South economic relations: Warsaw pact shift to military deals with developing world', *NATO Review* 33/2 April.

Golden, Kathie S. and Nelson, Daniel N. (1985) 'International Politica

Communications in the WTO: Crisis Reporting', paper prepared for delivery at the Southern Political Science Association annual meeting, Nashville, Tennessee, November.

Gorbachev, Mikhail (1988) *Perestroika* (London: Fontana/Collins).

Gormley, Dennis (1985) 'A New Dimension to Soviet Theatre Strategy', *Orbis*, Fall.

Grechko, A. A. (1977) *The Armed Forces of the Soviet Union* (Moscow: Progress).

Grechko, A. A. (1972) 'Boevoe armii sotsialisticheskikh stran', *Kommunist* (15) October.

Gribkov, A. General armii (1985a) 'Brat'ya po klassu, Brat'ya po oruzhiyu – k 30-letiyu Varshavskogo Dogovora', *Voennyi vestnik*, 5.

Gribkov, A. (1985b) '30 let na strazhe mira i sotsializma', *Voenno-istoricheskii zhurnal*, 5.

Gribkov, A. (1984) 'Ukreplenie voenno-politicheskogo edinstva stran Varshavskogo Dogovora na sovremennom etape' *Voenno-istoricheskii zhurnal* 5.

Gromyko, Andrei (1969) 'USSR Supreme Soviet: Questions concerning the international situation and Soviet foreign policy: report by Foreign Minister Andrei Gromyko', *Soviet News* 5499, 15 July.

Grzybowski, Kazimierz (1964) *The Socialist Commonwealth of Nations: Organizations and Institutions* (New Haven/London: Yale University Press).

Hanson, Philip (1985) 'No Resting Place?', *Detente 3*, May.

Hardenbergh, Chalmers 'News of Negotiations', *ADIU Report* (a regular feature).

Harmel Pierre (1987) 'Forty years of East-West relations. Hopes, fears, and challenges', *NATO Review* 35/4 August.

Hecht, Leo (1982) *The USSR Today: facts and interpretations* (Springfield, VA: 'Scholasticus' Publications).

Hedlin, Myron (1984) 'Moscow's Line on Arms Control', *Problems of Communism* vol. XXXIII/3, May–June.

Hegedüs András (1955) *Statement* [to the Moscow Conference, 1954], supplement to *New Hungary* 22, January.

Herrick, R. Waring (1968) 'The Soviet Military Intervention: terms of the Soviet troop-stationing treaty imposed on Prague', *Radio Liberty Research Bulletin* 24(2469) (CRD 379/68) 23 October.

Herrick, R. Waring (1970) 'Warsaw Pact Restructuring Strengthens Principle of National Control', *Radio Liberty Research Bulletin* 10(2540) (CRD 72/70) 11 March.

Herspring, Dale R. (1985) 'Technology and the Soviet System', *Problems of Communism*, January–February.

Herspring, Dale R. (1980) 'The Warsaw Pact at 25', *Problems of Communism* September–October.

HMSO (1983) *Russian-English Military Dictionary* (London: HMSO).

Hofman, Michal (1985) 'Firm Foundations' *Polish Perspectives* (Warsaw) vol. XXVIII/3, Summer.

Holden, Gerard (1985) 'The Politics of the Warsaw Pact', *Sanity* January.

Holloway, David (1978) 'Foreign and Defence Policy', in Archie Brown and Michael Kaser (eds) *The Soviet Union Since the Fall of Khrushchev* (London: Macmillan).

Holloway, David (1984) *The Soviet Union and the Arms Race* (New Haven/London: Yale University Press).

Holloway, David and Sharp, Jane M. O. (eds) (1984) *The Warsaw Pact Alliance in Transition?* (London: Macmillan Press).

How to Avert the Threat to Europe (1983) (Moscow: Progress).

Howe, Sir Geoffrey (1987) 'The Atlantic Alliance and the security of Europe', *NATO Review* 35/2 April.

Hunt, Kenneth and Murphy, Bill (1984) 'The "Counterdeployments" in Eastern Europe: military and political implications', *Radio Liberty Research* RL 32/84, 18 January.

Hutchings, Robert L. (1985) *Foreign and Security Policy Co-ordination in the Warsaw Pact* (Köln: Bundesinstitut für ostwissenschaftliche und internationale Studien, February 15).

Iovchuk, S. and Andreyev, V. (1985) 'Socialist Community: 40 Years of Peaceful Construction and Fraternal Co-operation', *International Affairs* (Moscow) 6.

Jain, J. P. (1973) *Documentary Study of the Warsaw Pact* (Bombay: Asia Publishing House).

Jamgotch, jr, Nish (1968) *Soviet-East European Dialogue – international relations of a new type?* (Stanford: Hoover Institute/Stanford University).

Jappie, Anne (1983) 'Co-operation, Security and Disarmament in Europe', *ADIU Report* vol. 5/6, November–December.

Johnson, A. Ross (1978) 'Soviet- East European Military Relations: An Overview', in Dale R. Herspring and Ivan Volgyes (eds) *Civil-Military Relations in Communist Systems* (Boulder, Co.: Westview Press/Folkestone: Dawson).

Johnson, A. Ross (1984) 'The Warsaw Pact: Soviet Military Policy in Eastern Europe', in Sarah Meiklejohn Terry, *Soviet Policy in Eastern Europe* (New Haven/London: Yale University Press).

Johnson, A. Ross; Dean, Robert W.; and Alexiev, Alexander (1981) 'The Armies of the Warsaw Pact Northern Tier', *Survival* vol. XXII/4, July–August.

Johnson, A. Ross; Dean, Robert W.; and Alexiev, Alexander (1982) *East European Military Establishments: The Warsaw Pact Northern Tier* (New York: Crane Russak).

Jones, Christopher D. (1986) 'Agencies of the Alliance: Multinational in Form, Bilateral in Content', in Jefrey Simon and Trong Gilberg (eds) *Security Implications of Nationalism in Eastern Europe* (Boulder, Co. and London: Westview Press).

Jones, Christopher D. (1984) 'The Political Administrations of the Warsaw Pact and the Reliability of the East-Bloc Armed Forces', in Daniel N. Nelson (ed.) *Soviet Allies . . .* (Boulder, Co.: Westview Press).

Jones, Christopher D. (1981) *Soviet Influence in Eastern Europe – political autonomy and the Warsaw Pact* (New York: Praeger).

Józsa Gyula (1985) *Hungary in the Crossfire of Criticism from Prague and Moscow* parts 1 and 2 (Köln: Bundesinstitut für ostwissenschaftliche und internationale Studien, 5, 6.

Katrich, A. (1985) 'Nadezhnyi shchit sotsialisticheskogo sodruzhestva' *Kommunist Vooruzhennykh Sil* 10.

Keesings Contemporary Archives.

Kirichenko, M. S. (1975) *Nadezhnyi strazh mira* (Minsk: Izdatel'stvo Belarusi).

Kobal, Daniel Andrew (1974) *Comecon and the Warsaw Treaty Organization: their political role since 1953* (University Microfilms International #7421698).

Kohl, Helmut (1985) 'Thirtieth anniversary of the accession of the Federal Republic of Germany to the North Atlantic Alliance', *NATO Review* 33/3 June.

Kolkowicz, Roman (ed.) (1969a) The Warsaw Pact: report on a conference on the Warsaw Treaty Organization held at the Institute for Defense Analyses, May 17–19, 1967 (Arlington, VA: Institute for Defense Analyses, 1969) (IDA Research Paper P–496).

Kolkowicz, Roman (1969b) 'Continuity and Change in the Warsaw Pact', introduction in Roman Kolkowicz (ed.) *The Warsaw Pact* (ibid.).

Korbonski, Andrzej (1969) *The Warsaw Pact* (New York: Carnegie Endowment for International Peace). (International Conciliation #573).

Korbonski, Andrzej (1982) 'The Warsaw Treaty after 25 Years: An Entangling Alliance or an Empty Shell?', in Robert W. Clawson and Lawrence S. Kaplan (eds) *The Warsaw Pact* (Wilmington, Delaware: Scholarly Resources Inc.).

Kozlov, General-Major S. N. (1977) *The Officer's Handbook* [Moscow, 1971] (Washington DC: US Government Printing Office) USAF 'Soviet Military Thought' vol. 13.

Kramer, Mark N. (1984–5) 'Civil-military relations in the Warsaw Pact: the East European component', *International Affairs* (London) vol. 61/1, Winter.

Krasinov, I. (1986) 'Soviet Foreign Policy Documents', *International Affairs* (Moscow) 3/1986.

Kruzhin, Peter (1985) 'Ogarkov Replacing Kulikov?', Radio Liberty *Research Bulletin* RL 242/85, 31(3340), 31 July.

Kulikov, V. (1980a) 'Chetvert' veka na strazhe zavoevanii sotsializma i mira' *Voenno-istoricheskii zhurnal* 5/1980

Kulikov, V. (1988) *The Doctrine of Peace: the military doctrine of the Warsaw Treaty member states* (Moscow: Novosti).

Kulikov, V. (1985) 'Nadezhnyi shchit mira' *Kommunist* 8/1985.

Kulikov, V. *et al.* (eds) (1980b) *Varshavskii Dogovor soyuz vo imya mira i sotsializma* (Moskva: Voenizdat/Ministerstvo Oborony SSSR).

Kusin, Vladimir V. (1985) 'Impending Renewal of the Warsaw Pact' Radio

Free Europe *Research* RAD Background Report/36 (Eastern Europe) 22 April.

Lachs, Professor M. (1955) 'The Warsaw Treaty Agreement and the Question of Collective Security in Europe', *International Affairs* (Moscow) 10/1955.

Lachs, Professor M. (1956) 'The Warsaw Treaty and the North Atlantic Treaty', *International Affairs* (Moscow) 2/1956.

Lewis, William J. (1982) *The Warsaw Pact: Arms, Doctrine, and Strategy* (—: McGraw-Hill Publications Co.).

Lewytzkyj, Borys (ed.) (1984) *Who's Who in the Soviet Union* (München: K G. Saur, 1984).

Lototskii, S. S. *et al.* (1971) *The Soviet Army* (Moscow: Progress).

Mackintosh, J. P. (1962) *Strategy and Tactics of Soviet Foreign Policy* (London: Oxford University Press).

Mackintosh, Malcolm (1982) 'Devolution in the Warsaw Treaty Organization', in Arlene Idol Broadhurst (ed.) *The Future of European Alliance Systems* (Boulder, Co.: Westview Press).

Mackintosh, Malcolm (1969) *The Evolution of the Warsaw Pact* (London: Institute for Strategic Studies, June) Adelphi Paper 58.

Mackintosh, Malcolm (1987) 'The Soviet Union under new rulers: Gorbachev's first two years', *NATO Review* 35/1 February.

Mackintosh, Malcolm (1974) 'The Warsaw Pact Today', *Survival* vol. XVI/3 May–June.

Maier, Anneli (1985) 'Romanian-Soviet Dispute', Radio Free Europe *Research*, vol. 10/34 (Romanian Situation Report/12) 23 August 1985.

Mal'tsev, V. F. *et al.* (1980) *Organizatsiya Varshavskogo Dogovora: dokumenty i materialy, 1955–1980* (Moskva: Politizdat).

Mal'tsev,V. F. (1986) *Organizatsiya Varshavskogo Dogovora 1955–1985: Dokumenty i materialy* (Moskva: Politizdat, 1986).

Marxism–Leninism on War and Army (1972) (Moscow: Progress).

Materialy XXVII *S'ezda* Kommunist*icheskoi Partii Sovetskogo Soyuza* (Moskva: Politizdat, 1986).

Meier, Christian and Oldenburg, Fred (1980) 'Soviet Policy in Eastern Europe', in *The Soviet Union 1978–79*, vol. 5 (New York/London: Holmes and Meier).

Meissner, Boris (1967) 'Die bilateralen Bündnisvertäge der osteuropäischen Länder', *Aussenpolitik* 10/1967 [translated for me by Niels Højberg].

Meissner, Boris (1966) 'The Soviet Union's Bilateral Pact System in Eastern Europe', in Kurt London (ed.) *Eastern Europe in Transition* (Baltimore, MD: Johns Hopkins Press).

Meissner, Boris (1979) 'Specific Changes in the East Pact System', *Aussenpolitik* vol. 30/3.

Meissner, Boris (1983) 'Warsaw Treaty Organization', in R. Berhardt (ed.) *Encyclopedia of Public International Law Instalment* 6 (Amsterdam/New York/Oxford: North-Holland).

Menzhinskii, V. I. *et al.* (eds) (1980) *Mezhdunarodniye organizatsii sotsialisticheskikh gosudarstv: spravochnik* (Moskva: Mezhdunarodniye otnosheniya).

Merezhko, A. (1980) 'Nadezhnyi shchit sotsializma i mira k 25-letiyu Organizatsiya Varshavskogo Dogovora', *Kommunist Vooruzhennykh Sil*, 1980/9.

Mertes, Alois (1985) 'East-West Relations: the political dimension', *NATO Review* vol. 33/1, February.

Mikhailov, Yu. (1986) 'The Main Potential of Peace (the results of the meeting of the Political Consultative Committee of the Warsaw Treaty member-states)', *International Affairs* (Moscow) 1/1986.

Ministry of Defence (1985) *British Defence Policy* (London: Ministry of Defence).

MISON (1985) *30-letie Varshavskogo Dogovora – ukazatel' literatury 1970–1984 gg* (Moskva: Mezhdunarodnaya informatsionnaya sistema po obshchestvennym naukam).

Mladenov, Petur (1985) 'Bulgaria in the Socialist Community's Efforts for Peace and European Security', *International Affairs* (Moscow) 6/1985.

Monks, Alfred L. (1984) *Soviet Military Doctrine: 1960 to the present* (New York: Irvington Publishers, Inc.).

Murphy, Bill (1984) 'Political-Military Relations in the USSR', Radio Liberty *Research* RL 397/84, 23 October.

Murphy, Bill (1984) 'Soviet Press Hints that SS–22 Missiles Have Been Deployed in Eastern Europe', Radio Liberty *Research* RL 37/84, 20 January 1984.

Mututshika, Sigeo (1986) 'Fundamental Directions of Romanian Foreign Policy for the Strengthening of its National Sovereignty', *Revue Roumaine d'Etudes Internationales XX*, 5(85) (Bucharest).

Nahaylo, Bohdan (1985) 'Soviet Foreign Policy Since Gorbachev Took Over', Radio Liberty *Research* RL 202/85, 25 June.

NATO Information Service (1984) *NATO and the Warsaw Pact: Force Comparisons* (Brussels: NATO Information Service).

Nekrasov, Vadim (1984) *The Roots of European Security – 40 years after the Yalta and Potsdam Conferences (1945)* (Moscow: Novosti).

Nelson, Daniel N. 'Burden-sharing in the Warsaw Pact' [draft paper].

Nelson, Daniel N. (1986a) 'Military Policy and Military Politics in Ceauşescu's Romania', [unpublished paper, 1986a; forthcoming to *Survey*]

Nelson, Daniel N. (1984) (ed.) *Soviet Allies: the Warsaw Pact and the Issue of Reliability* (Boulder, Co.: Westview).

Nelson, Daniel N. (1986b) *Alliance Behavior in the Warsaw Pact* (Boulder, Co.: Westview).

Nelson, Harold D. (1983/1984) *Poland: a country study* (Washington, DC: US Government Printing Office– Area Handbook series).

Nezhinsky, L. (1985) 'An Alliance for World Peace and Security. (On the 30th Anniversary of the Warsaw Treaty Organization), *International Affairs* (Moscow) 6/1985.

Odom, William E. (1985) 'Soviet Force Posture: Dilemmas and Directions', *Problems of Communism* vol. XXXIV/4, July–August.

Ogarkov, N. V. *et al.* (eds) (1983) *Voennyi entsiklopedicheskii slovar'*, (Moskva: Voenizdat).

Pick, Otto (1988) 'Perestroika and the Warsaw Pact', *NATO Review* 36/5 October.

Ponomarev, Boris (1985a) 'The Role of Scientists in Strengthening International Security', in P. N. Fedoseyev, *et al.* (eds) *Peace and Disarmament, Academic Studies 1984* (Moscow: Progress).

Ponomarev, Boris (1985b) *Winning for Peace: the Great Victory – its world impact* (Moscow: Progress).

Proektor, D. M. (1984) *The Foundations of Peace in Europe* (Moscow: Nauka).

Rakowska-Harmstone, Teresa; Jones, Christopher D.; Jaworsky, John; and Sylvain, Ivan (1984) *Warsaw Pact: the Question of Cohesion Phase II*, vol. 1 'The Greater Socialist Army: Integration and Reliability', ORAE Extra-Mural Paper 29 (Ottawa: Operational Research and Analysis Establishment/Department of National Defence, February).

Rakowska-Harmstone, Teresa; Sylvain, Ivan; and Abonyi, Arpad (1981) *Warsaw Pact: The question of cohesion, Phase 1*, ORAE Extra-Mural Paper 19 (Ottawa: Operational Research and Analysis Establishment/ Department of National Defence, December).

Reisch, Alfred (1984) 'New HSWP Interpretation of Communist National and International Interests', Radio Free Europe *Research*, 16 February.

Reissmüller, Johann Georg (1985) 'The Soviet Union comes to sense the discomfort of its European allies', *The German Tribune* 1178, 12 May.

Remington, Robin Alison (1967) *The Changing Soviet Perception of the Warsaw Pact* (Cambridge, Mass: Center for International Studies/MIT).

Remington, Robin Alison (1971) *The Warsaw Pact: case studies in communist conflict resolution* (Cambridge, Mass.: MIT Press) (Studies in Communism, revisionism, and revolution 17).

Renaud, Jean-Claude (1985) 'Eastern Europe: Economic problems and prospects', *NATO Review* 33/6 December.

Rice, Condoleezza (1984) 'Defence Burden Sharing', in David Holloway and Jane M. O. Sharp (eds) *The Warsaw Pact: Alliance in Transition* (London: Macmillan).

Rice, Condoleezza (1985a) 'Nuclear Weapons and the Warsaw Pact', in Jeffrey D. Boutwell, Paul Doty and Gregory F. Treverton *The Nuclear Confrontation in Europe* (Beckenham, Kent: Croom Helm).

Rice, Condoleezza (1985b) *Political-Military Relations in the Soviet Union* paper prepared for the Conference of the National Association for Soviet and East European Studies, 23–25 March).

Roberts, Adam (1983) 'The Warsaw Pact: the Parts and the Whole', *Survival* vol. XXV/6 November–December.

Rodionov, N. N. *et al.* (eds) (1975) *Organizatsiya Varshavskogo Dogovora 1955–1975: dokumenty i materialy* (Moskva: Politizdat).

Rosenau, William (1984) 'NATO vs Warsaw Pact: Is Massive Rearmament Necessary?', Council on Economic Priorities *Newsletter* February (New York: CEP Publication N84–2).

Rühle, Hans (1985) 'Gorbachev's "Star Wars"', *NATO Review*, vol. 33/4, August.

Rumanian Workers' Party Central Committee (1967) 'Statement on the Stand of the Rumanian Workers' Party Concerning the Problems of the International Communist and Working-Class Movement' Adopted by the Enlarged Plenum of the Central Committee of the RWP held in April 1964, in William E. Griffith (ed.) *Sino-Soviet Relations*, 1964–1965 (Cambridge, Mass./London: MIT Press).

Sanakoyev, S. 'Soviet Foreign Policy (1976) a vital factor of change on the international scene', *Socialism: theory and practice* 7/1976.

Sapir, Jacques (1982) 'Soviet Military Superiority: A Myth of the 1980s?', *World View 1983* (London: Pluto Press).

Savinov, Konstantin Ivanovich (1980) *Moguchii faktor mira i stabil'nosti v mezhdunarodnikh otnosheniyakh* (Moskva: Mezhdunarodnie otnosheniya).

Savinov, Konstantin Ivanovich (1977) *Sovmestnyi vklad sotsialisticheskikh stran v delo mira i progressa* (Moskva: Znanie).

Savinov, Konstantin Ivanovich (1986) *Varshavskii Dogovor faktor mira, shchit sotsializma* (Moskva: mezhdunarodnaya Otnosheniya).

Selucky, Radoslav (1985) *The Present Dilemma of Soviet-East European Integration* (München: Research Project 'Crises in Soviet-style Systems').

Shafir, Michael (1985) *Romania: Politics, Economics, and Society* (London: Frances Pinter).

Shakhnazarov, G. K. (1979) *The Destiny of the World: the Socialist Shape of Things to Come* (Moscow: Progress).

Shenfield, Stephen (1985) 'Star Wars – a Soviet view', *Detente* 3, May.

Shevchenko, Arkady N. (1985) *Breaking With Moscow* (London: Cape).

Shevchenko, E. S. (1971) 'Warsaw Treaty 1955', in *Bol'shaya Sovetskaya Entsiklopediya* 3rd edn., vol. 4, Moscow, pp. 314–16..

Shkarovskii, Viktor Stepanovich (1985) *Na Strazhe Mira i Sotsializma – k 30-letiyu Organizatsii Vartshavskogo Dogovora* (Moskva: Planeta).

Shtemenko, General Sergei (1976) 'The Warsaw Pact System', *Survival* vol. XVIII/4, July–August.

Shytikov, Alexei (1973) 'M.P.s Have A Great Part to Play in Strengthening European Security', *Soviet News* 5673, 30 January.

Silin, E. (1986) 'Ways of Safeguarding European Security', *International Affairs* (Moscow) 3/1986.

Simon, Jeffrey (1985) *Warsaw Pact Forces: problems of command and control* (Boulder/London: Westview Press).

Simon, Jeffrey and Gilberg, Trong (eds) (1986) *Security Implications of Nationalism in Eastern Europe* (Boulder, Co./London: Westview).

Skilling, H. Gordon (1985) 'Independent Currents in Czechoslovakia', *Problems of Communism*, January–February.

Skorodenko, P. Polkovnik (1983) 'Vozrastianie roli kommunisticheskikh partii v ukreplenii boevogo sodruzhestva bratskikh armii', *Voenno-istoricheskii zhurnal* 5/1983.

Skorodenko, P. P. (1985a) 'Nadezhnyi shchit mirnogo truda', *Kommunist Ukrainy* 5/1985a.

Skorodenko, P. P. (1985b) *Vo glave boevogo soyuza: Kommunisticheskie partii – sozdateli i rukovoditeli Organizatsii Varshavskogo Dogovora* (Moskva: Voenizdat).

Slavyanov, M. (1955/56) 'Firm Foundation of European and Universal Security (the Warsaw conference)', *International Affairs* (Moscow) 1955/6.

Smorigo, N. (1985) 'Varshavskii Dogovor – nadezhnyi instrument ukrepleniya mezhdunarodnoi bezopasnosti', *Partiinaya zhizn* 10/1985.

Socor, Vladimir (1985) 'Warsaw Pact Summit Renews the Warsaw Treaty', RAD Background Report/53 (Eastern Europe) Radio Free Europe *Research* 19 June.

Spravochnik Politrabotnika (1985) (Moskva: Voenizdat).

Starr, Richard F. (1982) *Communist Regimes in Eastern Europe* (Stanford, CA: Hoover Institute Press/Stanford University).

Starr, Richard F. (1982) 'East Central Europe and Soviet Foreign Policy', in Milorad M. Drachkovitch (ed.) *East Central Europe: Yesterday, Today, Tomorrow* (Stanford, CA: Hoover Institute Press).

Starr, Richard F. (1985) *USSR Foreign Policy After Detente* (Stanford, CA: Hoover Institute Press/Stanford University).

Strategic Survey 1970 Institute of Strategic Studies publication.

Stewart, James Moray (1985) 'Conventional Defence Improvements: where is the Alliance going?', *NATO Review* 33/2 April.

Sulzberger, S. L. (1955) 'NATO Through the Soviet Looking Glass', *New York Times*, 12 December, p. 30.

Stepaniuk, I. (1972) 'Na strazhe bezopasnosti narodov', *Krasnaya Zvezda* 15 May.

Svetlov, A. (1985) 'Varshavskii Dogovor na sluzhbe mira i bezopasnosti', *MEMO* 5/1985.

Szawlowski, Richard (1976) *The System of the International Organizations of the Communist Countries* (—: A. W. Sijthoff, Leyden).

Szűrős Mátyás (1985) 'Hungarian foreign policy in the mid-1980s', *Külpolitika* (Budapest) 4/1985.

Tiedke, Jutta and Stephan (1978) 'The Soviet Union's internal problems and the development of the Warsaw Treaty Organsiation', in Egbert Jain (ed.) *Soviet Foreign Policy – its social and economic conditions* (London: Allison and Busby).

Tismaneanu, Vladimir (1985) 'Ceauşescu's Socialism', *Problems of Communism* January–February.

Tolkunov, L. (1986) 'Parliaments and the Preservation of Peace', *International Affairs* (Moscow) 2/1986.

Treverton, Gregory (1981) *Nuclear Weapons in Europe* (London:International Institute of Strategic Studies) Adelphi Paper 168.

Tyranowski, Jerzy (1973) 'The Warsaw Treaty', in *Polish Yearbook of*

International Law (Wroclaw: Zaclad Narodnowy Imenia Ossolinskich Wydawnictwo Polskiej Akademia Nauk) – (Polish Academy of Science Institute of Legal Science) IV (1971), Wroclaw.

Tyushkevich, S. A. *et al.* (?1985) *The Soviet Armed Forces: A History of their Organizational Development* (Washington, DC: US Government Printing Office, ?1985) 'Soviet Military Thought 19'.

Urban, Josef (1977) *The Warsaw Treaty Organization – A Bulwark of Peace* (Prague: the Orbis Press Agency).

US Department of Defense (1981/1983/1984/1985) *Soviet Military Power* (Washington, DC: US Government Printing Office).

V interesakh ukrepleniya mira i bezopasnosti narodov' (1955) [editorial] *Kommunist* 8/1955.

van der Beugal, Ernst hans (1986) 'The Atlantic family – managing its problems' *NATO Review* 34/1 February 1986.

Vizit General'nogo Sekretarya TsK KPSS M. S. Gorbacheva vo Frantsiyu (1985) (2–5 oktyabrya 1985 g. – dokumenty i materialy) (Moskva: Politizdat).

Vladimirov, O. (1985) 'Questions of Theory: the Leading Factor on the World Revolutionary Process', from *Pravda* 21 June 1984, pp. 3–4, in *Current Digest of the Soviet Press* vol. XXXVII/25, 17 July.

Vladimirov, S. and Teplov, L. (1979) *Varshavskii Dogovor i NATO: dva kursa, dve politiki* (Moskva: Mezhdunarodnye otnosheniya).

Vladimirov, S. A. and Teplov, L. B. (1980) *Varshavskomy Dogovory – chetvert' veka* (Moskva: Znanie).

Volgyes, Ivan (1982) 'The Warsaw Pact – a study of vulnerabilites, tension, and reliability', in Arlene Idol Broadhurst (ed.) *The Future of European Alliance Systems* (Boulder, Co.: Westview).

Völkerrecht Teil 2 (1982) ([East] Berlin: Staatsverlag der Deutschen Demokratiischen Republik) section of WTO structure translated for me by Stephen Reville.

Volkogonova, D. A. *et al.* (1985) (eds) *Armii stran Varshavskogo Dogovora: spravochnik* (Moskva: Voenizdat).

Volkogonova, D. A. (1977) *Voina i armiya: filosofsko-sotsiologicheskii ocherk* (Moskva: Voenizdat).

Voslensky, Michael (1984) '35 years since Stalin's "turning point in the history of Europe"', *The German Tribune* 1153, 14 October.

Walker, Gregory (ed.) (1982) *Official Publications of the Soviet Union and Eastern Europe*, 1945–1980 (London: Mansell Publications Ltd.).

Warsaw *Treaty Organization and North Atlantic Treaty Organization: correlation of forces in Europe* (1989) (Moscow: Novosti).

The Warsaw *Treaty Organization: alliance for peace* (1984) (Moscow: Novosti).

Weickhardt, George G. (1985) 'Ogarkov's Latest Fulminations on Vigilance' Radio Liberty *Research Bulletin* RL 325/85, 27 September.

Weickhardt, George G. (1985) 'Ustinov versus Ogarkov', *Problems of Communism* January–February.

Wettig, Gerhard (1985) *The Smaller Warsaw Pact States in East-West Relations* (Köln: Bundesinstitut für ostwissenschaftliche und internationale Studien,1985/39).

Wettig, Gerhard (1984) *The Soviet Union and Arms Control* (Köln: Bundesinstitut für ostwissenschaftliche und internationale Studien, 1984/56).

White, Stephen; Gardner, John; and Schöpflin, George (1982) *Communist Political Systems: an introduction* (London: Macmillan).

Wiener, Friedrich (1981) *The Armies of the Warsaw Pact Nations* (Vienna: Carl Ueberreuter Publishers) 3rd edn.

Wolfe, Thomas W. (1965) *The Evolving Nature of the Warsaw Pact* (Santa Monica, CA: Rand Corporation) Memorandum RM-4835-PR.

Wolfe, Thomas W. (1973) *Role of the Warsaw Pact in Soviet Policy* (Santa Monica, CA: Rand Corporation) P-4973.

Wolfe, Thomas W. (1966) 'The Warsaw Pact in Evolution', in Kurt London (ed.) *Eastern Europe in Transition* (Baltimore, MD: John Hopkins Press).

Yakovlev, A. (1985) 'Mezhdunarodnoe znachenie Varshavskogo Dogovora', *MEMO*, 7/1985.

Yakubovskii, I. I. (1971) 'Bastion mira i bezopasnosti narodov', *Voenno-istoricheskii zhurnal* 3/1971.

Yakubovskii, I. I. (1975a) 'Boevoe sodruzhestvo armii sotsialisticheskikh gosudarstv', *Voenno-istoricheskii zhurnal* 5/1975-a.

Yakubovskii, I. I. (1975b) *Boevoe sodruzhestvo bratskikh narodov i armii* (Moskva: Voenizdat).

Yakubovskii, I. I. (1976) 'Boevoe sodruzhestvo', in A. A. Gretchko *et al.* (eds) *Sovetskaya voennaya entsiklopediya* (Moskva: Voenizdat).

Yakubovskii, I. I. (1969) 'Na strazhe mira i sotsializma', *Pravda* 14 May.

Zamascikov, Sergei (1982) *Political Organizations in the Soviet Armed Forces – the role of the Party and Komsomol* (Falls Church, VA: Delphic Associates, Inc.).

Zamyatin, S. (1984) 'Vo imya bol'shaya tsel' *Krasnaya Zvezda*, 31 March.

Zanone, Valerio (1988) 'Europe's rôle in NATO', *NATO Review* 36/2 April.

Zhilin, P. A. *et al.* (eds) (1984) *Stroitel'stvo Armii Evropeiskikh Stran Sotsialisticheskogo Sodruzhestva*, 1949–1980 (Moskva: Nauka).

Index

Note: Figures are italicised; Ap and n after a page number denotes references in the Appendixes or Notes, respectively.